THE AMERICAN VOTER

BOOKS BY A. CAMPBELL, P. E. CONVERSE,
W. E. MILLER AND D. E. STOKES

The American Voter
The American Voter: An Abridgement

THE

AMERICAN

VOTER

AN ABRIDGMENT

ANGUS CAMPBELL
PHILIP E. CONVERSE
WARREN E. MILLER
DONALD E. STOKES

SURVEY RESEARCH CENTER, UNIVERSITY OF MICHIGAN

JOHN WILEY & SONS, INC., NEW YORK · LONDON · SYDNEY

Preface to the Abridgment

This abridgment of *The American Voter* seeks to preserve in less extensive form the essential content of the original volume. The fact that this objective is achieved to a remarkable degree is due entirely to the editorial skill and good judgment of Professor Bernard C. Cohen of the Department of Political Science of The University of Wisconsin, who was responsible for the condensation. It is sobering to the authors to find how much of what they had to say in the original text could be maintained in only half as many pages, but they can only admire Professor Cohen's dexterity in bringing about this feat of distillation.

Ann Arbor, Michigan
March 1964

ANGUS CAMPBELL
PHILIP E. CONVERSE
WARREN E. MILLER
DONALD E. STOKES

Preface to the First Edition

This book issues from a program of research on the American electorate that extends back to 1948. In that year the Survey Research Center conducted a national study of the presidential election, and four additional election studies followed in the next ten years. Moreover, other studies conducted by the Center in this period, although not directly concerned with voting, have added to our understanding of the national electorate.

Although we have drawn primarily on election surveys carried out in 1952 and 1956, this book is actually an outgrowth of all the political studies in which the Center has been engaged. Since numerous members of the Survey Research Center staff, many of them no longer associated with the Center, participated in those studies, we would like to acknowledge their contributions here. These members include George M. Belknap, Homer C. Cooper, Burton R. Fisher, Gerald Gurin, Robert L. Kahn, Robert O. McWilliams, and Stephen B. Withey.

The program has also had the assistance of Charles F. Cannell, who has been in charge of the Center's excellent field staff throughout this period, of Leslie Kish, who has directed the sampling operations of the Center since 1951, and of Charlotte Winter, director of the Center's coding section. Rensis Likert, director of the Institute for Social Research, of which the Center is a part, has maintained a continuing interest in the program. Needless to say, the program has also depended on the services of the hundreds of interviewers, coders, IBM operators, and statistical clerks who are inevitably involved in research operations of this magnitude. Their names are seldom seen in published reports, but their work provides the basis from which all further analysis follows.

The Survey Research Center is fortunate in having a close and supportive relationship with many of the departments and schools of The University of Michigan. We are particularly indebted to an Advisory Committee of interested faculty members who worked with the Center staff in reviewing plans and progress as the studies developed. We wish to acknowledge the valuable assistance given us by the members of this committee: Arthur W. Bromage, Samuel J. Eldersveld, Amos H. Hawley, Daniel Katz, Theodore M. Newcomb, and James K. Pollock.

A number of scholars at other universities have also contributed to the development of this program of research. Particularly important are the members of the Social Science Research Council's Committee on Political Behavior. The Committee was closely associated with the planning of the 1952 study, and its members have shown a helpful interest in the Center's work ever since that time. During this period this group has included Conrad Arensberg, Robert A. Dahl, Alfred de Grazia, Oliver Garceau, Alexander Heard, V. O. Key, Jr., Avery Leiserson, Dayton McKean, M. Brewster Smith, and David B. Truman. Pendleton Herring, President of the Social Science Research Council, through his effective stimulation of research on political behavior has had an important influence on this entire area of inquiry.

The two major studies with which we are primarily concerned were made possible by support from private foundations. In 1952 the Carnegie Corporation of New York enabled the Center to carry through its study of the 1952 election. In 1956 the Center received a grant from the Rockefeller Foundation, which made possible our study in that year. We greatly appreciate the support of these two organizations. Neither the Carnegie Corporation nor the Rockefeller Foundation is in any way responsible for this publication, nor does either organization necessarily support the views expressed herein.

Finally we wish to acknowledge the contribution made to the preparation of this book by our research assistants: Natalie Brody, Aage Clausen, Harry Crockett, Jon Faily, Jerome Green, Nancy Working Mendelsohn, and Linda Wilcox. Marion T. Wirick, secretary to the program, and her assistant, Virginia Nye, likewise have contributed their services to the preparation. To all these people we are deeply indebted.

Because of the length of this book, we have not included the usual appendices containing the questionnaires, statements of sample design and sampling errors, and notes on statistical methods. These documents may be obtained upon request from the Survey Research Center of the University of Michigan.

Ann Arbor, Michigan
March 1960

ANGUS CAMPBELL
PHILIP E. CONVERSE
WARREN E. MILLER
DONALD E. STOKES

Contents

x ★ *Contents*

⭐ **SECTION I**
INTRODUCTION

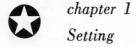

chapter 1

Setting

In the contemporary world the activity of voting is rivaled only by the market as a means of reaching collective decisions from individual choices. Voting is used by parliaments and bridge clubs, by courts, consistories, and leagues of nations, and, most remarkably, it has provided the modern state with a way of connecting the actions of government with the preferences of a mass citizenry. The casting of votes as a means of decision is a practice of extraordinarily wide currency in human society, and this type of action has been of growing interest in the study of the social life of men.

Indeed, anyone who reads the literature of voting research must be impressed by its proliferation in recent years. Those who would add to the literature of voting have a responsibility to place their work in a broader setting. Two ways of locating our work seem to us particularly important. First, the voting behavior of a mass electorate can be seen within the context of a larger political system. The electoral process is a means of decision that lies within a broader political order, and in research on voting it is valuable to have explicitly in view the wider political system in which the electoral process is found. Second, the empirical materials of our own work lie within a particular historical setting. The work reported here has extended through more than eight years; yet the fact that it deals with a specific historical era affects in countless ways the theoretical problems we have selected for treatment and the character of our empirical results. These effects may be better understood if certain characteristics of this historical period are kept before us.

VOTING AND THE POLITICAL SYSTEM

Voting behavior has been of interest to so many of the social sciences that the political importance of what is studied is sometimes lost from view. The varied theoretical concerns of investigators of voting ought not to obscure the fact that in the modern state the electoral process is of greatest interest because of its importance in the wider political system. However much voting may tell about the psychology and sociology of human choice, it is important because of the importance of the decisions to which it leads. Electoral behavior would not have attracted the attention that it has, were it not that the collective vote decision is of great significance in many political systems. Therefore, this study of voting is also concerned with a fundamental process of political decision, and we begin by emphasizing this fact.

It would be difficult to overstate the significance of popular elections for democratic theory and practice. If politics has to do with "who gets what, when, and how," the free, competitive election has proven an essential means of insuring that the current solution of this problem enjoys the broad consent of the governed. A regime in which leaders are subject to regularized and effective control by nonleaders has been possible in the modern world only when power is granted to some and withheld from others in periodic electoral contests. No democratic state has ever been governed by direct democracy. But popular election combined with representation has greatly expanded the distribution of political power, and it has offered a creative solution to the age-old problem of transferring authority without violence.

The importance of elections in democratic government may be elaborated in terms of decision making. Conceived in these terms, the political system can be idealized as a collection of processes for the taking of decisions. We often speak of the legislative process, the judicial process, the electoral process, and so forth. Each of these processes involves a group of actors, one or more decision rules, which have at least an indirect legal or constitutional basis, and a set of effective influences to which the actors respond in reaching a decision. No one of these decision processes is independent of the rest, and some of the most interesting problems of empirical analysis in politics are posed by the interrelation of the several decision points of the political system. Decisions of the electoral process have important effects on decisions taken elsewhere in the system. What the electorate decides may determine which actors will have the power of decision, and the outcomes of past and future elections generate important influences to which these actors respond. The holders of elective or appointive office in democratic government are guided in many of their actions by a calculus of electoral effect.

The decision of who shall control the executive power of the state is of great importance in every political system. Certainly few decisions in American government rival in importance the choice of a President. In vesting the power to make this choice in a mass electorate, the American system follows a practice that is fairly rare among nations even today; and in this respect the electoral process assumes a wider importance in American government than it does in many other political systems. This question is not really one of whether the constitutional order is parliamentary or presidential. In many parliamentary nations control of the executive *is* determined, if only indirectly, by a mass electorate. It is more a question of whether the will of the electorate is manipulated or abrogated by coercive power and whether the party system presents the electorate with an effective choice. Of course, the doctrine of virtually every nation of the modern world supposes that control of the executive depends at least indirectly on popular consent. But doctrine and practice can be widely different, and examples are plentiful enough of political systems in which the electorate is deprived of an authentic choice.[1]

Although our study of voting is prompted in part by a sense of the impact of popular elections elsewhere in government, our research has focused on the electoral process itself and has not explored the relation of this process to the other decision processes of the political system. We begin with the choice of a President and look backward to the configuration of causal influences that have produced this decision rather than forward to its impact in other arenas of the political system. Our theoretical scheme takes the act of voting as the datum to be explained, and this assumption underlies most of the discussion in later chapters. Yet we confess to a lively interest in the place of the electoral process in the wider political system, and this interest will lead us in a final chapter to reopen the question of how decision making by the American electorate, as we have observed it, affects the process of government elsewhere in the system.

Viewing the electoral process as part of a wider political order leads to an interest not only in the effects of elections on other parts of the system but also in the effects on the electoral process of what happens elsewhere in government. The consequences of decisions taken by the President and the executive agencies, by the Congress, by the courts, and by other actors of the national government are an impor-

---

[1] Some writers, following Schumpeter, have made the free, competitive election the essential characteristic of a democratic system. For an elaboration of this view see Morris Janowitz and Dwaine Marvick, *Competitive Pressure and Democratic Consent* (*Michigan Governmental Studies No. 32*, Bureau of Government, Institute of Public Administration, The University of Michigan, Ann Arbor, Mich., 1956), especially the "criteria for competitive democracy," pp. 1–10.

tant part of the full set of influences to which the electorate responds in reaching its own decision. Popular attitudes on issues of public policy ought not to be treated, as they sometimes are, simply as reflections of personality factors, or group memberships, or fixed partisan loyalties. These attitudes should be studied for what they show about public response to actions taken at the decision points of government. Their causal antecedents do not lie wholly within the individual voter's psyche or within his primary group associations. They are influenced to an immense degree by the external realities of national politics and, as such, are factors that tie the electoral process to the other decision processes of American government.

In placing the subject of our work within the context of a larger political system we should be clear about two ways in which this research is restricted. First, this book is about voting behavior only as it occurs in the United States. Parallel studies in different nations might be useful in learning much more about the role of variables in the nature of the political system itself, variables which must be taken as constants when voting behavior within a single system is examined. However, systematic comparison falls beyond the scope of the work reported here.

It should be clear, too, that this is a study of voting in presidential elections. Because the choice of a President has been the most important decision issuing from the electoral process, it is natural that the presidential election should attract wider interest than any other; but in focusing on this decision we do not disparage the importance of other types of elections, and neither do we imply that voting behavior in presidential elections and other national elections is essentially the same. In some respects it is, and many of the findings set forth here can be generalized to nonpresidential elections. But in other respects the choice of a President differs a good deal from other decisions of the electoral process. If, for example, we compare the presidential election with the midterm congressional election, it is plain that more of the potential electorate joins in the choice of a President than in the selection of a Congress when a President is not chosen. And there is evidence that the motivation of those who participate in both choices may differ in the two campaigns. In the presidential election the individual voter is likely to have a better-developed image of the political actors he is asked to appraise. This is particularly true of his image of the candidates themselves; perceptions of the candidates play a measurably greater role in presidential elections than they do in elections for Congress in a nonpresidential year.

It is of course true that each presidential election has imbedded within it a congressional election and a host of state and local contests. As a result, a study of voting behavior in presidential elections is inescapably a study of voting in a variety of other electoral contests as well. But the choice of a President has sufficient impact on these lesser contests so that what we learn about them in a presidential year ought to be extended to other years only with caution.

THE HISTORICAL CONTEXT

Our primary aim in this research is to understand the voting decisions of the national electorate in a manner that transcends some of the specific elements of historical circumstance. But anyone who works with extensive data on a social process as important as a presidential election must feel a responsibility to provide some historical description. Accordingly, much of this volume serves a descriptive as well as a theoretical purpose. We have not felt any tension between these objectives. To the contrary, one of the primary uses of theory is to improve the quality of description. In somewhat severe language, theory may be characterized as a generalized statement of the interrelationships of a set of variables. In these terms, historical description may be said to be a statement of the values assumed by these variables through time. Both characterizations leave a good deal more to be said, but they emphasize the interplay of theory and description. All too often facts are selected for descriptive reporting on an *ad hoc* and impressionistic basis. An important function of systematic theory is that it can identify variables whose values should be reported in describing some aspect of the world of experience. If a theory is accompanied by methods for connecting it to observed data, as any successful theory must be, the theory may guide the descriptive reporter to observations he would not otherwise have made.

The contribution of theory to description may be illustrated by an example drawn from our findings about the political impact of identification with social class. The relationship of class identification to political attitudes and behavior is treated in our work not as a constant but as a variable that will change through time in response to changes in certain other political, social, and economic variables. As a result, we have observed this relationship not simply to show that class identifications and partisan preferences are in fact associated but rather to establish how strongly they are associated at several points in time. The variation we have found in the strength of this association is at once an important datum in the testing of hypotheses and a fact of considerable interest in the description of the presidential politics of this historical period.

If theory can guide historical descriptions, the historical context of most research on human behavior places clear limitations on the development of theory. In evolving and testing his theoretical hypotheses the social scientist usually must depend on what he is permitted to observe by the progress of history. The experimental scientist often escapes this problem, at least in verifying his theoretical statements, by manipulating the variables of his theory. But the variables of large-scale social processes can rarely be manipulated in research, and the historical reality with which the social scientist must deal typically yields data that are inadequate for developing and testing a fully elaborated theory. Their inadequacy has to do partly with the problem of controlling correlated factors: when he examines the relation of two or more variables a social scientist is seldom able to remove by experimental or statistical devices the effects of all additional factors that may influence the variables of immediate interest. But the inadequacy of "natural" data has to do also with what might be called the problem of limited variation. If we return to the idea that theory consists of statements of the interrelationships of variables, it is evident that variables of great importance in human affairs may exhibit little or no change in a given historical period. As a result, the investigator whose work falls in this period may not see the significance of these variables and may fail to incorporate them in his theoretical statements. Even if he does perceive their importance, the absence of variation will prevent a proper test of hypotheses that state the relation of these factors to other variables of his theory.

The data of our research have been collected on three presidential elections, primarily by interviews with people selected by probability sampling to represent the national electorate. This collection of data spans the period from 1948 to 1956, although our interviews are much less full for the Truman-Dewey campaign than for the two Eisenhower-Stevenson elections. Of course, people are able to recall more or less accurately what they have done in the past, and this allows us to extend the historical interval to which some of our data apply. In particular, recollections of past voting behavior and even of previous identifications with the parties can lead to suggestive findings. But the capacity for accurate recall is certainly limited, and most of what we want to know about prior attitudes and behavior is simply impossible to reconstruct. In the main our data have to do with the historical interval extending from Truman's surprise victory in 1948 to the reelection of Eisenhower in 1956.

How great was the political change of these years? It seems clear that some change in the political climate occurred between the election of 1948 and that of 1952. The campaign of Harry Truman and Thomas E. Dewey belonged in many ways to the era of the New Deal. The parties chose as their candidates in 1948 the man who had been Franklin Roosevelt's running mate and who succeeded to the presidency at Roosevelt's death and the man Roosevelt had defeated in his last election campaign. The political alignments of the prewar era had remained remarkably undisturbed through the Second World War, and with the end of the war attention shifted rapidly to the circle of domestic concerns that had absorbed the nation's interest prior to the war. Undoubtedly the salience of these issues was increased by widespread industrial strife, accenting as it did the dimensions of economic interest and social class. The content of differences between the Democratic President and the Republican Congress was strongly reminiscent of issues that had divided the nation in the Roosevelt years.

It is true that the end of the war did not bring peace, and the growing tensions of the conflict with the Soviet Union prevented the nation from insulating itself from the world in the manner of a generation before. In the late 1940's the Republican Party sought to arouse public feeling about the deterioration of America's position abroad, particularly in the Far East, but it was not until the outbreak of the Korean War that the international conflict generated political effects of great importance at home. America's involvement in this unusual war, with its overtones of defeat and slight prospects of victory, created a mood of criticism toward the leadership of the Democratic Administration. In this climate a narrow segment of the population accepted the extreme accusations of the McCarthy era, and a much wider public came to view the Democratic leadership as unable to cope effectively with our problems abroad. With war in the Far East and with evidence of corruption in certain offices of the executive branch in Washington, the feeling grew that the Democratic Administration deserved to be turned out of office.

The Eisenhower candidacy in 1952 seemed perfectly calculated to exploit the dissatisfactions of war and domestic corruption. Eisenhower brought hope of a solution in the Far East and of a change in Washington, and to these appeals he added his great personal popularity. In 1952 Stevenson, too, was perceived as a candidate of attractive personal qualities, and his connection with the sins of his party was thought to be slight. Yet he could hardly have been expected to leave as great an imprint on the public consciousness as did his opponent. The years from 1952 to 1956 apparently secured still further the bases of Eisenhower's electoral strength. The end of the Korean War enhanced his image as a military statesman who could assure peace. Public response to his personal qualities remained exceptionally favorable. And the force of Democratic appeals was reduced by the economic prosperity of Eisenhower's first term and the failure of his administration to disturb the basic social reforms of the New Deal.

The Eisenhower victory of 1952 extended even into the South, seeming to mark the end of an era. Yet it would be easy to overstate the extent of political change in the preceding four years. The events of these years had not swept away the appeal of the Democratic Party as the agent of economic recovery and social reform. In the election of 1952 the party's strength registered clearly in the size of its congressional vote. The Democrats restored their majorities in both houses of Congress in 1954 and two years later held this control under the pressure of Eisenhower's increased electoral majority. In the three presidential elections within the span of our research the Republican proportion of the total vote has varied by more than twelve percentage points. Yet the Republican proportion of the congressional vote in these same elections has not varied by as much as four percentage points. If the congressional vote reflects more faithfully the stable partisan loyalties of the electorate, the aggregate statistics of the period suggest that these loyalties have shifted relatively little.[2]

Despite the turnover of party control it seems likely that the stabilities of the years from 1948 to 1956 were more important than the aspects of change. Perhaps there were within this period the seeds of profound political change; we can only guess the full impact on American politics of the Supreme Court's decision in 1954 striking down segregation in the public schools. Yet we have not found in this interval what we take to be the mark of fundamental electoral change —an asymmetric shift of long-term partisan commitments by substantial numbers of people who have passed the years of early adulthood in which these allegiances usually become fixed. Though the data supporting this conclusion are reserved for a later chapter, the finding is worth mentioning here, since it states an important descriptive characteristic of the period under review and since it suggests a limitation

[2] For an evaluation of this premise in terms of survey data see Chapter 5, Table 5-1, and accompanying discussion.

that the historical context has imposed on our research. Because these stable party attachments are of far-reaching importance in the orientation of political attitudes and behavior, voting research must seek to state the conditions under which they will change. But identifications with party have shown little variation in the historical period of our work. Neither war, nor economic distress, nor the appeal of a compelling leader has disturbed the partisan allegiance of a wide segment of the electorate. As a result, our understanding of change must remain incomplete.

SECTION II
POLITICAL ATTITUDES AND THE VOTE

In unraveling the causal threads leading to the vote we begin with
the immediate psychological influences on the voting act. By casting
a vote the individual acts toward a political world whose objects he
perceives and evaluates in some fashion; the view he has formed of
the presidential candidates, of the two major parties, and of various
political issues and politically involved groups has a profound influence on his behavior. In Walter Lippmann's phrase, the voter has a
picture of the world of politics in his head, and the nature of this
picture is a key to understanding what he does at the polls.

The *content* of popular perceptions of national politics is the focus
of Chapter 2, where we examine the qualitative themes the electorate
has associated with the parties and candidates during the period of our
research. Because we have recorded these themes in successive elections, we are able to say how the public's image of the political world
has changed through time, and the description of change will be a
central feature of the chapter. This kind of account raises naturally
the question of how change is induced. Only a partial answer can
be given, but we are able to draw some inferences about the dynamics
of mass percepts by confronting the record of change in popular
perceptions with what we know has happened in the wider political
environment.

The significance of political perceptions for behavior depends largely
on their evaluative character. The popular image of parties and candidates is not neutral, and the fact that it is colored by positive and
negative feeling vests it with great motivational importance. This
motivational role will concern us in the two latter chapters of the
section. In Chapter 3 we treat the impact of political attitudes on
the individual's partisan choice at the polls. We will see that this
choice springs immediately from a matrix of psychological forces, and
that by taking account of attitudes toward six discernible elements of

politics we can explain quite well the individual's choice between rival parties or candidates. Moreover, we will see that the internal coherence of this system of attitude forces has a good deal of significance for other aspects of voting. In particular, by taking account of the extent of conflict in the individual's political attitudes we are able to say more surely whether his partisan choice will be made early or late and whether he will cast a straight or split-ticket ballot.

No aspect of voting is of more fundamental importance than the individual's decision whether to vote at all. In Chapter 4 we shift our attention from the partisan decision to influences on voting turnout. We will see that partisan preference and turnout are bound together by the fact that the attitude forces which influence the individual's partisan choice may influence his decision whether to vote. Yet the contribution of partisan attitude to the explanation of turnout is a limited one, and additional psychological factors are needed to account for this aspect of voting behavior. In seeking a better explanation of turnout we will focus primarily on the extent to which the individual is psychologically involved in politics. The emotional commitment that people have toward political affairs varies widely between individuals, and political involvement is of far-reaching importance for voting turnout. Chapter 4 will deal with several areas of the individual's orientation to politics, areas that reflect a common dimension of involvement yet which are in some measure distinct. The extent of a person's interest in the campaign, his concern over its outcome, his sense of political effectiveness, and his sense of citizen duty all will be seen to have a clear influence on whether he joins in the electoral process.

chapter 2

Perceptions of the Parties and Candidates

If we are to understand what leads the voter to his decision at the polls we must know how he sees the things to which this decision relates. In casting a vote the individual acts toward a world of politics in which he perceives the personalities, issues, and the parties and other groupings of a presidential contest. His image of these matters may seem at times exceedingly ill-formed, but his behavior makes sense subjectively in terms of the way these political objects appear to him. As a result, measuring perceptions and evaluations of the elements of politics is a first charge on our energies in the explanation of the voting act. Indeed, it would be difficult to overstate the importance of the perceptions formed by a mass electorate for the decisions it must periodically render. Hyman has written of this aspect of voting:

Men are urged to certain ends but the political scene in which they act is perceived and given meaning. Some cognitive map accompanies their movements toward their ends.[1]

It is the cognitive map of national politics held by the American electorate that is our concern here. Plainly the map is a colored one. The elements of politics that are visible to the electorate are not simply seen; they are evaluated as well. Evaluation is the stuff of political life, and the cognitive image formed by the individual of the political world tends to be positively and negatively toned in its several parts. This mixture of cognition and evaluation, of belief and attitude, of percept and affect is so complete that we will speak of the individual's *cognitive and affective map of politics*.

The flow of historical reality has enormous influence on the elec-

[1] Herbert Hyman, *Political Socialization* (The Free Press, Glencoe, Ill., 1959), p. 18.

torate's perceptions of its political environment. This chapter is concerned first of all with the way the changing political environment affects the public image of the parties and their candidates, the non-party groupings that are involved in the political process, and the issues of national policy. Yet percept and reality are not the same, and to gain an understanding of the way change in the external world of politics alters the popular image of political objects, we will ultimately have to consider not only the "real" properties of these objects but certain processes of individual psychology as well.

The motivational significance of these percepts is such that understanding the way a changing political environment can redraw the popular map of politics will explain a good deal of the dynamics of electoral change. This problem is so important that any extensive body of data on the changing image of politics held by the national electorate ought to be pressed hard for the insights it can yield.[2]

A CASE STUDY IN CHANGE

At the beginning of the Eisenhower years our interviews with a cross section of the electorate explored the public image of Eisenhower himself, of his Democratic opponent, of the Republican and Democratic Parties, and of the groups and issues that the parties and candidates were thought to affect. These materials were duplicated by interviews with a new sample of the electorate in the campaign of 1956, at the end of Eisenhower's first term.[3] By comparing interview responses at these two points in time we have a remarkable portrait of public feeling toward the elements of politics in this period and of changes in its content through an interval of four years. Percept and affect are freely mixed in the view of parties and candidates held by the

---

[2] Yet several characteristics of our data limit the inferences we are able to draw. Our observations have to do with the change of a relatively brief interval. The data of a single four-year period can suggest hypotheses; they can hardly supply their proof. Also, our interviews in this interval were taken at two points in time, four years apart. To unravel the problem of change we would want ideally to sample the opinions of the electorate more frequently. Lastly, our data describe only the dependent variable of the causal process that is of interest. What we have measured are public cognitions and evaluations of politics and not the elements of the wider political environment that we have cast in a causal role.

[3] For this purpose a standard set of eight free-answer questions was used in the preelection interviews of 1952 and 1956. For each of the parties, one question sought favorable responses and one unfavorable responses, and for each of the candidates, one question sought favorable comment and one unfavorable comment.

electorate, and the qualities attributed to these objects evoke strong evaluative feeling.

The first historical period to leave an unmistakable imprint upon these responses is that of the Great Depression. Three marks of the depression experience and its political aftermath are discernible in the responses given in the first Eisenhower-Stevenson election. First of all, the Democratic Party was widely perceived in 1952 as the party of prosperity and the Republican Party as the party of depression. Great numbers of responses in that year associated the Democrats with good times, the Republicans with economic distress. Secondly, there was in 1952 a broad measure of approval for the domestic policies of the New Deal and Fair Deal. Favorable references to the domestic policies arising out of the Roosevelt and Truman Administrations were quite frequent. And as a third legacy of the depression experience, there was in 1952 a strong sense of good feeling toward the Democratic Party and hostility toward the Republican Party on the basis of the groups each was thought to favor. The Democratic Party was widely perceived as the friend of lower status groups; the Republican Party in opposite terms.

We do not know to what extent these attitudes had lessened in force from the mid-Depression years. Yet it is remarkable how strongly they carried over into the 1950's despite the efforts of Republican presidential candidates in every election since 1936 to create a more liberal image of the party. With a Republican President elected at last, the events of 1952 to 1956, however, challenged several of the assumptions on which the attitudes of an earlier era had rested. In the first place, a Republican occupied the White House in these years without a serious break in the nation's good times. With the recession of 1957–1958 yet to be experienced, the influence on public attitude of the nation's high nonfarm prosperity during the first Eisenhower Administration is suggested by Table 2-1. References to prosperity and depression declined 50 per cent from 1952 to 1956. And four years of Republican good times destroyed most of a 14-1 margin the Democrats had had in the partisanship of these responses. After haunting every Republican candidate for President since 1932, memories of the Hoover Depression had receded, at least temporarily, as a direct force in American politics.

A second aspect of this four-year interval that might be expected to challenge the attitudes of the past was the willingness of the Eisenhower Administration to embrace most of the reforms of the New Deal. This disposition to accept and even extend the social welfare policies of the previous twenty years undoubtedly lessened an impor-

Table 2-1. References to Prosperity and Depression

	1952[a]	1956
Pro-Democratic and Anti-Republican	974	316
Pro-Republican and Anti-Democratic	70	213
Totals	1044	529

[a] In this and subsequent tables the number of responses in 1952 has been increased by the ratio of the size of the 1956 sample to the size of the 1952 sample to make possible a direct comparison of frequencies in the two years. The effect of the adjustment is to equate frequencies whose size relative to the size of their respective samples is the same. In reading these tables it should be kept in mind that one respondent could make more than one reference; hence the number of references may be larger than the number of individuals mentioning a given subject.

tant difference the public had perceived between the parties. The extent of this change is suggested by the summary of references to social welfare policies in Table 2-2. The references of policies of this sort was reduced by a third between these election campaigns, and the proportion of responses associating the Democrats favorably or the

Table 2-2. References to Social Welfare Policies[a]

	1952	1956
Pro-Democratic and Anti-Republican	421	259
Pro-Republican and Anti-Democratic	96	101
Totals	517	360

[a] This tabulation is limited to domestic policies clearly in the area of social welfare. References to farm policy, civil rights legislation, etc., are not included.

Republicans unfavorably with any of these policies declined substantially. As a token of this shift, the Democratic advantage on social security was reduced by two-thirds from 1952 to 1956.

The Eisenhower Administration was not equally successful, however, in dispelling the popular belief that the Republicans were the party of the great and the Democrats the party of the small. Despite the change in public attitude toward the Republican Party on matters of economic and social welfare, the years 1952 to 1956 did not lessen this aspect of the image of the parties fixed in the Depression era. A large number of responses in 1956 still approved of the Democratic

Party and disapproved of the Republican Party on the basis of the groups each was felt to support, as may be seen in Table 2-3. The Democrats were still thought to help groups primarily of lower status: the common people, working people, the laboring man,

Table 2-3. References to Groups

	1952	1956
Pro-Democratic and Anti-Republican	1438	1659
Pro-Republican and Anti-Democratic	256	294
Totals	1694	1953

Negroes, farmers, and (in 1956 only) the small businessman. The Republicans, on the other hand, were thought to help those of higher status: big businessmen, the upper class, the well-to-do.

Changes in these parts of the popular view of the parties show the impact that changes in the external world can have on political attitude. The forces underlying these changes may be more sharply defined if we consider the farm sector of the economy. The prosperity of the Eisenhower years was felt only uncertainly on the nation's farms, and the posture of the Administration toward farm problems aroused widespread opposition. As a result, the moderation of public attitude toward the economic and social welfare record of the Republican Party did not extend to matters of farm policy. References to farm policy increased markedly between 1952 and 1956 and were strongly Democratic in partisanship. Moreover, references linking the Republicans unfavorably or the Democrats favorably with the welfare of farmers as a group were much more frequent in the latter year.

Other elements of the historical setting from which the attitudes of these years evolved are apparent in the responses given in these campaigns. Events more recent than the Great Depression had received wide attention in the years preceding the 1952 election. The worldwide struggle with the Soviet Union had culminated in a limited war that was widely seen as having exposed the nation to a humiliating defeat without having gained any essential end. The years preceding the 1952 election were also marked by increasing publicity about evidences of corruption in the federal government. Each of these more contemporary sets of events left an impression clearly discernible in the responses of 1952. References to foreign policy and the Korean War were of high frequency and strongly Republican in partisanship. And great numbers of responses cited misdeeds of the Democratic Administration and the need for a change in party control of the executive branch.

The attitudes, too, were modified by the unfolding of events from 1952 to 1956. Several changes in the external political world are reflected in the perceptions of the parties and candidates held by the electorate. In the first place, the ending of the Korean War enhanced the impression that the Republicans were better able than the Democrats to assure peace. Mr. Eisenhower and his party were widely supported in 1952 in the belief that they might end the Korean conflict. Their success in doing so and in preventing the outbreak of hostilities involving the United States elsewhere in the world added to public confidence that the cause of peace would be better served if the Republicans were continued in office. References to war and peace in 1952 were pro-Republican or anti-Democratic by a ratio greater than seven

Table 2-4. References to War and Peace

	1952	1956
Pro-Democratic and Anti-Republican	68	15
Pro-Republican and Anti-Democratic	514	595
Totals	582	610

to one. By 1956 the ratio had increased five times, owing to the virtual disappearance of comments favorable to the Democrats or unfavorable to the Republicans.

Through the first Eisenhower Administration, moreover, the Republican advantage in foreign affairs came to center much more completely on questions of war and peace. The finding of fault with the Democratic handling of the early cold war conflict, particularly in eastern Europe and China, seemed to lessen with the passage of time. And there was apparently a greater sense that what a Republican Administration might be able to do in these troubled areas was not widely different from what had been done by a Democratic Administration. The trend of these responses is shown in Table 2-5.

Table 2-5. References to Other Foreign Issues

	1952	1956
Pro-Democratic and Anti-Republican	143	145
Pro-Republican and Anti-Democratic	567	342
Totals	710	487

It is noteworthy that the total volume of comment about war and peace and other issues of foreign affairs was small relative to the level of other sorts of responses in these years. The Second World War as well as the Korean War had intervened between the experience of the Depression and the years 1952 to 1956. Yet the number of responses reflecting the Great Depression and its political aftermath was much greater than the number referring to issues raised by these wars or any other aspect of foreign affairs. Neither conflict seems to have had a great and lasting impact on popular political attitudes. By comparison with the impact of the Civil War, the effect of the wars of the twentieth century seems slight indeed.

Public concern about the corruption issue subsided rapidly with the Democratic Party out of power. However strong the sense of Democratic sin four years earlier, the party's loss of power seems to

Table 2-6. References to Corruption and "Time for a Change" Theme

	1952	1956
Pro-Republican references to corruption	546	93
Pro-Republican references to need for a change	490	. . .
Pro-Democratic references to corruption	. . .	20
Pro-Democratic references to need for a change	. . .	23

have accomplished its expiation by 1956. The swift decline of comment of this sort suggests that mismanagement and corruption are not issues that are easily kept alive after a change in control of the government.

At least one aspect of our recent political history is notable for the relatively slight extent to which it influenced public attitude toward parties and candidates in these years. In view of the enormous furor over internal subversion and the conduct of Senator McCarthy, it is astonishing to discover that the issue of domestic Communism was little mentioned by the public in 1952. The third element of the slogan reminding the electorate of "Corruption, Korea, and Communism" apparently was wide of the mark. Corruption and Korea were salient partisan issues for the electorate in that year. Communism, in the sense of domestic subversion, was not. Fewer responses touched the issue of domestic Communism in 1952 than referred to such esoteric subjects as the Point Four program and foreign economic aid and Mr. Stevenson's marital problems. By 1956 the issue had virtually disappeared.

Of the elements of politics that had emerged relatively recently as objects of partisan feeling, none was of greater importance in these years than the presidential candidates. The fact that the great prize of American politics is won by popular endorsement of a single man means that the appearance of new candidates may alter by a good deal an existing balance of electoral strength between the parties. An inspection of popular response to the candidates in these years suggests the correctness of the Republican strategy of using a figure who had won immense public esteem outside politics to overturn a long-established Democratic majority. The content of this response tells something, too, about the changes that may occur in public reaction to the figures of presidential politics.

An inspection of references to matters of group interest and to domestic issues in 1952 and 1956 makes clear that response of this

Table 2-7. References to Groups

	1952	1956
Associated with the Republican Party	563	663
Associated with the Democratic Party	855	886
Associated with Eisenhower	112	219
Associated with Stevenson	164	185
Totals	1694	1953

sort was associated more with the parties than it was with either of the candidates. A summary of these references strongly suggests that the attitudes they reflect were for the most part formed prior to the entry of Mr. Eisenhower and Mr. Stevenson into the political arena. In 1952 neither of these men was perceived in these terms to any significant degree. Although each candidate evoked somewhat more responses of this sort four years later, the numbers of responses connecting either with group interest or issues of domestic policy were still small by comparison with the volumes of comment on these mat-

Table 2-8. References to Domestic Issues

	1952	1956
Associated with the Republican Party	1276	898
Associated with the Democratic Party	1825	1001
Associated with Eisenhower	164	322
Associated with Stevenson	162	357
Totals	3427	2578

ters associated with the two parties. With respect to Mr. Eisenhower, this result was due in part to a moderation in domestic controversy during his first Administration. But it must also be an extraordinary comment on the way Mr. Eisenhower had interpreted his office. In view of the enormous responsibilities for legislative, partisan, and executive leadership that attach to the presidency, it is difficult to believe that a man could serve four years in this office and yet be associated with domestic issues to as slight a degree as an opponent who was wholly without public office in the same period.

Mr. Eisenhower was of course much more widely associated with issues of foreign affairs. Owing to his background, somewhat more than a third of all references to war and peace and to other foreign issues in 1952 were associated with Eisenhower. In 1956, with a smaller volume of total comment about foreign affairs, this fraction

Table 2-9. References to Foreign Issues

	1952	1956
Associated with the Republican Party	336	329
Associated with the Democratic Party	420	183
Associated with Eisenhower	546	481
Associated with Stevenson	62	58
Totals	1364	1051

was increased to nearly one-half. Both major parties were frequently linked with foreign issues in the first of these elections, but with the Democratic Party's record receding in time, relatively fewer of these comments referred to the Democrats in the second campaign. In neither year did Mr. Stevenson make any marked impression on the electorate in relation to foreign affairs. In view of his great concern with foreign policy, the attention he gave to foreign issues in his campaign addresses, and his travels abroad between these elections, this fact suggests how deep may be the gulf that separates the public's view of a candidate and the image he seeks to project. Mr. Stevenson probably had had more contact with foreign affairs than most presidential candidates. Yet this contact failed to cross the threshold of public awareness.

We have already called attention to the likelihood that a new figure in national politics will be evaluated by the public partly in terms of his connection with his party. This was true of both Mr. Eisenhower and Mr. Stevenson in these years. In each campaign, references were made to the fact that a candidate was the representative of his party and bore the party symbol. The extent to which Eisenhower and Stevenson were evaluated in these terms may be seen in Table 2-10. These figures make clear that the tendency to evaluate the candidates in terms of party was less pronounced in the second of these elections.

Table 2-10.　References to Candidates in Terms of Party

	1952	1956
Favorable to Eisenhower	121	57
Unfavorable to Eisenhower	220	162
Favorable to Stevenson	264	202
Unfavorable to Stevenson	360	64
Totals	965	485

Although a candidate is likely to be seen partly in terms of his connection with party and with issues of public policy and matters of group interest, he will be evaluated as well in terms of personal attributes. In the presidential elections of the 1950's most references to the candidates dealt with their record and experience, their abilities, and their personal characteristics. Since General Eisenhower entered politics as an established public figure, it is not surprising that his personal attributes were much more fully described in public response than were those of Governor Stevenson. In the campaign of 1952 references of this sort to Eisenhower exceeded in number references to personal qualities of Stevenson by more than sixty per cent. The figures of Table 2-11 indicate that at the end of Eisenhower's first term his personal characteristics were far better known to the public than were those of Mr. Stevenson. Nonetheless, a profound change in public attitude toward Stevenson is evident in these data. The perception of Stevenson's personal characteristics was less full in 1952 than

Table 2-11.　References to Personal Attributes of the Candidates

	1952	1956
Favorable to Eisenhower	2256	2226
Unfavorable to Eisenhower	906	854
Totals	3162	3080
Favorable to Stevenson	1416	1045
Unfavorable to Stevenson	555	1184
Totals	1971	2229

that of Eisenhower's; but it was warmly favorable. By 1956 the response to Stevenson was much less approving. More than half the references to his personal attributes in the latter year were unfavorable.

A finer analysis of response to the candidates brings to light a number of changes in their public images between the two campaigns.

Table 2-12. Favorable References to Eisenhower and Stevenson[a]

	Eisenhower		Stevenson	
	1952	1956	1952	1956
Generally good man, capable, experienced	301	330	200	190
Record and experience				
Military experience	202	111	—	—
Record in Europe	250	94	—	—
Political and other experience	57	106	354	115
Qualifications and abilities				
Good leader, knows how to handle people	138	107	19	20
Good administrator	64	26	36	10
Strong, decisive	53	32	7	11
Independent	70	17	32	21
Educated	97	62	149	180
Good speaker	31	42	141	100
Personal qualities				
Integrity, ideals	271	291	111	77
Sense of duty, patriotism	70	74	25	20
Inspiring, inspires confidence	53	39	14	4
Religious	19	85	7	2
Kind, warm	11	41	11	8
Sincere	63	126	33	33
Likeable, nice personality, I like him	220	363	91	77
Good family life	26	57	9	4

[a] Since a number of minor categories have been omitted from Table 2-12, the totals are somewhat smaller than the entries of Table 2-11.

The character of these changes suggests several clues to the forces shaping perceptions of the candidates in these years. A full classification of references to Eisenhower suggests that his appeal, already strongly personal in 1952, became overwhelmingly so in 1956. In the earlier campaign, Eisenhower's military experience and record in

Europe were clearly remembered. By 1956 these themes had receded, without the substitution of nearly as many references to his record and experience as president. Moreover, references to his skills as leader and administrator were fewer in 1956 than before. It was the response to personal qualities—to his sincerity, his integrity and sense of duty, his virtue as a family man, his religious devotion, and his sheer likeableness—that rose substantially in the second campaign. These frequencies leave the strong impression that in 1956 Eisenhower was honored not so much for his performance as President as for the quality of his person.

The flaws in the Eisenhower image were few, and in neither campaign were they matters for which the candidate could be held entirely accountable. In 1952 a large number of references cited Eisenhower's background as a military man (446) and his lack of experience in civil government (198). Presumably his induction as President and subsequent nonmilitary bearing quieted most of these doubts (only 16 references to lack of experience in 1956), though comments on his military background were still given in 1956 (63 references). Critical response in the latter year dealt primarily with the issue of his health (386) and his capacity to be a full-time president (64). Other than this the only unfavorable reference of any frequency was the doubt that Eisenhower as President was wholly his own man (73).

The popular response to Stevenson showed a general lessening of enchantment in his second appeal to the electorate, but several details of this loss in esteem stand out. The benefit to Mr. Stevenson of having been Governor of Illinois, as measured by references to his record and experience, seems largely to have been dissipated after four years. References to his experience in public service dropped quite low in 1956, and comments about his lack of experience increased over the four-year period from 25 to 72. Also, references to Stevenson's personal qualities, which had been substantially favorable in his first campaign, were much less so in his second. Responses like "I don't like him" increased from 34 to 159. Surprisingly, Stevenson's divorce seemed more on the public's mind in the latter year (from 85 to 137 references). Finally, the response to Mr. Stevenson's campaign performance was much more critical in 1956 (261 references) than in 1952 (103 references).

THE DYNAMICS OF MASS PERCEPTS

The materials we have reviewed disclose the elements of presidential politics, not as they were, but as the public perceived them in the

Eisenhower years. Taken together, the cognitive and affective themes recorded in our interviews suggest the "sense" the electorate made of the objects it acted toward in two elections. When they are laid against what we know of the objects themselves, the images found in these interviews suggest, too, some general ideas about the factors that have shaped their content.

Generalization and the Permanence of Objects. The individual voter sees the several elements of national politics as more than a collection of discrete, unrelated objects. After all, they are parts of one political system and are connected in the real world by a variety of relations that are visible in some degree to the electorate. A *candidate* is the nominee of his *party;* party and candidate are oriented to the same *issues* or *groups,* and so forth. Moreover, we may assume that the individual strives to give order and coherence to his image of these objects. As a means of achieving order, the transfer of cognitive attributes and affective values from one object to another undoubtedly plays an important role. A good deal of psychological research leads us to assume that under certain conditions the properties that one political element is perceived to have will be generalized to another, or that the emotion directed toward one object will be extended to a second. The "conditions" of this transfer may be exceedingly simple—as two elements bearing the same party label—although in the intellective processes of the most sophisticated, politically involved portion of the electorate they are probably very complex.

The fact that one element of politics may color another in both a cognitive and an affective sense is of especial importance because political objects enter public awareness at different times and have greatly different degrees of permanence. The world of politics is full of novelty, yet some of its elements persist for relatively long periods. Moreover, the features of these objects that are most widely known may heighten the sense of their unchanging character. At the simplest level, the elements of politics, like so much else in the external world, are known to the individual by name, and these symbols are of considerable cognitive importance to the electorate. What is more, a good deal else about the objects of politics may be characterized by symbols, such as the terms "New Deal" or "Fair Deal," whose persistence through time may give the objects an unchanging aspect despite wide changes in their "real" properties.

The most enduring objects of the political environment are of course the Republican and Democratic Parties, and the relative permanence of our major parties has two main consequences for the dynamics of popular attitude. First, the novel objects of presidential politics may receive a marked initial coloration by reason of their association with one or the other of the parties. The frequencies of Table 2-10 show that nearly a thousand references to party were among the responses to the two new candidates for President in 1952. Second, perception and feeling that were initially associated with other objects may survive in the image of the parties after the elements from which they arose have left the political environment. To a great extent the image of the Republican and Democratic Parties in 1952 and 1956 *was* the public's response to issues and events of the past generation, whereas popular perceptions of Eisenhower and Stevenson seemed to be fashioned of more current materials.

The Threshold of Awareness. A great deal of change in the electorate's map of politics can be explained in terms of what has and what has not penetrated the public consciousness.[4] In the electorate as a whole the level of attention to politics is so low that what the public is exposed to must be highly visible—even stark—if it is to have an impact on opinion. The evidential basis of this remark must await the discussion of later chapters, but its correctness is strongly implied by some of the frequencies we have examined. For example, despite a concentration on foreign issues by Mr. Stevenson, which must have been at least as great as that of any candidate in this country, the public was largely unaware of his positions. Nor in some respects did Mr. Eisenhower fare better as President. Despite the fact that his action or inaction as Chief Executive had wide impact on the course of our affairs at home, the public connected him with issues of domestic policy only to a slight degree in 1956.

Some implications of the low salience that most of national politics has for the electorate may seem fairly novel. For example, it is not unlikely that most new Presidents take office without their stance toward issues or groups having had much impact on popular attitude. What perceptions the public has are likely to be highly derivative carry-overs from perceptions of the President's party. In this respect the extent in 1952 of public knowledge of Eisenhower's orientation in world affairs, arising as it did out of the impact of his career as a soldier-diplomat, must have been quite unusual. It is largely *after*

---

[4] It is here that information is most needed on communication variables. Awareness is partly a matter of motivation and predisposition: the individual is aware of things he wants to attend. But it is also a matter of sheer currency or visibility, as the success of modern advertising suggests. Hence, the decisions of those who control communication are partial determinants of public awareness, and more information is needed about them.

the President has taken office and has assumed the position of match-less visibility in American politics that his image begins to acquire the large number of issue themes we might expect. The acquisition may be dramatically sudden, as it probably was in the case of Roosevelt; it may be slow and uneven, as it clearly was in the case of Eisenhower.

The Social Bases of Stability. The stability of mass percepts de-pends importantly on how well they are bound into the social fabric. To make this point clear let us return to the problem of the impact on subsequent attitude of the wars in which America has been in-volved. We have remarked that the world wars of the twentieth century did surprisingly little to remake the partisan perceptions held by the electorate. Of course these wars had a deep impress on American thinking in a variety of ways. But they left in their wake relatively few issues that would continue to divide the electorate, and, what is most important, except perhaps for the alienation of those of German ethnicity[5] from the administration party, these issues failed to coincide well with stable groupings within the population. The impact of the Civil War was very different, opening as it did issues of intense partisan contest, which coincided very closely with enduring regional and racial fissures in the social order. The stability of percepts arising out of the Civil War experience undoubtedly was greatly reinforced by the fact that they became enmeshed in conflict between enduring social groupings.

Additional weight is lent this view if we consider the group themes associated with the parties and candidates in the Eisenhower years. We have said that these references usually implied a status dimension: the Democratic Party was approved for championing lower status groups, the Republican Party disapproved for failing to do so or for favoring high status groups. The group themes associated with the two parties actually increased in vitality between 1952 and 1956; the vitality of these group-related percepts may be due in part to the fact that they are supported by the mechanisms that conserve social norms. Here the group may serve not only as an element of politics to which parties and candidates adopt some attitude; it may also serve as a reference group whose perceived opinion reinforces the individual's own perception of what is the stance toward the group of other actors in the political environment.

To say this much is to raise the broader question of how perceptions

[5] For evidence on this point see Samuel Lubell, *The Future of American Politics* (Harper and Brothers, New York, 1951), especially Chapter 7, "The Myth of Isolationism," pp. 129–157.

of the political world differ between the groupings that make up the whole electorate. The measurements of this chapter have been of the composite image held by the total population, but the fact of differences between groups is clear enough. Although a survey of these differences is beyond the scope of discussion here, we may note that the stability of the partisan perceptions dividing the electorate will depend in part on the extent to which these divisions coincide with enduring social groupings.

chapter 3
Partisan Choice

The cluster of percepts and feelings that make up the popular image of the parties and candidates are ultimately of interest for their effect on what the electorate does. When the public must act toward the elements of politics, as it must every four years in choosing a President, evaluations of these subjects are of fundamental importance as guides to the electorate's choice. The popular image of politics is continuously changing, at least in its detail, with changes in the wider political environment and in the circumstances of individuals and groups within the electorate. Yet as the moment of decision arrives periodically, the image as currently formed has a profound influence on public choice.

In assessing the impact on behavior of the public's cognitive and affective map of politics we will have to describe this map in terms of *individual* attitude. In this chapter we will conceive the individual's evaluative orientations toward the several elements of politics as a system of partisan attitudes and examine the place of this system among the psychological forces governing behavior.

The motivational role of perceptions of the wider political environment deserves greater attention than it has received in electoral research. It is not true that attitudes toward the several elements of politics are only reflections of party loyalty or group memberships or of other factors that may lead to perceptual distortion. To suppose that they are is to understate the importance of changes in the properties of what the individual sees in his environment. Changes in the external realities of politics can have effects on popular feeling within every partisan or social grouping in the electorate. The truth of this statement is easily seen if we observe that attitudes toward the objects of politics, varying through time, can explain short-term fluctuations in partisan division of the vote, whereas party loyalties and social characteristics, which are relatively inert through time, account but poorly for these shifts.

PSYCHOLOGICAL FORCES ON BEHAVIOR

However important more remote factors may be in the causation of behavior, if we limit our inquiry to their relation to the vote we miss important elements of motivation. For this reason we begin our search for causality at the psychological level and conceive of the voting act as the resultant of attitudinal forces. The effect of all factors leading to behavior is finally expressed in the direction and intensity of the forces of a psychological field, in which the individual's attitudes toward the elements of politics have a central place. The elements of national politics—the presidential candidates, questions of group interest, the issues of domestic and foreign policy, the performance of the parties in the conduct of government—are not simply perceived by the individual; they are evaluated as well. Orientations to these objects, seen by the voter as positive or negative, comprise a system of partisan attitudes that is of primary importance for the voting act. The nature of this system and its significance for behavior concern us here.

Of course these partisan attitudes do not exhaust the set of psychological forces that may affect the voting act. For most persons, the partisan decision at the polls depends largely on attitudes of this sort, and a good deal of evidence on this point will be offered here. But for other persons additional forces, such as the perceived preferences of primary group associates, come to bear, as they do in the case of a wife who votes her husband's preferences either against her own inclinations or without developing perceptions of her political environment. In saying this we are not raising the question of what the antecedents of the partisan attitudes may be. In *most* cases information picked up through face-to-face contact with family, work associates, and friends will have some influence on the individual's attitudes toward the elements of presidential politics. We are speaking rather of the cases in which psychological forces other than the partisan attitudes —or even contradicting these attitudes—are of greater importance for behavior.

To assess the impact of the partisan attitudes on behavior we need to reshape the materials on perceptions of politics to measure the psychological forces acting on the individual. From our knowledge of what political objects are visible to the public and the characteristics of attitude toward these objects we have defined six dimensions of individual partisan feeling. In the elections of 1952 and 1956 the elements of politics that seemed most clearly to be objects of popular attitude were these: the personal attributes of Stevenson; the personal attributes of Eisenhower; the groups involved in politics and the questions of group interest affecting them; the issues of domestic policy; the issues of foreign policy; and the comparative record of the two parties in managing the affairs of government. We have conceived evaluative orientations toward these classes of things as six dimensions of partisan attitude. Of course not everyone articulated feeling about each; most people in our samples expressed attitudes toward less than the full set.

To locate the individual on these dimensions of attitude we have used the same sequence of free-answer questions about the parties and candidates that elicited the responses analyzed in Chapter 2. By classifying each answer according to the type of object involved we were able to allocate all the responses given by our samples in 1952 and 1956 and to construct six measures of individual partisan feeling. The measures were designed to show the partisan *direction* of an individual's attitude toward a given element of politics—that is, they were constructed to tell us whether a person's attitude was pro-Republican, neutral, or pro-Democratic—and to show the *intensity* of partisan attitude—i.e., for other than neutral feeling, they were fashioned to tell us how strongly pro-Republican or pro-Democratic was the affect directed toward a political object. With measures having these properties we are able to examine the influence of these psychological forces on the voting act.

We will consider several characteristics of the vote that seem to depend on the presence or absence of conflict between the partisan attitudes. A person may form distinct but conflicting evaluations of the several elements of politics, and the consequences of this conflict for electoral behavior are of substantial importance.

PARTISAN ATTITUDE AND VOTING CHOICE

That the partisan decision of the individual is profoundly affected by the psychological forces we have measured seems clear in the data of several election campaigns. To illustrate the extent of the dependence of this choice on each dimension of partisan feeling, let us examine the behavior of voters in 1956 according to the direction and intensity of their feeling toward the personal attributes of Eisenhower. The variation of behavior across this dimension of attitudes was almost as great as possible, as may be seen in Table 3-1. At the negative end of the scale, those whose image of Eisenhower was quite unfavorable voted Democratic in nearly every case. Among those whose attitude

Table 3-1. Relation of Attitude toward Eisenhower
to Party Division of the Vote, 1956

	Attitude toward Eisenhower								
	Unfavorable				Favorable				
									+
							+	+
	−					+	+	+
	−	−			+	+	+	+
	−	−	−	0	+	+	+	+	+
Voted Democratic	94%	81%	79%	56%	31%	21%	14%	6%	2%
Voted Republican	6	19	21	44	69	79	86	94	98
	100%	100%	100%	100%	100%	100%	100%	100%	100%
Number of cases	35	73	151	275	232	216	139	99	46

toward Eisenhower was more favorable, the Republican proportion of the vote was greater, increasing without exception as we move toward the other end of the scale. When the extreme positive end is reached, those whose image of Eisenhower was strongly favorable voted Republican in virtually every case. In the extreme differences of partisan behavior it discloses, Table 3-1 is quite representative of the associations we have found between each dimension of attitude and the individual's partisan choice.

Yet we may easily exaggerate how well public attitude toward any single element of presidential politics, such as the Republican candidate, can account for the voting act. Table 3-1 does show that the individual's evaluation, positive or negative, of one of the candidates could be of such strength that it would insure a vote in the same partisan direction. But only a slight fraction of the electorate had feelings toward Eisenhower that were extremely strong. The frequencies given in the bottom row of the table indicate that most of the electorate had less intense attitudes and fell in the scale categories where behavior was far less unidirectional. The extreme differences in behavior between the ends of the scale need to be coupled with the fact that most of the electorate was nearer the middle of the scale, if we are to get a correct idea of how well this dimension of attitude alone could explain the choices of individual voters in 1956.

The increase of our power to explain the voting act by taking account of attitude toward more than a single element of politics may be shown by combining a second dimension of feeling with attitude toward Eisenhower and observing the joint effects of two psychological forces on behavior. For this purpose let us consider the joint relation to the vote in 1956 of attitude toward Eisenhower and partisan feeling related to issues of domestic policy. Table 3-2 shows the proportion

Table 3-2. Relation of Attitude toward Eisenhower and Attitude on Domestic Issues to Per Cent Voting Republican, 1956[a]

Attitude toward Eisenhower[b]	Attitude on Domestic Issues[b] — Extent to Which Attitude Favors Republicans							
	− − − −	− − −	− −	−	0	+ +	+ + +	+ + + +
Favorable								
++++	...	...	...	79	97	97	100	100
+++	...	...	63	83	85	96	100	89
++	...	...	47	61	83	87	85	100
+	...	18	47	64	79	83	87	...
0	0	8	16	37	48	75	64	92
Unfavorable								
−	0	0	18	6	23	67	...	...
− −	0	8	10	11	25	40	...	...

[a] Entries give per cent voting Republican for each combination of attitude toward Eisenhower and attitude on domestic issues.

[b] Both the scale of attitude toward Eisenhower and the scale of attitude on domestic issues assumed more values than are shown in the table. In order to lessen the sampling variability associated with low frequencies, many of the extreme cells have been combined. Hence the percentages at the first and last of each row or column include cases falling in more extreme cells.

of the vote cast for the Republican candidate across these two dimensions of attitude at once. In the table the horizontal dimension is attitude on domestic issues, the vertical dimension attitude toward Eisenhower. Hence each row indicates how the behavior of individuals of the same attitude toward Eisenhower varied with the partisan direction and intensity of their attitude on domestic issues; and each column shows how the behavior of those of the same partisan feeling on domestic issues varied with their attitude toward Eisenhower. It is clear that measuring a second psychological force enhances our ability to account for the vote. The entries of Table 3-2 are quite representative of those we would obtain by displaying the relation to the voting act of orientations toward any two of our six elements of presidential politics.

From these specimen findings with two dimensions of attitude it requires only a change of technical procedures to consider the combined effects on the partisan decision of all six dimensions of partisan feeling.[1] Our hypothesis that the voting act depends in an immediate sense on the individual voter's evaluative orientations toward *several* objects of politics ought to be tested by an examination of the influence of all these orientations at once. When this test is made for the presidential elections of 1952 and 1956, the findings are consistent with the motivational hypothesis. In these years the individual's partisan decision could be predicted from his evaluations of the elements of national politics with a relatively slight error both in the sense of statistical estimation and of statistical discrimination.

Across the full national electorate the multiple correlation of the six dimensions of attitude with the partisan decision was greater than 0.7 both in 1952 and 1956, and the magnitude of these coefficients is the more impressive if we keep in mind that they have been depressed by errors of measurement and other factors that are not contradictory to our theoretical hypothesis. But it is the capacity of these attitudes to discriminate the actual Republican voter from the actual Democratic voter that perhaps best suggests their explanatory power. The test of our theoretical hypothesis in terms of statistical discrimination is shown in Fig. 3-1. Figure 3-1a gives the distribution of all major-party voters in our 1952 and 1956 sample according to the probability of their voting Republican, as we have estimated this probability from the direction and intensity of their attitudes toward the several elements of national politics.[2] Individuals toward the left of this distribution have a low probability of voting Republican (hence, a high probability of voting Democratic), those toward the right a high probability of voting Republican. To predict actual behavior from these probabilities we would select the value of 0.5 as a point of dis-

---

[1] Examination of the relation of the vote to *two* dimensions of attitude by inspecting multivariate frequency distributions presses the number of cases in a sample of well over a thousand persons. To examine the relation of the vote to *six* dimensions by the same method is plainly out of the question. For this reason we have fitted a statistical model to our data and have examined the relation of the voting act to the six partisan attitudes by the methods of multiple regression and of statistical discrimination.

[2] The probabilities are computed by the methods of multiple linear regression by assigning a score of 0 to a Democratic vote and a score of 1 to a Republican vote and treating the equation giving the regression of voting choice on the six partisan attitudes as a linear probability function.

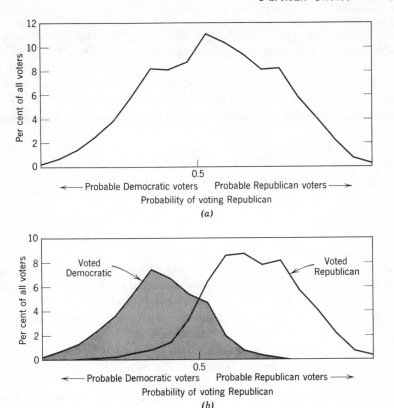

FIG. 3-1. *The prediction of voting choice from all partisan attitudes, 1952 and 1956 combined.* (a) *Distribution of all respondents by probability of voting Republican;* (b) *distribution of actual Democratic and Republican voters by probability of voting Republican.*

crimination and predict that those with a probability less than 0.5 of voting Republican would in fact cast their votes for the Republican candidate.

The success of these predictions in the elections of 1952 and 1956 is shown in Fig. 3-1b, which gives separately the distributions of probability scores for *actual* Democratic and Republican voters. The overlap of the Democratic and Republican curves indicates the error of our predictions; the overlap here is quite small relative to the total area under the two curves. Both in 1952 and in 1956 the behavior of more than 85 per cent of the electorate is consistent with our theoretical hypothesis.[3] This percentage may have sharper meaning if we observe that it is actually larger than the percentage of voters in these samples who were able before the election *to predict correctly their own behavior.* That is, the number of our respondents whose votes we are able to foretell from what we know of their partisan attitude is greater than the number who were able to foretell their own votes. The greater success of the psychological forces we have considered here is of course chiefly due to their greater immediacy to behavior. But it is remarkable that *any* explanatory factors can be found which surpass self-prediction in their capacity to distinguish those who will actually vote Republican from those who will vote Democratic.

The Components of Error. The very success of the partisan attitudes in accounting for behavior leads to a consideration of the deviant case. What factors can explain the partisan choices of those for whom we were in error, particularly when behavior seems strongly to have contradicted the direction of partisan attitude? A close inspection of the interview protocols suggests several components of error, and certain of these are factors of theoretical importance in the total field of forces leading to the voting act.

As one might expect, some errors are of measurement and do not contradict our theoretical hypothesis. The slight overreport of votes for the winning candidate in the Eisenhower elections suggests that a few of our respondents have falsely reported their behavior in the postelection interview.[4] Moreover, with interviews as early as six weeks before the election, in some cases attitude change can occur between the interview and election day. Our data suggest strongly that eleventh-hour events such as the Suez War in 1956 and the offer of Eisenhower to go to Korea in 1952 could not possibly have had the great impact on the whole electorate with which they are often

---

[3] The greater predictive power of the full set of six dimensions of partisan attitude may be summarized as follows for the election of 1956:

When Prediction Is From:	Correlation of Predictors with Voting Choice	Proportion Correctly Classified
Attitude toward Eisenhower only	0.52	75%
Attitude toward Eisenhower and attitude on domestic issues	0.59	79%
All six dimensions of partisan attitude	0.71	86%

[4] However, both in 1952 and 1956 the division of the vote reported by our samples was less than 3 per cent more Republican than the true division of the votes cast, as recorded in official election statistics.

credited. But there is little doubt that some errors of prediction are due to attitude change induced by events after our preelection interview.

Paralleling errors of measurement are those arising from the nature of our statistical methods. The probability model we have fitted to the interview data from a national sample assigns weights to the several partisan attitudes according to the strength of their association with the voting act across the entire electorate. But these statistical averages may distort the relative importance of the several forces in the decision of a single individual. For example, a Southern respondent in 1956 had formed a favorable estimate of Eisenhower, of Republican foreign policy, and of the success of the Republican administration in cleaning up the "mess" in Washington. But he "knew" that Eisenhower and the Republicans were wrong on a single domestic issue—the issue of segregation—and so he unhesitatingly cast his vote for a Democratic candidate he did not like.

There is occasional error of another type that appears traceable to direct interpersonal influence. Our interviews suggest that the dynamics of face-to-face associations are capable of generating forces that may negate the force of the individual's own evaluations of the elements of politics. Probably this happens most often in the relations of husband and wife, but an analysis of error provides many other illustrations of this influence as well. For example, one respondent traced an abrupt reversal of his vote intention to the arrival of a brother-in-law from California; another, to the pressures he felt from work associates; another, to face-to-face badgering by a precinct committeeman.

Important as primary group influence may be in informing or contradicting partisan attitude, an interview survey of widely separated individuals is not well suited to its study. The small group setting of attitude and behavior is one of great significance, but estimates in survey studies of its importance for voting typically have had to depend on what respondents tell about the partisan preferences of their family, work, and friendship groups. The degree of homogeneity suggested by these reports is impressive. Among respondents in our 1952 sample who voted Republican or Democratic and who ascribed a partisan color to one or another of their primary groups, the agreement reported between own preference and that of primary group associates was very high. The difficulty with figures such as these is that they cannot be checked against independent observations of the preferences of these groups. Until they can be checked, we will not be sure how much the reported agreement rests on perceptual distortion. Yet this difficulty does not lessen our qualitative sense of the importance of the small group setting of partisan attitude and the partisan choice. And it does not obscure the finding, from an analysis of errors of prediction, that primary group associations may in the exceptional case introduce forces in the individual's psychological field that are of sufficient strength to produce behavior that contradicts his evaluations of political objects.

THE EFFECTS OF ATTITUDE CONFLICT

In many cases attitudes toward the elements of presidential politics are well formed before the campaign opens. The associations found in the preceding chapter between changes in the external political world and popular feeling toward the elements of that world suggest that important shifts of attitude occur *between* campaigns. For example, the transformation of political mood associated with the Korean War and the "mess" in Washington almost certainly antedated the campaign of 1952, as did the origin of favorable attitudes toward Eisenhower. Nevertheless, politics is more salient to a good deal of the electorate during an election campaign, and the weeks of the presidential contest heighten the intensity of partisan attitude in most individuals. Moreover, response to the candidate who is not familiar to the public may be formed largely during the campaign and its immediate prelude.

A Problem to Be Explained: Motivational Differences by Time of Vote Decision. A description of shifts in attitude through the campaign has not been a main objective of our research. In each election year we have assessed the psychological forces acting on the individual by means of a single preelection interview; we have not sought the repeated interviews that would be needed to measure short-term change within a single campaign. And neither have we asked our respondents to recollect these changes, owing to the uncertain nature of this type of recall information.

Yet we have asked those interviewed in each election year to tell us when it was that their vote decision crystallized.[5] The answers to this question, too, are subject to the hazards of recall, but the responses undoubtedly give a sense of the location in time of individual choices. They are summarized for the elections of 1952 and 1956 in Table 3-3. The entries of the table confirm the judgment that the psychological

[5] The question used was: "How long before the election did you decide that you were going to vote the way you did?"

Table 3-3. Reported Time of Vote Decision

	1952	1956
Knew all along how they would vote	30%	44%
Decided when Eisenhower or Stevenson became a candidate or at time of conventions	35	32
Decided after conventions, during campaign	20	11
Decided within two weeks of election	9	7
Decided on election day	2	2
Do not remember	1	1
Not ascertained	3	3
Totals	100%	100%
Number of cases	1195	1291

forces guiding behavior arise before the campaign opens. In each of these elections fewer than two voters in five felt they had decided in the course of the campaign proper. Apparently this proportion was somewhat less in 1956 than it had been even in 1952. In the rematch of Eisenhower and Stevenson only 20 per cent of the voters felt they had reached their decision while the campaign was in progress.

The distribution through time of individual choices tells something about the background of partisan attitude, but a more revealing finding emerges when the relation of attitudes to the voting act is examined according to the timing of the individual's partisan decision. The remarkable pattern of differences that is found when our samples are divided according to the reported time of vote decision is shown in Fig. 3-2. Among persons indicating they knew all along how they would vote the joint relation of the several attitudes to the partisan decision was very high in both 1952 and 1956. Among those who reported deciding before or during the conventions this relation was somewhat lower. Among those who said they decided in mid-campaign, the relation was lower still. And among those who told us they decided within two weeks of the election or on election day, the relation was found to be fairly slight. In both the elections of 1952 and those of 1956 the proportion of the variance of voting choice explained by these psychological forces was more than seven times greater among persons who knew all along than it was among those who decided in the final days of the campaign.

The extraordinary differences of Fig. 3-2 make clear that the psychological forces we have measured influence the time at which the vote decision is made. But to interpret the nature of this effect more information is needed than is supplied by the figure. What explains

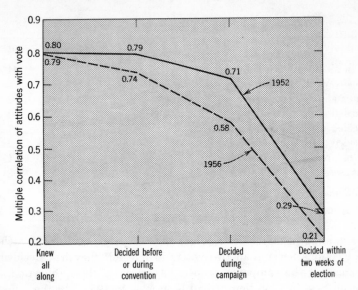

FIG. 3-2. Relation of reported time of decision to ability of partisan attitudes to explain vote.

the extreme variation of the relation of the partisan attitudes to behavior that appears when our samples are divided in this way? The answer lies largely in the presence or absence of conflict among the several psychological forces acting on behavior. Although the near-random behavior of those deciding late in the campaign is not to be explained altogether in terms of conflict, persons who reported deciding early are distinguished from those who reported deciding late primarily in the degree to which they experienced conflict in their evaluations of the several elements of national politics. In raising the question of attitude consistency, Fig. 3-2 leads to a problem that transcends in importance the explanation of the time of the individual's vote decision.

Psychological Conflict and Social Cross-Pressures. Cross-pressures have been treated in our work primarily in terms of attitude conflict. Conflict within the individual's psychological field may result from politically heterogeneous memberships, and we will give one example of a connection, albeit a fairly weak one, between psychological conflict and social cross-pressures. Yet conflicts of psychological forces may arise for quite different reasons than this, and most of our discussion will proceed without inquiring into what has led to attitudinal cross-pressures. It is the effect, rather than the cause, of conflict that is of primary interest.

In devising our measures of partisan attitude we have sought to reduce to a minimum what the investigator must infer to establish the fact of psychological conflict. The portion of our interview schedules used to assess these attitudes presents the individual with the objects of the political world and elicits responses that *the individual himself* identifies as being positive or negative, pro-Republican or pro-Democratic, and so forth. As a result, we can easily tell whether the individual's attitudes toward the several objects of his feeling are consistent in their partisan direction. Referring once more to the dimensions of attitude used illustratively in Table 3-2, we may say that the person who likes Eisenhower and also the Republican position on domestic issues is consistent in his attitudes toward these things, and so is the person who dislikes Eisenhower and Republican domestic policies. But the individual who likes Eisenhower and dislikes the Republican position or who dislikes Eisenhower but approves his party's stands may be said to experience some conflict in preparing his voting act.

We have noted before that not everyone in our samples showed clear evaluative feelings toward all six classes of objects we have considered. Indeed, most of those interviewed in 1952 and 1956 appeared to be neutral on one or more dimension either by showing a balance of feeling toward a given object or by showing no feeling toward the object at all. Because the meaning of conflict can vary a good deal according to the number of psychological forces acting on the individual, we will treat separately those having partisan feeling on two, three, four, or five dimensions. So few people had partisan feeling on all six dimensions that they are excluded from the analysis. Those who showed partisan feeling on one dimension or on none are also excluded, since they could hardly be thought to experience conflict as we define it here. Let us speak of the number of partisan attitudes as the individual's *attitude level*. It is clear that at the level of two, three, four, and five attitudes we can distinguish those whose feelings are fully consistent in the Democratic or Republican direction from those who exhibit some degree of conflict of partisan attitude.

THE EFFECTS OF ATTITUDE CONFLICT. Let us now return to the role of partisan attitudes in fixing the time of the individual's vote decision. If we examine the relation of attitude consistency to the reported time of decision at each attitude level, a clear set of differences is found, as is shown by Fig. 3-3. In the design of the figure each of the four curves is associated with a distinct level of attitude. The shape of each curve

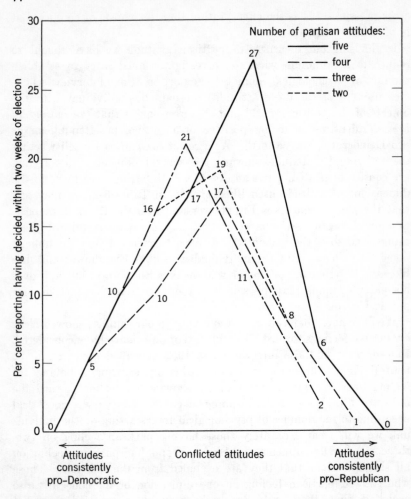

FIG. 3-3. *Relation of extent of attitude consistency to reported time of vote decision, 1956.*

shows the differing proportions of voters deciding late in the campaign as we move from full attitude consistency in the Democratic direction through various degrees of attitude conflict to full consistency in the Republican direction. The proportion deciding late *always* is greater as the degree of attitude conflict is greater; at any attitude level, those of a given degree of attitude consistency will have a larger proportion of late deciders than any group of greater consistency, and it will have a smaller proportion of late deciders than any group showing less

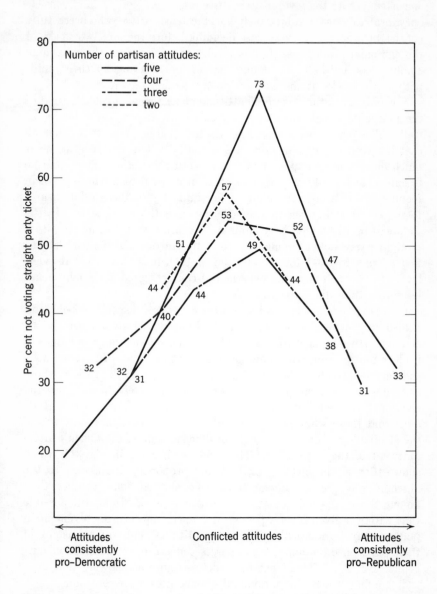

FIG. 3-4. Relation of extent of attitude consistency to degree of straight-ticket voting, 1956.

consistency. At the level of five attitudes, where conflict and consistency probably were subjectively most intense, those who were fully consistent reported in every case deciding before the last two weeks of the campaign; and those at this level who experienced the maximum conflict reported as often as one case in four making up their minds within two weeks of the election or on election day itself.

Not only does the degree of attitude consistency affect the time of the individual's vote decision; it affects other aspects of behavior as well. The person who experiences some degree of conflict tends to cast his vote for President with substantially less enthusiasm, he is much more prone to split his ticket in voting for other offices, and he is somewhat less likely to vote at all than is the person whose partisan feelings are entirely consistent. The similarity of these relationships to the relation between time of decision and the consistency of attitude can be illustrated by examining the proportion failing to vote a straight party ticket among those of different degrees of attitude conflict. From Fig. 3-4 for the election of 1956 it is clear that at every level of attitude those who experienced conflict voted a straight ticket less often than did those whose attitudes were consistent.

If attitude conflict leaves its impress on several aspects of behavior, it also influences what we will call the individual's involvement in the election. In our data from several presidential election campaigns it is clear that persons who show some degree of conflict of partisan attitude are less likely to be interested in the campaign than those whose attitudes are fully consistent, and they are less likely to care how the election turns out. We may look for evidence *within each attitude level* that those who experience conflict tend to become indifferent to the election's outcome as a means of defense against the difficult alternatives that they encounter. This evidence is given in Fig. 3-5, which shows that in the election of 1956 the proportion indifferent to the outcome was greater among those who showed some conflict than among those who did not at every attitude level. It is still possible that within a given level a person of deeper long-term involvement in politics may be more likely to form attitudes that are consistent in their partisan direction and to express concern over the election outcome. But it is difficult not to read this figure as showing that attitude conflict lessens the individual's concern over the outcome.

A TEST OF SOCIAL CROSS-PRESSURES. Having observed the impact of attitude conflict on the voting act and on the individual's orientation to the election, we may raise the question of the relation of these findings to prior research on social cross-pressures. What evidence can be found that would tie conflict within the individual's psychological

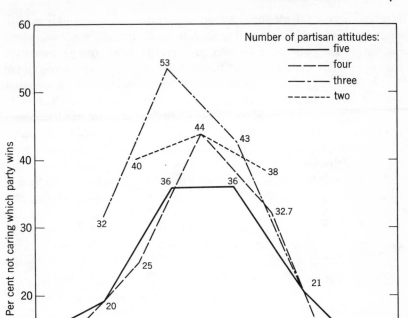

FIG. 3-5. *Relation of extent of attitude consistency to degree of indifference to election outcome.*

field to membership in social groupings of dissimilar political preferences? Some evidence of the sociological roots of the psychological
conflict we have measured can be found in a group suggested by the
Erie County study[6] as a clear example of social cross-pressures. Although the political homogeneity of Catholics is not nearly so great as

[6] Paul F. Lazarsfeld, Bernard Berelson, and Hazel Gaudet, *The People's Choice*
(Duell, Sloan and Pearce, New York, 1944).

is often supposed, Catholics do tend to perceive members of their faith as more Democratic than Republican in their political allegiance.[7] Similarly, the political differences of occupational groups are often overstated, but we may accept the fact that business and professional people are perceived as being pro-Republican, whereas blue-collar workers are perceived as being generally pro-Democratic. Therefore we would presume that white-collar Catholics are subjected to cross-pressures flowing from their religious and occupational groupings. These cross-pressures should be reflected in a less consistent field of partisan attitudes.

A test of this hypothesis for the election of 1956 is given in Table 3-4, which shows the per cent of Catholics in each occupational group and

Table 3-4. Proportion of Catholics Showing Some Conflict of Partisan Attitude by Occupation and Level of Attitude, 1956

	Two Partisan Attitudes	Three Partisan Attitudes	Four Partisan Attitudes	Five Partisan Attitudes
Blue Collar	15%	45%	45%	74%
Business or Professional	50%	47%	59%	85%

at each level of attitude who experienced some degree of conflict. The differences shown here are not large and are based on fairly small occupational and religious groupings, yet they are uniformly in the direction that leads us to accept the hypothesis. At every level of attitude, those who belong to the occupational group whose political coloration tends to be the same as that of their religious group show less conflict of partisan attitude than those who belong to the occupational group whose political preference tends to be opposite to that of Catholics as a whole. The relation is only of moderate strength, but the pattern of these data seems to suggest an interesting connection between widely separated factors that contribute to the voting act.

[7] Angus Campbell, Gerald Gurin, and Warren E. Miller, *The Voter Decides* (Row, Peterson and Co., Evanston, Ill., 1954), p. 214.

chapter 4
Voting Turnout

The act of voting requires the citizen to make not a single choice but two. He must choose between rival parties or candidates. He must also decide whether to vote at all. Since a partisan decision can be effective only if it is expressed at the polls, people's decisions whether or not to vote have great influence on party fortunes. Indeed, the dramatic turns of our electoral history have been accompanied as much by wide changes in turnout as they have by shifts in relative party strength. In percentage terms, the change in turnout between the 1948 and 1952 elections was greater than the change in relative party strength.

Citizen participation at the polls is highly valued in American society, and every national election campaign brings its spate of exhortations to vote. Because of the high value placed on turnout, a good deal of the attention given it in popular discussion has to do with why so many people fail to vote. Despite the great public interest aroused by a presidential contest, our national elections bring less than two thirds of the adult population to the polls.[1] Of course, in any year a great many people are kept from voting by legal barriers— most commonly, in a nation of movers, by the requirements of minimum residence in a state and its lesser divisions.[2] And many others are kept from voting by political or personal obstacles they could not reasonably overcome. But in each of our national elections millions

[1] For example, the 61,522,000 people who voted for President in 1952 constituted 62.7% of the 97,574,000 people the Census Bureau estimated to be civilians of voting age on November 1 of that year. In 1956, 62,027,000 voters comprised 60.4% of an estimated 102,179,000 civilians of voting age.

[2] A comparison of reported length of current residence with state and local residence requirements indicates that these requirements have prevented at least 3 per cent of our respondents from voting.

of people whose way toward registering and voting is relatively clear fail to do so, and this fact has excited wide comment.

Although accounting for nonvoting is important in understanding the turnout decision, we will conceive the problem of explanation too narrowly if we concentrate solely on failures to vote. The really extraordinary aspect of our presidential elections is that tens of millions of people *do* expend the energy required to reach their polling-places and register their votes. If we are to explain this type of behavior we must find the patterns of motivation that lead these people to vote, as we must find the conditions that keep others from doing so. The explanatory problem is just that of finding what it is that distinguishes the voter from the nonvoter, and we will see as the discussion proceeds that the deviant voter—the person we "expect" *not* to vote yet who does—is somewhat more difficult to explain than is the person we expect to vote who fails to do so.

We assume that the decision to vote, no less than the decision to vote for a given party, rests immediately on psychological forces, although nonpsychological barriers to action are more prominent among the causes of turnout than they are among the causes of partisan choice. Hence, our quest of understanding begins with an examination of motivational forces, and this chapter will describe a number of psychological influences that affect the likelihood the individual will vote. Yet we assume that the proximate causes of turnout, like the immediate determinants of partisan choice, are intervening variables that express the influence of a wide array of antecedent factors.

MODES OF POLITICAL PARTICIPATION

For most Americans voting is the sole act of participation in politics. Table 4-1 shows for the two Eisenhower elections the proportion of the electorate that was politically active in each of four elementary ways. The percentages of this table make clear that only small fractions of the public are connected with a party apparatus or help with the work and expense of a campaign. Moreover, since the groups in our samples who did report engaging in these activities are widely overlapping, the percentages cannot be added together to reach an estimate of the total number who were active.

Beyond these modes of participation there are several informal, less well-defined ways in which large numbers of people become "engaged" in a presidential contest. One of the most important of these is informal political discussion. In each of the Eisenhower elections about a fourth of the electorate reported having talked to other people and

Table 4-1. Popular Participation in Politics, 1952 and 1956[a]

	1952	1956
"Do you belong to any political club or organizations?"	2%	3%
"Did you give any money or buy tickets or anything to help the campaign for one of the parties or candidates?"	4%	10%
"Did you go to any political meetings, rallies, dinners, or things like that?"	7%	7%
"Did you do any other work for one of the parties or candidates?"	3%	3%

[a] Entries are proportions of total samples answering affirmatively.

having tried to persuade them to vote a given way.[3] The casual nature of this behavior should not conceal its importance either as an expression of individual motivation or as a means by which the final distribution of partisan preference in the electorate is achieved. Discussion of this sort is undoubtedly one of the most significant forms of political behavior by a mass public, even if it does not draw the individual directly into organized political activity.

Although it requires still less personal energy, following the campaign through the mass communications media might also be described as a type of informal participation. For some individuals, gleaning the political content of newspapers and magazines and of radio and television is a principal means of relating to politics. For others—presumably for a great majority of Americans—following the campaign in the mass media is a much more passive activity. Yet since the audiences of the media screen out vast amounts of their content, the individual plays at least a minimal role in deciding what he will and will not attend, and in this sense following an election campaign in the media may be called a form of participation.[4] In the Eisenhower elections only about one person in twenty said that the campaign had failed to reach him through any of the principal media of communication.

Since this book is concerned primarily with the act of voting itself, we will fix our attention on turnout rather than on other types of

[3] The question "Did you talk to any people and try to show them why they should vote for one of the parties or candidates?" was answered "yes" in 1952 by 27% of our respondents; in 1956 by 28%.
[4] See Angus Campbell, Gerald Gurin, and Warren E. Miller, "Television and the Election," *Scientific American*, 188 (May 1953), p. 47.

participation in politics. Yet in assessing the determinants of the voting act we are assessing factors which may underlie other modes of behavior by which the individual may participate in the political process. In one other respect the act of voting in a given election can be interpreted as an element of a broader dimension of behavior. It is plausible to think of voting as a type of conduct that is somewhat habitual and to suppose that as the individual develops a general orientation toward politics he comes to incorporate either voting or nonvoting as part of his normal behavior. Certainly we have found a pronounced association between what people tell us their past behavior has been and whether they vote in the elections we have studied. From this viewpoint our inquiry into the determinants of voting turnout is less a search for psychological forces that determine a decision made anew in each campaign than it is a search for the attitude correlates of voting and nonvoting from which these modes of behavior have emerged and by which they are presently supported. As the inquiry proceeds we will find that some of the dimensions of attitude that are most helpful in accounting for turnout appear to have the character of orientations to politics much more than they do the character of forces acting on a present decision.[5]

However useful it may be to distinguish turnout and partisan choice analytically, we ought not to suppose that these dimensions of the voting act appear distinct to the individual citizen. It is natural for the individual to perceive that he votes because he wants to make his preference between parties or candidates count, or that he fails to vote because he does not have a clear preference between partisan objects that he feels are equally appealing, unappealing, or without any affective content at all. Almost certainly this perception of the motives for voting overreaches the facts: we will see that the strength of preference only partially accounts for turnout. Yet the perception catches a clear element of motivation, and the relation of turnout to the intensity of preference is the first important fact we should establish in seeking to explain why some people have voted and others have not.

The evidence for this relation is readily seen if we classify people according to the intensity of their preference, and observe what proportion has voted at each level of intensity. Data of this sort from our combined samples of 1952 and 1956 are arrayed in Fig. 4-1. The pattern seen in the figure shows that the probability that a person will vote depends on the strength of his partisan preference. Across vir-

[5] For a discussion of the causal relation of participation behavior and various psychological dimensions see Heinz Eulau and Peter Schneider, "Dimensions of Political Involvement," *Public Opinion Quarterly*, XX (Spring 1956), 128–142.

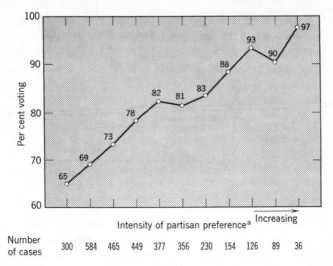

FIG. 4-1. Relation of intensity of partisan preference to voting turnout, 1952 and 1956.

tually the entire range of intensity found in these samples, the greater the strength of the individual's preference, the greater the likelihood he would vote. And the rate of voting at the highest levels of intensity shows that the individual's preference virtually insures his turnout.

Intensity of preference affects not only whether the individual votes; it affects how "strongly" he votes as well. A common observation is that people go to the polls with different degrees of concern about voting. For some the act is imbued with strong positive affect, whereas for others it is much more neutrally toned. To measure these differences we have asked each person who voted how much he cared about having voted, and we have used the answers to this question to identify people who cared a great deal and those who voted in a much more perfunctory way. The strength of voting is plainly associated with the intensity of preference; among those of low preference intensity, the proportion of perfunctory voters is a good deal larger than it is among those whose strength of preference is high.

This sketch of the influence of preference intensity is in one respect overly simple and needs to be complicated by the addition of a perceptual factor. Despite the immediacy of the impact that we would expect strength of preference to have on turnout, its motivational force seems to depend on how close the individual perceives the election to be. The interaction of these factors in the motivation of turn-

Table 4-2. Relation of Perceived Closeness of Election and Intensity of Partisan Preference to Voting Turnout, 1956

	Election Perceived to Be					
	One sided			Close		
	Intensity of Preference			Intensity of Preference		
	Weak	Medium	Strong	Weak	Medium	Strong
Voted	70%	71%	73%	71%	79%	89%
Did not vote	30	29	27	29	21	11
	100%	100%	100%	100%	100%	100%
Number of cases	130	170	88	301	360	226

out is shown in Table 4-2 for the election of 1956. In this table, the levels of intensity in Fig. 4-1 are combined into three broad categories, and the proportion voting in each of these categories is given separately for those who expected the election to be one sided and those who expected it to be close. What the entries of the table have to say about the motivation of turnout is quite clear. The person who thinks the outcome of the election is a foregone conclusion is not more likely to vote if his preference is strong. But the person who thinks the outcome is in doubt is more likely to vote if the intensity of his partisan preference is high. The power of partisan choice to motivate turnout evidently is contingent on the individual feeling, at least in some diffuse way, that his vote may "count."[6] To put the matter another way, the turnout behavior of a person of weak preference is not affected by whether he thinks the election will be close. But the behavior of someone of stronger preference is affected a good deal by his perception of how close the election will be.

The relation between strength of preference and turnout that is seen in our data needs to be interpreted with a greater time perspective. If our measures spanned a broader interval in the life of the individual we would expect to find that the strength of his preference in prior

---

[6] The questions we have used to classify respondents according to their expectations about the election have referred to the contest *in the nation as a whole*. Because presidential electors are chosen by states and because all of a state's electors are usually awarded to a single party, we might suppose that how close a person feels the presidential candidates are running in his own state would be of greater importance. But the analysis of answers to a question referring to the presidential race within the respondent's state indicates that it is the election *as a whole* that has cognitive and motivational significance, despite the existence of the Electoral College.

elections has an effect on the likelihood of his voting in later elections. In showing the relation of turnout to the strength of preference in single elections, our data undoubtedly understate the full impact of preference intensity on the decision to vote. A strong commitment to one side or the other in any election tends to involve the individual psychologically more deeply in politics. As a result, the probability of his participating in subsequent elections increases, even though his preference may be substantially less strong in the later campaigns. In this sense, the influence of partisan choice on turnout transcends that shown by the data we have presented here. Yet this secondary effect plainly involves intervening factors. The effect of intensity of preference in time past must be transmitted through forces that act on the individual at the moment of his present behavior.

The need to identify additional psychological forces on the turnout decision is strongly reinforced by a realistic appraisal of how well the intensity of current preference can explain this type of behavior. The findings we have given demonstrate that in a single election someone of strong preference is more likely to vote than is someone of weaker partisan dispositions. Yet Fig. 4-1 should dispel altogether the idea that the strength of partisan choice can by itself fully explain why some people go to the polls and others do not. The inadequacy of strength of preference in accounting for turnout is perhaps most clearly seen in its failure to explain the behavior of those of minimum partisan disposition. Although the proportion voting is lowest in the group having the slightest degree of preference, nearly two-thirds even of these people were found to have cast a vote.

TURNOUT AND POLITICAL INVOLVEMENT

The partial dependence of turnout on preference is of theoretical importance in large part because it implicates everything that may influence the intensity of preference as a possible influence on the disposition to vote. The fact that one basic dimension of voting is related to the other means that any element in the array of factors leading to partisan choice may lead to turnout as well. The truth of this is recognized at least implicitly in a number of discussions that have explained the disposition to vote in terms of what may strengthen or weaken the disposition to vote a given way.[7] Furthermore, many

---

[7] It is of central importance, for example, in the discussion of turnout appearing in Seymour M. Lipset *et al.*, "The Psychology of Voting: An Analysis of Political Behavior," *Handbook of Social Psychology*, ed. Gardner Lindzey (Addison-Wesley Publishing Co., Cambridge, Mass., 1954), II, 1124–1175.

discussions of the antecedents of partisan choice can throw light on the causes of turnout as well.

Our concern for the moment is not with the antecedents of the intensity of preference but rather with psychological influences on turnout that act apart from the effect of a disposition to vote a given way. In pressing this aspect of our research our major effort has been to relate turnout behavior to what we will call the individual's psychological involvement in politics. We have felt that the individual develops a characteristic degree of interest and involvement in political affairs, which varies widely among individuals but which exhibits a good deal of stability for the same person through successive election campaigns. Postulating a dimension of this sort leads naturally to the hypothesis that the stronger the individual's psychological involvement the more likely he is to participate in politics by voting. We have sought to design measures that would catch several aspects of the individual's psychological involvement in politics; in particular, we have measured two sorts of attitudes that describe the individual's orientation to a specific election and two additional attitudes that characterize his orientation to politics and elections more generally.

Interest in the Campaign. The first aspect of involvement we have sought to measure is the degree of a person's interest in the campaign. The presidential contest holds the attention of different people quite unequally, and the degree of interest has varied widely among the individuals we have interviewed in several election campaigns. The importance of this aspect of involvement for voting turnout is demonstrated by Table 4-3 with data drawn from the election of 1956. The entries of the table show that the rate of turnout among persons of high interest exceeded that among persons of low interest by nearly 30 per cent. What is more, the incidence of nonvoting among the third of the electorate that is lowest in interest is appreciably greater

Table 4-3. Relation of Degree of Interest in Campaign to Voting Turnout, 1956

	Degree of Interest in Campaign		
	Not Much Interested	Somewhat Interested	Very Much Interested
Voted	58%	72%	87%
Did not vote	42	28	13
	100%	100%	100%
Number of cases	540	695	520

than it is among the third that is lowest in strength of partisan preference, as shown by Fig. 4-1. Our measure of interest carries us further than the measure of partisan intensity in finding the conditions of nonvoting, although we still need to learn what brought to the polls more than half of those who tell us they are not much interested in the campaign.

Concern over the Election Outcome. A person's orientation to a specific election can be described also in terms of his concern over its outcome. Some people are deeply involved, psychologically speaking, in the electoral result, whereas others are relatively indifferent. Concern over the election result would seem intuitively to be somewhat distinct from political interest, and in our data it is by no means perfectly correlated with interest. Yet the association of the two suggests the influence of a more general involvement factor and leads us to concur in Lane's observation that "questions on 'interest' and 'concern' tend to select out the same populations and to be related to behavior in roughly the same way."[8] The relation we have found between the individual's concern over the outcome and the probability of his voting is shown in Table 4-4 for 1956. Here again, the effect of involvement on voting turnout seems very clear.

Table 4-4. Relation of Degree of Concern about Election Outcome to Voting Turnout, 1956

	Degree of Concern over Election Outcome			
	Don't Care at All	Don't Care Very Much	Care Somewhat	Care Very Much
Voted	52%	69%	76%	84%
Did not vote	48	31	24	16
	100%	100%	100%	100%
Number of cases	230	367	627	459

Sense of Political Efficacy. Our measures of interest and of concern over the election outcome refer explicitly to the election at hand. As such, they are likely to catch important short-term fluctuations of the individual's political involvement. These measures may tap more enduring orientations to politics as well. The individual does not react *de novo* to each election but tends rather to respond to the stimuli of a new campaign in terms of stable attitudes and disposi-

---

[8] Robert E. Lane, *Political Life* (The Free Press, Glencoe, Ill., 1959), p. 134.

tions he has toward politics generally. His social environment, immediate and distant, is composed of a number of areas that compete for his emotional energy and in which he comes to have a characteristic level of emotional involvement. Politics is such an area, and most adults have a relatively fixed degree of involvement in it, although their commitment to political affairs, as to work, family, religion, or sports, may vary somewhat over time. This characteristic level of involvement differs widely among people. A really intense commitment to politics probably is limited in American society to a small fraction of political activists, but even in the wider electorate we find substantial differences in the extent of emotional involvement in political affairs.

An important aspect of the individual's response to politics as a general area is the degree to which this response is passive in character. To some people politics is a distant and complex realm that is beyond the power of the common citizen to affect, whereas to others the affairs of government can be understood and influenced by individual citizens. We have assessed the effectiveness the individual feels in his relation to politics by using answers to several questions probing attitudes of this sort to develop a cumulative scale, on which we could array our samples. The influence this dimension of attitude has on the turnout decision is shown by Table 4-5 for the election of

Table 4-5. Relation of Sense of Political Efficacy to Voting Turnout, 1956

	Sense of Political Efficacy				
	Low				High
Voted	52%	60%	75%	84%	91%
Did not vote	48	40	25	16	9
	100%	100%	100%	100%	100%
Number of cases	263	343	461	501	196

1956. The rate of voting turnout was found to increase uniformly with the strength of the individual's sense of political efficacy, and more than 40 percentage points separated those whose sense was least developed from those whose sense of effectiveness was strongest.

Sense of Citizen Duty. The final aspect of involvement we have sought to measure also transcends a single election. Wide currency in American society is given the idea that the individual has a civic responsibility to vote. When this norm becomes a part of the value system of the individual, as it has for most of our citizens, it may be regarded as a force acting directly on the turnout decision. Of course its strength is not the same for everyone, and the degree to which the individual feels an obligation to vote is an important aspect of his orientation to politics. We have measured the strength of this attitude by constructing a cumulative scale from several questions about the responsibility to vote and classifying those we have interviewed into the categories of the scale. When the proportion voting is shown for each category, as it is in Table 4-6 for the election of 1956, it is clear that the strength of a person's sense of citizen duty has a very great influence on the likelihood of his voting.

Table 4-6. Relation of Sense of Citizen Duty to Voting Turnout, 1956

	Sense of Citizen Duty				
	Low				High
Voted	13%	42%	52%	74%	85%
Did not vote	87	58	48	26	15
	100%	100%	100%	100%	100%
Number of cases	89	78	146	639	812

The most striking entries of Table 4-6 are those indicating that voting is rare among people whose sense of citizen duty is least strong. In those whose sense of citizen duty is weakest we have found a small group whose motivation to participate in politics is so near zero that other forces inducing them to vote only rarely bring them to the polls.

Despite the evidence that the four aspects of political involvement we have measured share an important common component, we have considered separately their relation to turnout because each aspect contributes a distinctive element. However, we can assess how well involvement accounts for behavior only if we examine the joint relation to turnout of the four measures. In order to make entirely clear what we have *added* to our ability to account for the turnout decision by measuring these aspects of involvement, we will include strength of partisan preference among the explanatory variables so that their *combined* power to account for behavior may be compared directly with that of the intensity of preference alone, as shown in Fig. 4-1.

Such a comparison attests the fundamental role of involvement in motivating turnout behavior. As is seen in Fig. 4-2, the rate of turnout increases steadily with political involvement and partisan preference, and differs by more than 75 per cent from one extreme to the other,

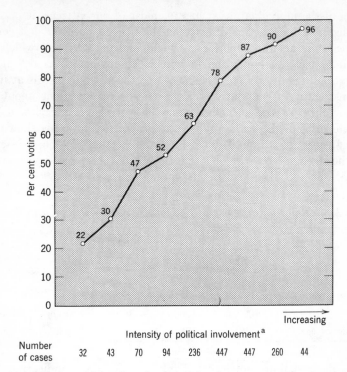

Number
of cases   32   43   70   94   236   447   447   260   44

FIG. 4-2. Relation of intensity of political involvement to voting turnout, 1956.

whereas the proportions voting at the extremes of low and high intensity of preference alone differed by less than half this much. The fact that persons of the highest involvement are more nearly unanimous in voting than are those of lowest involvement in not voting suggests that we are still beset more by the problem of the deviant *voter* than we are with that of the deviant *nonvoter.* And the existence of any group of similar motivation whose behavior is not homogeneous invites us to push further the quest for explanation.

Divergent Cases. Most of the variability in turnout that political involvement fails to explain is found in the middle categories of Fig. 4-2, where the psychological forces we have measured are neither so weak that the individual is highly unlikely to vote nor so strong that he is highly unlikely *not* to vote. In these middle categories other factors, some of them undoubtedly exogenous to our theoretical concerns, have determined whether the individual will vote. But the "error" in Fig. 4-2 that is most interesting is found at the extremes of political involvement, where we would expect to be able to predict with higher confidence whether the individual will in fact vote. The presence of error of this sort leads naturally to an intensive examination of divergent cases to learn why it is that our expectations have proven wrong.

We are better prepared, by the popular lore about voting, for error at the extreme of high involvement. Located here is the person of strong motivation who is kept from voting by personal circumstances he could not reasonably overcome, as the individual who was prevented from voting by a flat tire on his way to the polls. We doubt that this specific factor, which we would unhesitatingly declare exogenous, has had a very high incidence in American politics, but it suggests well the sort of barrier that may keep a highly motivated person from voting. An inspection of our interview protocols provides a number of such cases.

Located here, too, are the individuals of strong motivation who are barred from voting by legal disabilities. Some of our respondents living in states that make no provision for absentee balloting have been away from their homes on election day. Others have changed their residences too recently to satisfy the requirements of minimum residence. Nonregistration ought generally to be regarded as a legal barrier only with caution, since the failure to register may simply reflect the same motivational factors as the failure to vote. Yet in certain cases the impossibility of registering has stood as a clear barrier for those who were motivated to perform the voting act.

Deviant cases of the opposite sort, in which a person of slight motivation has voted, are less familiar in the common lore, except perhaps for what is known of party machines that have voted the dead. An analysis of interviews with people of very low motivation who have gone to the polls indicates that the most important force on their behavior is interpersonal influence, as we have found it to be in inducing deviant partisan behavior. Personal influence seems particularly important within the family group. Of the twelve voters in 1956 who had the least reason for going to the polls in terms of the psychological factors we have measured, nine were women who appeared to respond to the wishes of husbands or of other men in their immediate families.

It is the preferences of those who vote that are of primary importance in the wider political system. But the preferences of those who do not are by no means of trivial importance; indeed, in recording substantial shifts over time they prove to be of considerable theoretical interest. Let us examine the partisan preferences of nonvoters, as they have been assessed over a twenty-year period.

With the rise of public opinion polls in the 1930's the first systematic evidence began to appear that nonvoters—or at least people who expected not to vote—were more Democratic than the electorate as a whole. This evidence accumulated through the latter years of the New Deal and the Fair Deal until the generalization that nonvoters tend to be Democrats had worked itself into the popular understanding of politics. Since it was well known that both partisan preference and voting turnout were related to social class, an explanation of the strongly Democratic color of nonvoters was easily supplied.

The report of partisan preferences we obtained from a national sample interviewed after the election of 1948, the high-water mark of the Fair Deal, was consistent with this description of nonvoters. Whereas the preferences reported by voters were divided very nearly evenly between the parties, the preferences reported by non-voters favored the Democrats by a margin of more than 4–1. Were it not for the fact that the Truman vote exceeded the advance expectations, the closeness of the Democratic victory in 1948 relative to earlier years would probably have been explained in terms of the lower level of turnout.

If the report taken from those who failed to vote in 1948 supported the contention that non-voters tend to be Democrats, the postelection reports of 1952 and 1956 dealt this notion severe blows. In our interviews following the election of 1952 only about half of the nonvoters indicating a preference said they would have voted Democratic; in our interviews following the election of 1956 little more than a quarter of the nonvoters giving a preference said they would have voted Democratic. The extreme nature of this shift in the Democratic proportion over an eight-year period is shown by Table 4-7. Few statistics in all of our studies have shown so violent a change over time as this one.

What can explain so great a shift among nonvoters? Over a period in which the division of preference changed by little more than ten

Table 4-7. Postelection Preference of Nonvoters, 1948 to 1956[a]

	1948	1952	1956
Would have voted Democratic	82%	52%	28%
Would have voted Republican	18	48	72
Total	100%	100%	100%
Number of cases	192	417	429

[a] Among nonvoters giving a preference between major-party candidates.

per cent among voters it changed by more than 50 per cent among nonvoters. How are we to account for the difference? Undoubtedly a number of factors have been at work, but we believe that much of the observed change can be explained by a few central ideas. The major key to understanding is supplied by what we have found to distinguish nonvoters from voters: the nonvoter tends to be a person of lower involvement whose emotional investment in politics and its partisan decisions is on the average much less than that of the voter. As a result, we would expect the nonvoter to be less stable in his partisan inclinations than the voter and more responsive to the massive political stimuli that produce shifts of popular attitude over time. And we have little doubt that for the nonvoter a stimulus of great importance in this period, as in any other, was the fact of who was winning elections. For at least part of the way between his position of 1948 and his position of 1956 the nonvoter was riding a psychological bandwagon.

Several kinds of evidence can be marshalled in support of this general view. First of all, if we are right in thinking that the outcomes of these elections were stimuli of relatively greater importance for the nonvoter, we ought to find evidence of the fact in a comparison of the reported preferences of nonvoters before and after each election. We do not have the data to make this comparison for the election of 1948, but for each of the Eisenhower elections we may examine the nonvoter's report of preference in the first and second interviews of our brief panel studies spanning the elections. The division of preference among nonvoters shifted in the direction of the winner in each of these years; indeed, the postelection shift toward Eisenhower in 1956 (from 58% to 72%) was 14 percentage points—as great as the shift of preference among voters over the entire period from 1948 to 1956. We would suppose that the Truman victory had much the same effect on the preference of nonvoters—although in the opposite partisan direction—as the Eisenhower victories had in each of the elections that followed.

The most telling evidence for our characterization of change, however, is obtained by further dividing nonvoters according to the degree of their involvement in politics. In any election some individuals whose involvement is high and whose motivation is strong fail to vote. If we can separate these people from individuals who are weakly involved, we should have a clearer sense of the forces inducing change in preference over time. Table 4-8 makes such a separation for each of the Eisenhower elections by classifying nonvoters according to the extent of their interest in the campaign. Several observations that are

Table 4-8. Relation of Degree of Political Involvement to Change in Partisan Preference of Nonvoters[a]

	1952 Election		1956 Election	
	Before	After	Before	After
Very much interested	51%	54%	43%	37%
Somewhat interested	56%	57%	40%	37%
Not much interested	63%	52%	42%	24%

[a] Entries are percentages favoring Democrats of those giving a preference.

important for our formulation of change can be based on this table. First, it is clear for both the 1952 and 1956 elections that change in the Republican direction between the pre- and postelection interviews occurred more among the slightly involved than it did among those of greater involvement. Only the group least interested in the campaign shifted toward Eisenhower in his first victory; hence, the shift seen among nonvoters as a whole rests on the fact that most nonvoters are people of little involvement. Second, the fact that the Democratic percentage prior to the 1952 election was highest among those of slightest interest suggests that these people were most under the influence of past Democratic victories. Yet it is this same group that responded most strongly to the Eisenhower victories and shifted far enough that by the postelection interview of 1956 less than one-fourth of their number favored the Democrats.[9]

This unbroken swing in the Republican direction dissolves the generalization that nonvoters are pro-Democratic and calls attention in the most dramatic way to the importance of psychological involvement in explaining political behavior. We have treated in some detail the shifts of preference among those who fail to vote because these changes suggest the far-reaching effects on behavior of the low involvement that is the nonvoter's primary quality. Yet voters and nonvoters are by no means the only groups within the electorate that differ in the extent of their political involvement, and we shall have occasion in later chapters to examine the behavior of other groups as well for which involvement supplies a key to understanding.[10]

[9] Of course we have repeated measurements of the preferences of the same persons only within a single election and not over two or more elections. The assumption that the composition of the several involvement groups would be fairly stable over time cannot be validated with these data, and comparisons of their preferences between elections ought to be treated with caution.

[10] See particularly the discussion of agrarian voting behavior in Chapter 13.

Whether an event is political or nonpolitical depends on the meaning ascribed to it by the individual. For example, an economic fact such as the loss of a job becomes a political fact as well only when the actors involved perceive unemployment as a condition for which governments may be blamed or which governments may alleviate. The development of a perception that politics is relevant to pressures arising outside the political order is a psychological process that we call "political translation." An important accompaniment is the frequent perception that the political parties differ in their attitudes toward these pressures.

It is common to explain voting behavior in terms of roots that are in the first instance relatively contemporary and in the second largely nonpolitical. In the traditional view, democratic elections are periodic reviews of governmental conduct. Hence roots of behavior are sought within the time interval since the preceding election. Similarly, it is recognized that political behavior is instrumental behavior. The act of voting is not an end in itself; rather, it is a choice of means toward other ends. More often than not, these ends concern facets of human experience that are at core nonpolitical, involving problems of economic security, the disruptions of war, rights of minorities, the distribution of social status, and the like. These facts turn attention immediately to nonpolitical sources of the vote decision.

We have chosen instead to devote our initial attention to the purely political roots of attitudes proximal to the voting decision and of the voting act itself. For we find that the individual's current choice tends to have simple and direct roots in time prior to the current era, and that this past is, in no small measure, a *political* past. We have already seen that the images of the parties most firmly imbedded in the public mind represent a variety of political eras in time past as well as reflecting the immediate partisan controversies of the preceding

65

four years. Initial selection of a party may often be a response to nonpolitical pressures; but once made, partisan choice tends to be maintained long after its nonpolitical sources have faded into oblivion. Current pressures arising outside the political order continue to affect the evaluation process, and from time to time they may contribute to a critical margin of political victory. Yet for most of the people most of the time such contemporary forces turn out to be but minor terms in the decision equation.

We shall attempt, over the ensuing chapters, to document these assertions and suggest why they are so, given the nature of our political system and the psychological makeup of the individual. We shall consider in turn why the connectives with the partisan past are so strong and, on the other hand, why the intrusion of current nonpolitical forces is no more potent. Principal among connective mechanisms is a growing sense of identification with the party. The role of these enduring attachments in the genesis of the proximal attitudes is examined in Chapter 5. Chapter 6 inquires in some detail into the nature of these identifications as psychological phenomena, and traces their roots to more remote points in time past.

Such party loyalty, although it helps the individual to make sense out of politics, serves in a peculiar way to insulate him from nonpolitical pressures that might otherwise push him to more frequent partisan reevaluation. But review of this kind is infrequent as well because of the fallibility of the process of political translation. We shall consider the vicissitudes of this translation process in Chapters 7, 8, and 9. The most obvious bridges aiding the citizen to link nonpolitical conditions with partisan evaluation are to be found in claims of the parties for support on the basis of policies toward social, economic, and other problems. Thus our attention shifts here from the political parties to the political issues. We shall progress from a discussion of the role of issues at a level of relatively specific policy demands to the role of the most general dimensions of evaluation suggested by the term "ideology."

Other more elusive forces requiring conception in purely political terms shape behavior as well. We shall complete our discussion of the political context of the voting act by considering, in Chapter 10, the rules and norms for behavior that vary by political subcommunity across the national electorate. Although both formal and informal norms generally have been overlooked in analyses of individual responses, we shall find that both have interesting effects on behavior and that their impact may be strong or weak according to the motivational system of the individual actor.

chapter 5
The Impact of Party Identification

A general observation about the political behavior of Americans is that their partisan preferences show great stability between elections. Key speaks of the "standing decision" to support one party or the other, and this same phenomenon soon catches the eye of any student of electoral behavior. Its mark is readily seen in aggregate election statistics. For virtually any collection of states, counties, wards, precincts, or other political units one may care to examine, the correlation of the party division of the vote in successive elections is likely to be high. Often a change of candidates and a broad alteration in the nature of the issues disturb very little the relative partisanship of a set of electoral units, which suggests that great numbers of voters have party attachments that persist through time.

The fact that attachments of this sort are widely held is confirmed by survey data on individual people. In a survey interview most of our citizens freely classify themselves as Republicans or Democrats and indicate that these loyalties have persisted through a number of elections. Few factors are of greater importance for our national elections than the lasting attachment of tens of millions of Americans to one of the parties. These loyalties establish a basic division of electoral strength within which the competition of particular campaigns takes place. And they are an important factor in assuring the stability of the party system itself.

THE CONCEPT AND MEASUREMENT OF PARTY IDENTIFICATION

Only in the exceptional case does the sense of individual attachment to party reflect a formal membership or an active connection with a party apparatus. Nor does it simply denote a voting record, although the influence of party allegiance on electoral behavior is strong. Generally this tie is a psychological identification, which can persist without legal recognition or evidence of formal membership and even without a consistent record of party support. Most Americans have this sense of attachment with one party or the other. And for the individual who does, the strength and direction of party identification are facts of central importance in accounting for attitude and behavior.

The importance of stable partisan loyalties has been universally recognized in electoral studies, but the manner in which they should be defined and measured has been a subject of some disagreement. In keeping with the conception of party identification as a psychological tie, these orientations have been measured in our research by asking individuals to describe their own partisan loyalties. Some studies, however, have chosen to measure stable partisan orientations in terms of an individual's past voting record or in terms of his attitude on a set of partisan issues. We have not measured party attachments in terms of the vote or the evaluation of partisan issues precisely because we are interested in exploring the *influence* of party identification on voting behavior and its immediate determinants. When an independent measure of party identification is used, it is clear that even strong party adherents at times may think and act in contradiction to their party allegiance. We could never establish the conditions under which this will occur if lasting partisan orientations were measured in terms of the behavior they are thought to affect.

Our measurement of party identification rests fundamentally on self-classification. Since 1952 we have asked repeated cross sections of the national population a sequence of questions inviting the individual to state the direction and strength of his partisan orientation.[1] The dimension presupposed by these questions appears to have psychological reality for virtually the entire electorate. The partisan self-image of all but the few individuals who disclaim any involvement in politics permits us to place each person in these samples on a continuum of partisanship extending from strongly Republican to strongly Democratic. The sequence of questions we have asked also allows us to distinguish the Independents who lean toward one of the parties from

---

[1] The initial question was this: "Generally speaking, do you think of yourself as a Republican, a Democrat, an Independent, or what?" Those who classified themselves as Republicans or Democrats were also asked, "Would you call yourself a strong (Republican, Democrat) or a not very strong (Republican, Democrat)?" Those who classified themselves as Independents were asked this additional question: "Do you think of yourself as closer to the Republican or Democratic Party?" The concept itself was first discussed in George Belknap and Angus Campbell, "Political Party Identification and Attitudes toward Foreign Policy," *Public Opinion Quarterly*, XV (Winter 1952), 601–623.

those who think of themselves as having no partisan coloration whatever.

The measure these methods yield has served our analysis of party identification in a versatile fashion. To assess both the direction and intensity of partisan attachments it can be used to array our samples across the seven categories shown in Table 5-1, which gives the distri-

Table 5-1. The Distribution of Party Identification

	Oct. 1952	Sept. 1953	Oct. 1954	Apr. 1956	Oct. 1956	Nov. 1957	Oct. 1958
Strong Republicans	13%	15%	13%	14%	15%	10%	13%
Weak Republicans	14	15	14	18	14	16	16
Independent Republicans	7	6	6	6	8	6	4
Independents	5	4	7	3	9	8	8
Independent Democrats	10	8	9	6	7	7	7
Weak Democrats	25	23	25	24	23	26	24
Strong Democrats	22	22	22	19	21	21	23
Apolitical, don't know	4	7	4	10	3	6	5
Total	100%	100%	100%	100%	100%	100%	100%
Number of cases	1614	1023	1139	1731	1772	1488	1269

bution of party identification in the electorate during the years from 1952 to 1958.

In using these techniques of measurement we do not suppose that every person who describes himself as an Independent is indicating simply his lack of positive attraction to one of the parties. Some of these people undoubtedly are actually repelled by the parties or by partisanship itself and value their position as Independents. Certainly independence of party is an ideal of some currency in our society, and it seems likely that a portion of those who call themselves Independents are not merely reporting the absence of identification with one of the major parties.

Sometimes it is said that a good number of those who call themselves Independents have simply adopted a label that conceals a genuine psychological commitment to one party or the other. Accordingly, it is argued that a person's voting record gives a more accurate statement of his party attachment than does his own self-description. Our samples doubtless include some of these undercover partisans, and we have incorporated in our measure of party identification a means of distinguishing Independents who say they lean toward one of the parties from Independents who say they do not. We do not think that the problem of measurement presented by the concealed partisan is large.

Rather it seems to us much less troublesome than the problems that follow if psychological ties to party are measured in terms of the vote.

This question can be illuminated a good deal by an examination of the consistency of party voting among those of different degrees of party identification, as is done in Table 5-2. The proportion of persons consistently supporting one party varies by more than sixty per-

Table 5-2. Relation of Strength of Party Identification to Partisan Regularity in Voting for President, 1956[a]

	Strong Party Identifiers	Weak Party Identifiers	Independents Leaning to Party	Independents
Voted always or mostly for same party	82%	60%	36%	16%
Voted for different parties	18	40	64	84
Total	100%	100%	100%	100%
Number of cases	546	527	189	115

[a] The question used to establish party consistency of voting was this: "Have you always voted for the same party or have you voted for different parties for President?"

centage points between strong party identifiers and complete Independents. For the problem of the undercover partisan, the troublesome figure in Table 5-2 is the 16 per cent of full Independents who have voted for the candidates of one party only.[2] The importance of this figure diminishes when we remember that some of these persons have voted in very few presidential elections and could have supported one party consistently because of the way their votes fell, free of the influence of a genuine party tie.

A simple test of this hypothesis is made in Table 5-3 by separating persons who have come of voting age relatively recently from those

[2] In this discussion we assume that the concealed partisan is less likely to distort his voting record than his description of his party attachment; that is, we assume that what the undercover partisan values is chiefly the designation "Independent." To the extent this is untrue, the analysis of voting consistency by strength of party identification fails to enhance our understanding.

Table 5-3. Relation of Strength of Party Identification to Partisan Regularity in Voting for President, by Age Groups, 1956

Age	Strong Party Identifiers	Weak Party Identifiers	Independents Leaning to Party	Independents
21 to 34				
Voted always or mostly for same party	91%	78%	60%	33%
Voted for different parties	9	22	40	67
Total	100%	100%	100%	100%
Number of cases	104	120	53	21
35 and above				
Voted always or mostly for same party	80%	55%	26%	11%
Voted for different parties	20	45	74	89
Total	100%	100%	100%	100%
Number of cases	440	405	136	93

who have been of voting age for a greater number of elections. Plainly, the length of time a person has had to develop a variable voting record influences the likelihood that he will report that he has voted for the candidates of more than one party, whatever the strength of his party identification. But among complete Independents the proportion of people thirty-five years old or older who could reasonably be called concealed party identifiers is now reduced to 11 per cent. A detailed inspection of these cases shows that a number of these individuals have voted in relatively few elections and have had little opportunity to form an inconsistent voting record. When the frequency of voting turnout is considered, the proportion of extreme Independents who have voted only for the candidates of one party is not greater than we would expect it to be by chance alone.

The measurement of party identification in the period of our research shows how different a picture of partisan allegiance voting behavior and self-description can give. Despite the substantial Republican majorities in the elections of 1952 and 1956, the percentages of Table 5-1 make clear that the Democratic Party enjoyed a three-to-two advantage in the division of party identification within the electorate in these same years.[3] Moreover, Table 5-1 documents the stability of this division of party loyalty in a period whose electoral history might suggest widespread change. Except for the shifting size of the group of respondents refusing to be assigned any position on the party scale, there is not a single variation between successive distributions of party identification that could not be laid to sampling error.

The great stability of partisan loyalties is supported, too, by what we can learn from recall data about the personal history of party identification. We have asked successive samples of the electorate a series of questions permitting us to reconstruct whether an individual who accepts a party designation has experienced a prior change in his party identification. The responses give impressive evidence of the constancy of party allegiance.

The fact that nearly everyone in our samples could be placed on a unitary dimension of party identification and that the idea of prior movements on this dimension was immediately understood are themselves important findings about the nature of party support within the electorate. In view of the loose, federated structure of American parties it was not obvious in advance that people could respond to party in these undifferentiated terms. Apparently the positive and negative feelings that millions of individuals have toward the parties are the result of orientations of a diffuse and generalized character that have a common psychological meaning even though there may be a good deal of variation in the way party is perceived.

PARTY IDENTIFICATION AND POLITICAL ATTITUDE

The psychological function of party identification undoubtedly varies among individuals. Our interest here centers primarily on the role of party as a supplier of cues by which the individual may evaluate the elements of politics. The fact that most elements of national politics are far removed from the world of the common citizen forces the individual to depend on sources of information from which he may learn indirectly what he cannot know as a matter of direct experience. Moreover, the complexities of politics and government increase the importance of having relatively simple cues to evaluate what cannot be matters of personal knowledge.

[3] Because Republican identifiers voted with somewhat greater frequency than Democratic identifiers in these years, the Democratic edge in party allegiance was slightly less among voters.

In the competition of voices reaching the individual the political party is an opinion-forming agency of great importance. This is not to say that party leaders are able as a matter of deliberate technique to transmit an elaborate defense of their position to those in the electorate who identify with the party. To the contrary, some of the most striking instances of party influence occur with only the simplest kind of information reaching the party's mass support. For example, a party undoubtedly furnishes a powerful set of cues about a political leader just by nominating him for President. Merely associating the party symbol with his name encourages those identifying with the party to develop a more favorable image of his record and experience, his abilities, and his other personal attributes. Likewise, this association encourages supporters of the opposite party to take a less favorable view of these same personal qualities. Partisans in each camp may incorporate into their view of the candidates whatever detailed information they can, and the highly-involved may develop an elaborate and carefully-drawn portrait. But the impact of the party symbol seems to be none the less strong on those who absorb little of politics and whose image of the candidates is extremely diffuse.

Apparently party has a profound influence across the full range of political objects to which the individual voter responds. The strength of relationship between party identification and the dimensions of partisan attitude suggests that responses to each element of national politics are deeply affected by the individual's enduring party attachments. If we return to the attitude forces of Chapter 3 and examine their strength and direction across the party identification scale, a remarkable pattern is seen. Figures 5-1 and 5-2, respectively, show this pattern as it appeared in 1952 and 1956 by displaying the mean of each attitude in each of five groups spanning the party dimension.[4] In the design of these figures the vertical dimension indicates the intensity and direction of attitude partisanship, the horizontal dimension the strength and direction of party identification. If we take any group along the party identification scale, it will be *more* pro-Republican in all its attitudes than the group immediately to its left and it will be *less* pro-Republican in all its attitudes than the group immediately to its right, except of course as a group may fall at the

[4] In each case the mean of an attitude factor for a party identification group has been divided by the standard deviation of the factor for the group in order to express the mean in standard units about the zero point. The effect of this normalization is to lessen differences in the means that are attributable simply to differences in the number (rather than the relative partisanship) of references a party identification group has made to a given element of national politics.

end of the party scale. The fact that without exception these attitude forces become steadily more pro-Republican as we move from the Democratic to the Republican end of the party dimension suggests the

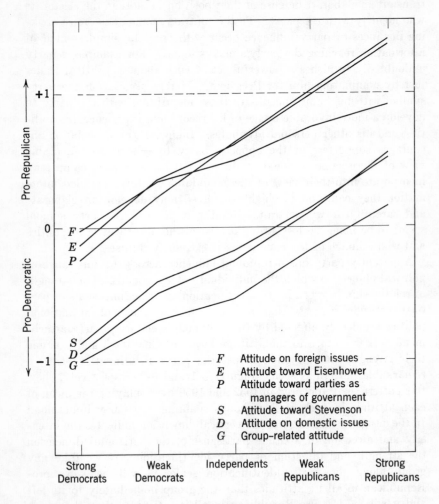

FIG. 5-1. Relation of party identification to partisan evaluations of elements of national politics, 1952.

extent of the party's impact on the electorate's evaluations of the elements of politics.

Of course party identification cannot account for all the observed variation of political attitude. However great its impact, partisan loyalty does not by any means express the total influence of factors antecedent in a causal sense to the attitudes we have studied. Paradoxically, the very data that show the enormous influence of party

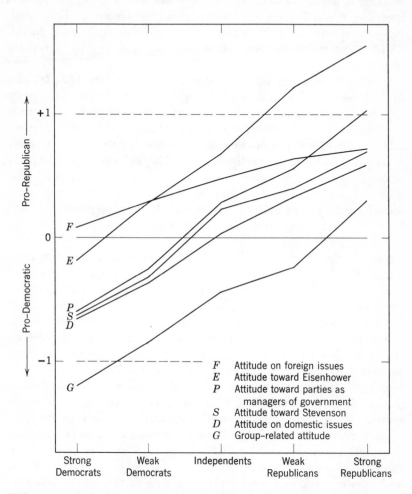

FIG. 5-2. Relation of party identification to partisan evaluations of elements of national politics, 1956.

allegiance on political attitude in these elections show also the limits of its explanatory power. In Figs. 5-1 and 5-2 we may note that some attitudes are more favorable than others to one of the parties *across the entire party identification scale.* For example, in each of these elections the Republicans fared better with the public on foreign issues than on domestic issues in each of the groups defined by our measure of party identification. And between the two elections this difference in attitude partisanship diminished in every one of these groups by a lessening of pro-Democratic feeling on domestic policy. These findings plainly have to be explained in terms of antecedent causal factors whose effects were independent of what is measured by our party identification scale.

If party identification deeply influences the partisan character of a field of psychological forces, it also will have marked effects on the internal consistency of the field. Our conception of the role of partisan loyalties leads us to expect this result. Identification with a party raises a perceptual screen through which the individual tends to see what is favorable to his partisan orientation. The stronger the party bond, the more exaggerated the process of selection and perceptual distortion will be. Without this psychological tie, or perhaps with commitments to symbols of another kind, the Independent is less likely to develop consistent partisan attitudes.

The earlier discussion of attitude conflict is readily extended to give empirical support to this view. We will take a person's attitudes toward the several elements of politics to be fully consistent here if each attitude that is not politically neutral has the same partisan direction. The entries of Table 5-4 show the great significance of party identification for the internal consistency of attitude. If the number of people we would expect to have consistent attitudes by chance is taken as a suitable zero, a slight tendency toward consistent partisanship is seen even among extreme Independents. But the tendency is much more marked among Independents who lean toward one of the parties and among weak party identifiers, and it is vastly greater among those who describe their party allegiance as strong.

The patterns of relationship found in cross-sectional data ought not to suggest too simple an idea of the connection between party identification and attitudes toward the elements of politics. A relation that may appear static and unidirectional in data of this sort is undoubtedly fairly complex, and several more things need to be said about it if our formulation is to do justice to psychological realities. In particular, it should be clear that the influence of party identification on attitudes toward political objects extends through time. The relationships found in the interviews of a relatively brief campaign period reflect a process of opinion formation and change that may go back over many months or years. Hence the explanatory problem we confront is a dynamic one; we need to understand the causal pri-

*Table 5-4. Party Identification as an Influence
on Partisan Consistency of Attitude, 1956*[a]

	Strong Party Identifiers	Weak Party Identifiers	Independents Leaning to Party	Independents
Number expected to have consistent attitudes	107	122	47	31
Number observed to have consistent attitudes	358	259	94	43
Increase of observed over expected number	235%	112%	100%	39%
Number of cases	597	558	230	117

[a] This tabulation includes only individuals having at least two non-neutral attitudes; that is, only respondents for whom the notion of consistent or inconsistent attitude could be given meaning. For two, three, four, five, or six non-neutral attitudes the probabilities of someone's having attitude consistency by chance alone are easily calculated, assuming the probability is 0.5 that a particular attitude will have a given partisan sign. The probabilities so calculated may be combined with what we know about the number of people in each of the four party identification groups who have each of the possible numbers of non-neutral attitudes. From this combination we obtain the number of people of each degree of party identification that we would expect to have consistent attitudes by chance. The difference between these expected frequencies and the actual frequencies of consistent individuals in each group seems an appropriate statistic for assessing the importance of strength of party identification as an influence on consistency of attitudes.

orities of a process extending through time and not just the direction of influence at a given moment. It seems likely that at the peak of a presidential campaign the causal relation of party identification to attitudes toward the things that are seen in national politics is two-directional. If the individual has formed attitudes that are consistent with his party allegiance, that allegiance will continue to support the attitudes it has shaped. But these attitudes in turn comprise an important defense of the individual's fixed partisan commitment, one that may well give service in discussions with face-to-face associates during the campaign. If the individual has developed attitudes *not* consistent with his party allegiance, that allegiance presumably will work to undo the contrary opinions. But they in turn must exert some pressure on the individual's basic partisan commitment. If this pressure is intense enough, a stable partisan identification may actually be changed. When such a change occurs in a considerable part of the electorate, as it has at rare moments of our political history, the great realignments occur that change the course of electoral politics for years to come.

In the period of our studies the influence of party identification on attitudes toward the perceived elements of politics has been far more important than the influence of these attitudes on party identification itself. We are convinced that the relationships in our data reflect primarily the role of enduring partisan commitments in shaping attitudes toward political objects. Our conviction on this point is rooted in what we know of the relative stability and priority in time of party identification and the attitudes it may affect. We know that persons who identify with one of the parties typically have held the same partisan tie for all or almost all of their adult lives. But within their experience since coming of voting age many of the elements of politics have changed. For example, the 1952 campaign brought two new candidates to presidential politics and a set of issues arising very recently from the Korean War and the charges of corruption during the later Truman years. Yet the reactions to the personalities of Eisenhower and Stevenson, to the issues of the Far Eastern war, and to the probity of the Democratic Administration differed markedly according to the individual's party allegiance. If we are to trust the evidence on the stability of party identification, these differences must be attributed to the capacity of a general partisan orientation to color responses to particular political objects.

What is more, even the elements of politics that carry over from one election to another may be evaluated anew in later campaigns by part of the electorate. The involvement of many Americans in politics is slight enough that they may respond *de novo* to issues and personalities that have been present in earlier elections but that are salient to them only at the height of a presidential campaign. For many voters the details of the political landscape may be quite blurred until they are brought more into focus during the campaign period. The formative influence of party identification on these re-evaluations would not be essentially different from its influence on responses to newer elements of politics.

Because the influence of party identification extends through time, its workings cannot be fully disclosed by the relationships seen at a particular moment. For this reason, our statement of causal priorities is in the end an inference, but one for which the evidence is strong. If the inference is correct, the differences in attitude between those of differing partisan loyalties enlarge considerably our understanding of the configuration of forces leading to behavior. We have seen in Chapter 3 that the voting act can be explained in an immediate sense by the strength and direction and consistency of attitudes toward the political objects this act touches. We find now that an important part of the variation in the partisanship and internal coherence of these attitudes may in turn be accounted for by stable partisan identifications.

This causal paradigm requires one additional amendment. Our hypothesis that party identification influences the voting act by influencing attitudes toward the objects to which this act relates needs to be modified for the person who has only the faintest image of these objects. If someone has little perception of the candidates, of the record of the parties, of public issues or questions of group interest, his attitudes toward these things may play a less important intervening role between party identification and the vote. Like the automobile buyer who knows nothing of cars except that he prefers a given make, the voter who knows simply that he is a Republican or Democrat responds directly to his stable allegiance without the mediating influence of perceptions he has formed of the objects he must choose between.

PARTY IDENTIFICATION AND ELECTORAL CHOICE

The role of general partisan orientations in molding attitudes toward the elements of politics is thus very clear. As a consequence of this role, party identification has a profound impact on behavior. A sense of its impact may be gained if we return to the statistical model used in Chapter 3 to express the probability that a given individual would vote in a given partisan direction. From the strength and direction of attitudes toward the various elements of politics we could order the individuals in our samples according to the probability of their voting Republican. That is, we could form an array extending from those most likely to vote Democratic to those most likely to vote Republican. Let us now make explicit the impact party identification has on behavior through its influence on attitude, by showing a separate array for each of five groups defined by our party identification scale. For each of the distributions shown in Fig. 5-3 the horizontal dimension is the probability an individual will vote Republican; to the left this probability is low (that is, the likelihood the individual will vote Democratic is high), and to the right the probability that the individual will vote Republican is high. The effect of party is seen at once in the changing location of the distributions along this prob-

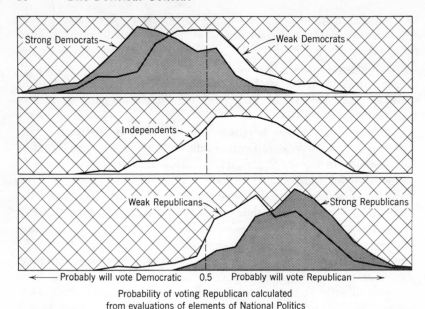

←——— Probably will vote Democratic   0.5   Probably will vote Republican ——→

Probability of voting Republican calculated
from evaluations of elements of National Politics

FIG. 5-3. Probable direction of vote by party identification groups, 1956.

ability dimension as we consider successively Strong Democrats, Weak Democrats, Independents, Weak Republicans, and Strong Republicans. The moving positions of these arrays show clearly the impact of party identification on the forces governing behavior.

The properties of Fig. 5-3 serve also to demonstrate once again that party allegiance is not the sole determinant of the attitudes supporting behavior. In the election of 1956 all five of these arrays were "biased" in the Republican direction in the sense that many more strong or weak Democrats than strong or weak Republicans are seen to be probable voters for the opposite party and fewer Independents are probable Democratic voters than are probable Republican voters. Evidently in this election powerful antecedent factors other than party allegiance influenced in a direction favorable to the Republican Party the psychological forces acting on behavior.

The distributions of Fig. 5-3 foreshadow the division of the presidential vote within the several party identification groups in the election of 1956. In view of the dependence of voting choice on the psychological forces we have treated, these probability arrays lead us to expect extreme differences in the division of the vote across the party groups. They lead us to expect, too, that the Republican Party had an advantage in this election in securing the votes of Independents and of persons identifying with the opposite party. Both these expectations are confirmed by Table 5-5.

Table 5-5. Relation of Party Identification to Presidential Vote

	Strong Demo- crats	Weak Demo- crats	Inde- pendents	Weak Repub- licans	Strong Repub- licans
1952					
Republican	16%	38%	67%	94%	99%
Democratic	84	62	33	6	1
	100%	100%	100%	100%	100%
Number of cases	262	274	269	171	199
1956					
Republican	15%	37%	73%	93%	99%
Democratic	85	63	27	7	1
	100%	100%	100%	100%	100%
Number of cases	286	270	305	194	211

Differences in the motivational forces acting on voters of contrasting party loyalties lead us to expect wide differences between party groups in the division of the presidential vote. Yet the variability of the vote shown in Table 5-5 is so extreme that it naturally raises the question whether party identification does not have a residual effect on behavior apart from its impact through the attitudes it influences so profoundly. That this residual effect is small is indicated by the fact that adding party identification to the set of attitude variables from which we have predicted behavior brings only a slight improvement in explanation of either the sense of statistical estimation or that of the discrimination of actual Republican voters from actual Democratic voters.[5] The improvement that *is* found we attribute primarily to the role of party identification in motivating directly the behavior of persons who are without a well-developed image of the things to which their vote relates. For them, the connection of party identification and behavior may not be mediated by attitudes toward the political objects

[5] Incorporating party identification in the statistical model used for prediction in Chapter 3 increases the multiple correlation with voting choice from 0.72 to 0.74 in the election of 1952 and from 0.71 to 0.73 in the election of 1956. In each year the addition of this factor raises less than 2 per cent the number of persons who could be correctly classified as Republican or Democratic voters.

this behavior concerns. As a result, knowing their stable partisan loyalties improves our ability to predict behavior more than it does for individuals who have formed stronger evaluations of the things toward which the vote is directed.

The nature of this difference—and of our conception of the place of party identification in the forces leading to the vote—can be made clearer if we examine, in Table 5-6, the behavior of individuals whose attitudes toward the current elements of politics contradict their sense

Table 5-6. Relation of Degree of Attitude Development to Direction in Which Conflict of Party Identification and Partisan Evaluations Is Resolved in Voting[a]

| | Those Who Have Formed Evaluations | | Those Who Have Formed No Evaluations at All |
	That Are Well-Developed	That Are Poorly Developed	
Vote agrees with party identification	20%	47%	75%
Vote fails to agree with party identification	80	53	25
Total	100%	100%	100%
Number of cases	143	164	36

[a] Figures in this table are based on a combination of data from the 1952 and 1956 election samples.

of party identification. Among those who have a strong evaluative image of the elements of presidential politics, behavior coincides with these evaluations in 80 per cent of the cases. The fact that party allegiance prevails in only one-fifth of these cases is the more remarkable if we keep in mind the very strong relationship of party identification to the vote across the electorate as a whole. Among those who have a less clear evaluative image of the objects of politics, behavior coincides with party identification in a much greater proportion of cases. For these people the relation of party allegiance to behavior does seem to be mediated less by evaluations of political objects, although a good half of even these persons act in accord with the evaluations they have formed, rather than in accord with their party loyalties. Table 5-6 also describes the behavior of the very small group of individuals in our samples who identify with one of the parties yet who appear on our standard measures to have no perceptions of current political objects whatever. This is the group for which we would expect the causal sequence connecting party allegiance, attitudes toward the elements of politics, and the voting act to be most severely truncated. With evaluations of political objects playing no apparent intervening role between partisan allegiance and behavior, 75 per cent of these people simply vote their party loyalties at the polls.

PARTY IDENTIFICATION AND POLITICAL INVOLVEMENT

Our discussion of the impact of party identification should not close without some consideration of the relation of party allegiance to the dimension of political involvement introduced in Chapter 4. It is not accidental that the individual's general partisan orientation and the extent of his involvement in politics, either of which may influence a wide set of attitudinal and behavioral characteristics, are related to each other. Although our causal understanding of this relation is far from sure, the fact of association is clear enough: the stronger the individual's sense of attachment to one of the parties, the greater his psychological involvement in political affairs.

The association is easily missed in popular accounts of electoral behavior. The ideal of the Independent citizen, attentive to politics, concerned with the course of government, who weighs the rival appeals of a campaign and reaches a judgment that is unswayed by partisan prejudice, has had such a vigorous history in the tradition of political reform—and has such a hold on civic education today—that one could easily suppose that the habitual partisan has the more limited interest and concern with politics. But if the usual image of the Independent voter is intended as more than a normative ideal, it fits poorly the characteristics of the Independents in our samples. Far from being more attentive, interested, and informed, Independents tend as a group to be somewhat less involved in politics. They have somewhat poorer knowledge of the issues, their image of the candidates is fainter, their interest in the campaign is less, their concern over the outcome is relatively slight, and their choice between competing candidates, although it is indeed made later in the campaign, seems much less to spring from discoverable evaluations of the elements of national politics.

These differences may be illustrated in terms of two of the measures of involvement used in Chapter 4. When those of strong partisan identifications are compared with those who call themselves Inde-

Table 5-7. Relation of Strength of Party Identification to Interest in Campaign, 1956

	Strong Party Identifiers	Weak Party Identifiers	Independents
Very much interested	42%	23%	25%
Somewhat interested	38	42	43
Not much interested	20	35	32
Total	100%	100%	100%
Number of cases	624	651	415

pendents, the partisan tends both in his interest in the campaign and his concern over the outcome to be more involved than the political Independent, as Tables 5-7 and 5-8 indicate. What is more, a further division of the Independent group would show in each case that those

Table 5-8. Relation of Strength of Party Identification to Concern over Outcome, 1956

	Strong Party Identifiers	Weak Party Identifiers	Independents
Care very much or care pretty much	82%	62%	51%
Don't care very much or don't care at all	18	38	49
Total	100%	100%	100%
Number of cases	609	621	395

who refused to say they were closer to one party or the other are even less involved then other Independents.

It is by no means clear what causal interpretation should be given the association of strength of party identification and degree of political involvement found in the interviews taken at single points in time. For the moment we may suppose that a person's location on either of these fundamental dimensions will influence his location on the other. The individual who has a strong and continuing involvement in politics is more likely to develop a commitment to one or the other of the major parties. And the individual who has such a commitment is likely to have his interest and concern with politics sustained at a higher level. But we may suppose, too, that the relation of partisanship and involvement is to be explained in part by common antecedents. Discovering what it is in the individual's life experience that could account both for his party allegiance and his political involvement leads naturally to a consideration of the development of party identification.

★ chapter 6
The Development of Party Identification

ORIGINS OF PARTY IDENTIFICATION

When we examine the evidence on the manner in which party attachment develops and changes during the lifetime of the individual citizen, we find a picture characterized more by stability than by change— not by rigid, immutable fixation on one party rather than the other, but by a persistent adherence and a resistance to contrary influence.

Early Politicization. At the time we meet the respondents of our surveys they have reached the minimum voting age, and most of them are considerably beyond it. The only information we can obtain about their political experience in their pre-adult years depends on their recall. Hyman's review of the literature on "political socialization" brings together the available data to extend our understanding of this important stage of political growth.[1] It is apparent from his presentation that an orientation toward political affairs typically begins before the individual attains voting age and that this orientation strongly reflects his immediate social milieu, in particular his family.

Our own data are entirely consistent with this conclusion. The high degree of correspondence between the partisan preference of our respondents with that which they report for their parents may be taken as a rough measure of the extent to which partisanship is passed from one generation to the next.[2] This correspondence is somewhat higher among those people who report one or both of their parents as having been "actively concerned" with politics than among those whose parents were not politically active. If we make the reasonable

---

[1] Herbert Hyman, *Political Socialization* (The Free Press, Glencoe, Ill., 1959).
[2] There are obvious weaknesses in this measure. Some of our respondents had undoubtedly carried an "inherited" party identification into early adulthood but had changed by the time we interviewed them.

assumption that in the "active" homes the political views of the parents were more frequently and intensely cognized by the children than in the inactive homes, we should of course expect to find these views more faithfully reproduced in these children when they reach adult years. In contrast, we find that persons from inactive homes, especially those with no clear political orientation, tend strongly toward nonpartisan positions themselves. For a large proportion of the electorate the orientation toward politics expressed in our measure of party identification has its origins in the early family years. We are not able to trace the history of these families to find an explanation of why the homes of some people were politically oriented and others were not. Such homes appear to exist in all social strata, less frequently in some than in others, of course.

The Persistence of Partisanship. The extent to which pre-adult experience shapes the individual's political future may be judged from the constancy with which most people hold to the partisan orientation they have at the time they enter the electorate. When we ask people to recall their first presidential vote, for example, we discover that of those who can remember their first vote for President two thirds still identify with the same party they first voted for. A majority (56 per cent) of these presidential voters have never crossed party lines; they have always supported their party's candidate.

A direct assessment of the stability with which the average citizen holds to his political orientation may be obtained from his report on whether he has ever identified himself differently than he does at present. The picture is generally one of firm but not immovable attachment. The greatest mobility (32%) is found among those people whose party attachment is weakest; the strongly identified are least likely to have changed sides (only 7% of strong Democrats, and 15% of strong Republicans).

It is apparent from these various pieces of evidence that identification with political parties, once established, is an attachment which is not easily changed. Some members of the electorate do not form strong party attachments, however, and they make up a sufficiently large proportion of the population to permit the short-term influence of political forces associated with issues and candidates to play a significant role in determining the outcome of specific elections. Even strong identifiers are not impervious to such influences, and, as we shall see, occasional cataclysmic national events have had the power to produce substantial realignment in long-standing divisions of political sentiment.

FLUCTUATIONS IN PARTY IDENTIFICATION

Changes in public attitudes may be classified according to the type of stimulus that produces them. We may speak of *personal forces,* which move individuals selectively without reference to the larger social categories to which they belong, or of *social forces,* which move large sections of the population more or less simultaneously. Personal forces produce changes that vary in an uncorrelated way from individual to individual and do not have a significant impact on the prevailing pattern of attitudes, even though the total proportion of people shifting their position may be sizable. Social forces influence large numbers of people in similar ways and may produce substantial realignments of the total distribution of attitudes.[3]

Changes Produced by Personal Forces. A variety of circumstances in the life of the ordinary citizen have political significance for him as a person without having any accompanying implications for broader groups. When we examine the reports of those of our respondents who shifted parties for reasons that appear to be entirely individual, we find that their change in partisanship tended to be associated with a change in their social milieu. A marriage, a new job, or a change in neighborhood may place a person under strong social pressure to conform to political values different from his own. Close personal relationships are usually associated with common political identifications in American society, and discrepancies tend to create strain, especially if the conflicting political views are strongly held.

Of the 20 per cent of our respondents who say they have changed party affiliation during their lifetime only about one in six explains this change as a result of personal influence. Considering the high degree of mobility in American society, one might have anticipated that changes of this kind would be more numerous. The movements of large numbers of people from the farm to the city, from the city to the suburbs, from region to region, and from one employment situation to another undoubtedly result in profound differences in their manner of living. But none of these movements necessarily implies a change in one's immediate surroundings. As we know, there are large representations of both parties at virtually all social and occupational levels and it would not be surprising for a person of either

---

[3] This formulation closely resembles a model for the explanation of attitude changes developed by George Katona. See his "Attitude Change: Instability of Response and Acquisition of Experience" (*"Psychological Monographs,"* Vol. 72, No. 10; Washington, D. C.: American Psychological Association, Inc., 1958).

political persuasion to find himself among copartisans in almost any new situation into which he moved. We would, in fact, expect him to seek out such associates. Only in certain special groups, such as labor union members in mass industry in Northern metropolitan centers or high income business owners and executives, do we find such strong consensus of political belief that a dissenter might find himself in a lonely position.

Changes Produced by Social Forces. Although the changes resulting from purely personal circumstances may be expected to occur about as often in one partisan direction as the other, changes brought about by experiences shared in common are likely to be cumulative. If these experiences are sufficiently intense and sufficiently widespread, their political consequences may be profound.

Social forces create cumulative changes, but these changes need not disturb the prevailing balance of party strength. If the stimulus to which the public is subjected strikes different segments of the electorate in ways that have contrasting political implications, the resulting shifts in partisanship may change the makeup of each party's support without altering the relative proportions supporting each party. The impact of social forces may also have quite a different character, producing systematic movements from one party to the other that are not offset by movements in the opposite direction. There are two general types of public experience that appear to have this quality: those experiences associated with great national crises and, less obviously, those associated with progress through the life cycle. There have been two occasions when national crises have shaken prevailing political loyalties so violently that they reversed the balance of party strength throughout the country.

The political upheaval associated with the Civil War imposed a regional dimension on the partisan attachments of the American electorate. The violent reaction in the East and Midwest to the passage of the Kansas-Nebraska Act in 1854 led to the creation of the Republican Party, committed to resisting the extension of the "great moral, social, and political evil" of slavery. The Free Soil movement, taken up as a major principle by the Republican Party, and the Homestead Act of 1862 created a resource of rural Republican strength throughout the Northern and Western areas. Within a short period the political contours of the nation had been drastically reshaped. The South, which in prewar years had divided its votes in proportions similar to those of the North, became the Solid South. Northern communities that had been Democratic turned Republican and remained so for decades. The distribution of partisan attachments in the nation today, a century after the Civil War, follows the same regional lines laid down at that time.

The second national crisis that reshaped the political profile of the nation took place during the lifetime of most of our respondents, and we can see directly the impact of that event in their lives. The economic collapse that befell the nation during the administration of Herbert Hoover swept out of office a party that had dominated national politics since the election of William McKinley in 1896. The scope of the reversal of the party fortunes that followed 1932 is amply documented by the election statistics. In the early years of the New Deal there was a swing to the Democratic ticket, which was felt in varying degrees throughout the country. The tide then receded, and those areas that had been centers of Republican strength returned to Republican majorities. But the Republican Party did not regain the national majority that it had obviously had prior to 1932. When we ask from what levels of society the Democratic Party drew this new strength, we find from our survey data and from the aggregative election figures that the impact of the events of that period appears to have been felt most strongly by the youth, the economically underprivileged, and the minority groups.

YOUTH. Our inquiries into the political histories of our respondents lead us to believe that a larger component of the Democratic gain came from young voters entering the electorate and older people who had previously failed to vote than from Republicans who defected from their party.

A demonstration of the impact of the depression on the people reaching voting age at that time is given in Fig. 6-1. We have here arrayed our respondents by age group according to the party identification they reported at the time of our interview with them. Those members of the present electorate who came of age during the 1920's have a lower proportion of Democratic identifiers than do any of the groups that entered the electorate in later years. The sharp increase in Democratic identification among those who reached their majority at the end of this decade or during the early 1930's does not represent the total shift toward the Democratic Party at that time, but it does show the proportion of that shift that has persisted over the intervening years to the present time.

ECONOMIC GROUPS. The appeal of the New Deal was unquestionably strongly economic in character; it had, after all, been brought into being in the midst of the greatest economic catastrophe in American history. Mr. Roosevelt spoke about the "forgotten man" and spon-

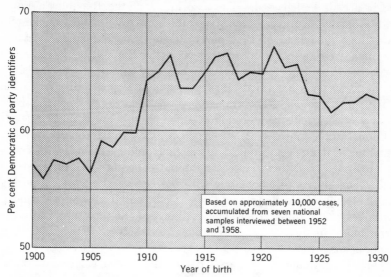

FIG. 6-1. *Party identification of party identifiers born between 1900 and 1930.*

sored a program of social legislation that his critics regarded as outright socialism. It is difficult to estimate how much influence all this had on the economic composition of the followings of the two parties, but it can be said with assurance that the economic and class distinctions between the two parties increased during this period. Such associations as had existed prior to the Depression between the less favored sections of the electorate and the Democratic Party were undoubtedly greatly enhanced.

On the basis of extensive analysis of the election returns from 1932 and 1936 Key offers these "educated guesses." "The policies of the New Deal brought in 1936 substantial new support from their beneficiaries. Metropolitan, industrial workers turned in heavy Democratic majorities. The unemployed, and those who feared they might become unemployed, voted Democratic in higher degree. Organized labor moved more solidly into the Democratic ranks."[4]

Our surveys do not go backward in time sufficiently for us to follow the political changes at the various economic levels during the Depression period, but the impact of the Depression is unmistakable in the images of the parties that we find in the public mind long after that

[4] V. O. Key, *Politics, Parties and Pressure Groups* (4th ed., Thomas Y. Crowell Company, New York, 1958), p. 578.

tragic decade had passed. The association of the Republican Party with economic depression was one of the strongest features of the picture the public held of that party at the time of our 1952 study. Through their twenty years out of office the Republican Party could not erase the memory that lingered in many minds of the hardships of the Depression nor rid itself of the onus of responsibility for them.

MINORITY GROUPS. The impact of the Depression and the New Deal was not exclusively economic. The philosophy of the Roosevelt Administration contained a strong element of social equalitarianism, which gave it a special appeal to religious and racial minorities who had reason to feel themselves discriminated against. Catholics have had a long history of association with the Democratic Party. During the Eisenhower elections there were substantial defections among Catholics to the Republican nominee, but even at that time Catholics were more likely (5–2) to consider themselves Democrats than Republicans.

The Jewish minority comprises one of the most Democratic groups to be found in the electorate; Democratic Jews outnumber Republican Jews in the order of 4–1. During the 1920's the vote in heavily Jewish districts of the Eastern metropolises ran as high as 80 per cent Republican.[5] Although vote is not the same as party identification, it can scarcely be doubted that the orientation of this group toward the two parties was substantially altered during the 1930's. We may surmise that the rise of the Nazi dictatorship in Germany and the opposition of the Roosevelt Administration to it must have played an important role in this change. Whatever the cause, the shift of Jewish allegiances to the Democratic Party was one of the most impressive of the several group movements in political preference during the Roosevelt period.

Prior to the 1930's, so far as we can tell from election statistics, the prevailing political preference among Negroes was Republican. This was a consequence, of course, of the Civil War and the attachment of Negroes to the party of Lincoln. During the 1930's politics took on a different significance to the Negro tenth of the electorate. It is impossible to know whether the shift of Negro allegiances to the Democratic standard from the traditions inherited from earlier generations occurred as the reactions of individual Negroes to the personalities and events of the times or as a mass movement resulting

[5] Lawrence H. Fuchs, *The Political Behavior of American Jews* (The Free Press, Glencoe, Ill., 1956), p. 56. See also Oscar Handlin, *The Uprooted* (Boston, Mass.: Little Brown, 1951), 216.

largely from the mobilization of Negro sentiment by an articulate leadership. No doubt both of these circumstances were present. In any case, the conversion of Negroes to the Democratic Party was very substantial. During the Eisenhower period Democratically identified Negroes outnumbered Republican Negroes by a margin of 3–1.

We turn now to a class of changes in party identification that does not depend on the dramatic impact of national catastrophes but on the gradual and commonplace changes in life situations that occur as one grows older. The fact that the successive phases of the life cycle are associated with a certain degree of common experience for most members of our society means that we may expect to find systematic changes in attitudes and behavior associated with changes in age. Such age-related changes are clearly present in the political orientation of the American electorate.

INTENSITY OF IDENTIFICATION. We find a steady increase in strong party attachments as we move through successive age levels, demonstrating the presence of age-related influences that are obviously not random. Young people, just entering the electorate, are more likely than any of the older age groups to call themselves Independents. This proportion drops among people in their late twenties and thirties and is accompanied by a proportionate increase in the number of strong identifiers. The older half of the electorate are clearly more likely to show a strong party attachment, with the most extreme position of all held by those people over 65 years old, a group that now constitutes approximately one twelfth of our adult population; 50 per cent of this age group are strong party identifiers, compared with 24 per cent of those 21 to 24 years of age.

We may now consider the way in which identification with political parties develops over the lifetime of the individual elector. Most people learn the party labels and something of what they mean during the early years when they are living with their parents. As young adults they are not overly interested in politics, they are indifferent voters, and they do not typically regard themselves as strongly attached to the political parties. As the young adult passes through the early egocentric years, however, the salience that political matters have in his life gradually increases. This happens for a variety of reasons. He is, for one thing, drawn into close association with social groups of one kind or another, some of which may have strong political orientations. He becomes aware of their political interests and he absorbs their interests as his own. It is also likely that as he becomes a more fully integrated community member he becomes more aware of the immediate implications for him of political decisions.

In addition, since political affairs become more familiar to a person as he matures, they seem less distant and unrealistic. The number of people who become politically active themselves, either as candidates or as party workers of one kind or another, is very small, but a much larger number of people acquire a certain familiarity with political goings on, and it seems likely that this fact is associated with an increasing identification of oneself with the party symbols.

Finally, for some people politics and parties may take on reality only as the result of some personal or national crisis. For example, many apparently inert people were stimulated to vote for the first time during the early years of the Great Depression. The Korean War appears to have activated several million people who had sat out the previous elections. On a more personal basis a business failure, a bad crop year, the loss of a job, or an encounter with the law may create a need for action and a sharpening of interest in what can be accomplished through political channels. Crises of large or small magnitude occur repeatedly during the lifetime of the ordinary citizen and serve to keep him alive to his role in the total political process.

Once a person has acquired some embyronic party attachment, it is easy for him to discover that most events in the ambiguous world of politics redound to the credit of his chosen party. As his perception of his party's virtue gains momentum in this manner, so his loyalty to it strengthens, and this fact in turn increases the probability that future events will be interpreted in a fashion that supports his partisan inclination. There are limits on the extent to which reality can be distorted to fit expectations and preferences, and exceptionally critical circumstances may induce a party identifier to cross party lines for a single election in the spirit of "time for a change." It is even possible that the flow of events may place his party in such an unfavorable position as to bring an actual change in his identification. But this is unusual; more typically party identification is not only sustained but strengthened by the passing show of political acts and actors.

It is matter of particular interest that party identification does not decline in significance in the later years of life; on the contrary, strong party attachment is more common among people of retirement age than it is at any other period. A close look at the comparatively few people who have changed their party identification during adulthood has given us reason to believe that intensity of party identification is directly related to the length of time a person has felt some degree of attachment to his party. As we move through the successive age cohorts we are consequently more and more likely to find people who have had a long unbroken experience of party identification. Older people have had more time to accumulate tenure in their party association, even those who in their earlier years moved from one party to the other. As they settle in their ultimate choice and their tenure with it grows, they become increasingly rigidly attached to it and less and less susceptible to cross-party pressures.

PARTISANSHIP OF IDENTIFICATION. It remains now to consider one further aspect of the relationship of age to political orientation. Republican identification increases progressively from the younger to the older age groups; 8 per cent of the 21–24 age group were strong Republican identifiers, compared with 24 per cent of those over 65 years old.

This peculiarity of the distribution of party identification presents an interesting question that we cannot fully answer. Is the Republican Party gradually aging and being replaced by a party that has captured the bulk of the young people coming into the electorate? If party identification is typically a life-long commitment, changed on the national scale only by major social cataclysms, it would be reasonable to conclude that the present age division in party identification is the consequence of the Depression and the New Deal and that the present Republican following must inevitably decrease as time replaces the older age groups with the younger groups in which people of Democratic commitment are more numerous.

To this explanation, however, one may oppose the hypothesis that the two parties have different appeals to people of different ages, and although the Democratic Party may have an advantage in its appeal to young people, this advantage may be gradually dissipated as these young Democrats grow older and respond differently to political stimuli. It would seem likely in a society in which the Republican Party was widely perceived as conservative and middle-class and the Democratic Party as liberal and working-class that the two parties would not be equally attractive to the older and younger members of the electorate.

If we examine in detail the reports of individual political history, we find that there was a substantial shift of party attachments during the New Deal period, most of it toward the Democratic Party. In each of the four-year periods during the last twenty years, however, there has been additional shifting, balancing out in each case to a relatively small advantage to the Republican Party. These findings lead us to doubt the proposition that either of the major parties is likely to expire as the result of old age. The great break toward the Democratic Party at the beginning of the Depression undoubtedly split the electorate along age lines. This split appears to have been maintained in the ensuing years by the heavy proportion of young people who declared themselves for the Democratic Party as they entered the electorate, but it has been offset by the Republican advantage in cross-party conversions among those in the older age brackets. During the 1950's these two components of the total following of the two parties appeared to balance each other very closely. Both the proportions of the electorate identifying themselves with each party and the age composition of each party's adherents remained constant throughout this period.

chapter 7
Public Policy and Political Preference

Just as the citizen's political behavior may be taken to affect, in one degree or another, the course of public policy, so questions of public policy may be presumed to affect the citizen's political behavior. The substance of partisan debate forms one of the most visible aspects of the political context in which voting decisions are made. For this reason we have conceived of issues as one of the major classes of political objects, and have included issue perceptions explicitly among our six partisan attitudes. A "proper" issue position taken by the candidate or party is a major source of favorable evaluation.

The process whereby issues are created and come to be endowed with partisan meaning over a mass electorate is as fascinating as it is complex. Party loyalty plays no small role in the formation of attitudes on specific policy matters. The identifier who sees his party take up a new issue is likely to be influenced thereby. On the other hand, if the individual has intense feelings about an issue before partisan alignments form, and his party's subsequent policy conflicts with such belief, they may act as important forces toward partisan change.

We have no adequate method for determining which of these sequences has led to an observed congruence between the individual's issue position and that of his current party. However, we do know that this congruence is less prevalent than commonly assumed; and we know that the mass electorate encounters difficulties in translating issue feelings into partisan motivations.

THE CONDITIONS OF ISSUE-ORIENTED POLITICAL BEHAVIOR

The role that any specific issue may play in ultimate partisan choice is limited in several directions. Only rarely does a single policy belief comprise the sole force in the psychological field as the voting decision is made. Except in the referendum, votes are cast directly for candidates and parties. Not only do these objects represent numerous issue positions at once; they also have properties of their own independent of any issue significance. Reactions to these properties, as we have argued, token further forces on behavior.

More important for our current purposes are the circumstances under which we could not legitimately expect a specific issue to exert any force in the individual's field. We may specify at least three conditions to be fulfilled if an issue is to bear upon a person's vote decision:

1. The issue must be cognized in some form.
2. It must arouse some minimal intensity of feeling.
3. It must be accompanied by some perception that one party represents the person's own position better than do the other parties.

If an issue is to motivate a voter, he must be aware of its existence and must have an opinion about it. Although this statement is obvious, it draws our attention to the fact that many people know of the existence of few if any of the major issues of policy. One of the greatest limitations on civic participation is imposed by sheer ignorance of the existence of major social and economic problems. From the viewpoint of social action, the problem of creating familiarity with issues is the first task; from the viewpoint of social analysis, understanding the evolution of public familiarity with issues is also a necessary beginning step.

The second condition requires that there be some sense of the importance of an issue, for involvement cannot be assumed on the basis of familiarity alone. Intensity of opinions may vary widely from voter to voter, but when opinions are relatively intense we have another important indication that they will have some bearing on the voter's ultimate decision.

An issue may be recognized, and recognized as important, without having serious consequences for the voter's partisan preference unless the final condition is fulfilled. Intense feeling about an issue must be translated into a partisan motivation, and this process can only be completed if the individual has some sense that the parties will handle things differently. In short, he must perceive that the political system offers alternatives, and he must be able to determine which of them matches his own position most closely.

These three conditions are entirely obvious ones. Yet their simplicity should not deceive us into assuming that they are generally fulfilled across the electorate. Instead, large portions of the adult population fail to meet each succeeding condition on a wide variety of prominent issues. It is important to note, therefore, that we take these three conditions as necessary rather than sufficient conditions, if issues are to affect the vote decision. If any of these conditions is *not* met, we can hardly expect the issues involved to bear in any meaningful way upon partisan preference. On the other hand, all three conditions may be fulfilled without giving us genuine assurance that the issue has played any major role in determining the voter's choice.

ISSUE FAMILIARITY

If we wish to know how familiar an issue is to the members of an electorate, we soon find that most of the traditional cues are as likely to be misleading as they are to be enlightening. The amount of public attention paid an issue by political leaders is an unreliable index of public familiarity. Similarly, it is seldom wise to rely on even the most rigorous study of the mass media for indications of the public's familiarity with any specific issue. In general, public officials and people involved in public relations tend to overestimate the impact that contemporary issues have on the public. They find it difficult to believe that the reams of newspaper copy and the hours of television and radio time could be ignored by any normal person within the reach of those media. The fact seems to be, however, that the human perceptorium is highly selective, and unless it happens to be tuned to a particular wavelength, the message transmitted over that wavelength will be received only as noise. This perceptual screening seems to protect the individual citizen from too strenuous an overload of incoming information.

An example of public indifference to an issue that was given heavy emphasis by political leaders is provided by the role of the Taft-Hartley Act in the 1948 election. The Democratic Party chose this piece of labor legislation as a major point of attack in the 1948 campaign. Yet almost seven out of every ten adult Americans saw the curtain fall on the presidential election of 1948 without knowing whether Taft-Hartley was the name of a hero or a villain.

Components of Familiarity with an Issue. To gather better information about public familiarity with issues of politics, a set of questions on public policy was posed for a cross section of the 1956 electorate. The questions were deliberately presented in such a manner as to yield an indication of the variation in public familiarity with these issues. The presentation of each policy item was prefaced with the direct suggestion that it was quite proper for the person to respond by telling us that he (or she) did not happen to have an opinion on the question.

Our 1956 data illustrate the extent of variation in public familiarity with issues. About one-fourth of the national population claimed familiarity with fewer than one out of every two issues presented to them. At the other extreme we find almost one-third who claimed enough familiarity with the issues to give us statements of attitudes on at least fourteen out of sixteen issues posed for them. It is likely that our list included most of the better-known issues and could have been extended only by adding items familiar to fewer and fewer persons. If this is true, the previously given estimates may overstate the average level of familiarity with specific issues in 1956. For many purposes of political analysis it is useful to introduce a further criterion in a discussion of public familiarity with issues. The possession of an opinion about governmental policy is of greatest interest to us when the person holding the opinion can and does relate it to a pertinent part of the political system. Therefore, it was important to ascertain whether the person had any notion of what the federal government was doing with respect to the policy in question. The person's accuracy in evaluating the performance of the government is not pertinent here. Familiarity is intended to refer only to the existence of an opinion that is given some sort of political meaning by its possessor; it is not confined to the existence of "accurate" opinions that are "correctly" related to the "reality" of the political world.

Use of both criteria of familiarity over a variety of issues leads to the results summarized in Table 7-1. On the average, about one respondent out of every three failed to survive these two hurdles for any issue. There is some variation according to the nature of the issue. When the item involves some general posture that this nation might adopt, such as "being friendly with the other countries of the world," there appears to be more likelihood of an opinion's being expressed and some perception of what the government is doing. Where an item deals with more specific programs such as aid to neutrals, however, fewer perceptions emerge. It is clear that the level of specificity is not the only determinant of familiarity; relatively specific programs of social welfare that have been under debate for some time appear more familiar to the public. But it seems that the specificity with which the issue is formulated does play some role in responses.

Table 7-1. Public Familiarity with Selected Issues, 1956

Issue	No Opin-ion	Hold Opinion but Do Not Know What Gov't Is Doing	Hold Opinion and Know What Gov't Is Doing	Total
Foreign Policy				
Give aid to neutral countries	28%	19	53	100%
Send soldiers abroad	20%	13	67	100%
Economic aid to foreign countries	17%	16	67	100%
Act tough toward Russia, China	20%	11	69	100%
Avoid foreign involvement	14%	15	71	100%
Friendliness toward other nations	12%	10	78	100%
Domestic Policy				
Firing of suspected Communists	16%	39	45	100%
Leave electricity, housing to private industry	30%	19	51	100%
Segregation of schools	12%	34	54	100%
Influence of big business in government	28%	18	54	100%
Influence of unions in government	25%	20	55	100%
Insure medical care	12%	29	59	100%
Cutting taxes	19%	18	63	100%
Government guarantee of jobs	10%	23	67	100%
Racial equality in jobs and housing	14%	19	67	100%
Government aid to education	10%	23	67	100%

The Development of Issue Familiarity. The existence of an opinion on an issue depends on both cognitive and affective factors. In the first case, the person who fails to cognize the basic components involved in a policy question will not have any great familiarity with the question as a political issue. Table **7-2** shows a direct relationship between increasing years of schooling and increasing familiarity with our selection of issues.

Table 7-2. Relation of Education to Familiarity with Issues, 1956

Familiarity with Issues	From No Formal Schooling to Completion of 8 Grades	High School, Some or Completion	College, Some or Degree
High	21%	31%	50%
Medium	37	47	44
Low	42	22	6
	100%	100%	100%
Number of cases	543	890	331

Sheer awareness of a problem is, of course, not enough to bring an opinion into being. An attitude takes shape as cognitions become related in some manner to values held by the person. Unless various states of affairs associated with an issue are evaluated as good or bad, desirable or undesirable, a person will not express an opinion about the issue. Thus, if he sees neither good nor bad in the vigorous enforcement of fair employment practices he may show no feeling about the matter, even though he may have more than enough information to classify as "aware" of the issue.

THE INTENSITY OF ISSUE OPINION

The second important component of issue involvement that may lead to issue-oriented political behavior is, then, the extent to which the issue arouses intense feelings. In the context of elections, an issue that creates only mild sentiments of support and opposition is not a politically important issue, regardless of its actual importance to the national welfare. At first glance it might seem difficult to disentangle the properties of familiarity and intensity. Yet even our restricted selection of public issues contains clear examples of a distinct lack of congruence between these properties. The question of the role of the federal government in electric power production and housing construction provoked almost as large a proportion of extreme opinions as did the education question, but it was familiar to many fewer persons. Both questions were the object of intense opinions, but one question was known to two thirds of the population, whereas the other was familiar to little more than half of the people. The item advocating "economic help to the poorer countries of the world even if they can't pay for it" was widely known but was the object of only mild expression of opinion. Although almost seven out of every ten persons showed some familiarity with the issue, less than half of them expressed strong or intense opinions.

Variation of Intensity. In defining intensity we work within the context of familiarity: among persons who are familiar with an issue, what variation can be observed in a quantitative measure of intensity, extremity, or strength of opinion? It should be remembered that we have specified two essential components of familiarity, one cognitive and the other evaluative. It is the latter that is most clearly subject to variation in intensity.

The factor governing the intensity of a person's opinions is not merely the absolute importance of values that are thought to be relevant to a policy question, but also the discrepancy in importance between values that will be realized and values that will be thwarted under alternative resolutions of the policy question. In the simple case, enactment of policy may result in goal achievement for a person; failure to enact will result in the failure to achieve. The importance of the value that is enhanced by achievement or denied by nonachievement will determine the intensity of opinion.

Questions of governmental policy, however, more commonly involve conflict and competition among goals. If policy A is pursued, goal X is achieved but goal Y is denied; if the policy is not pursued, Y will be achieved and not X. If the goals are equally important, the opinion on policy A may be extremely mild, really a matter of indifference. But if goal Y is much more highly valued than goal X, the opinion will be one of opposition to policy A. The intensity of the opposition will depend on *how much more important* Y is than X; that is, it will depend on the discrepancy in importance of the values which are in conflict.

A second major source of variation in intensity springs from the fact that some people find an issue more relevant for their values than do others holding the same values. The manner in which values caught by an issue lead to more intense opinions may be readily illustrated by responses to our issue items. A striking example is provided by White and Negro attitudes on the question of the government "helping Negroes get jobs and housing." Of course the division of opinion on this issue between the racial groups conforms to our expectations. Whereas White respondents gave strong support to the policy of governmental aid to Negroes, the Negroes themselves were virtually unanimous in their approval. However, our interest here lies not

in the division of opinion but in the relative frequency of strong statements of policy position as opposed to milder expressions of feeling.[1]
Although the White members of the population lined up 66 to 34, intense to moderate, on the question, Negroes divided 94 to 6. This
differential undoubtedly reflects the greater importance to Negroes of
the values involved. Completely comparable differences between opinions of White and Negro citizens were found both in the South and in
the non-Southern states.

Other things equal, then:

1. Persons for whom a value is more important will be more likely
   to express intense opinions than will persons for whom the same
   value is less important.
2. Persons who perceive issues to be more relevant for their values
   will be more likely to express intense opinions.

THE PERCEPTION OF PARTY DIFFERENCES ON ISSUES

When the individual sees the parties to be in conflict on an issue
that concerns him, there is usually little further problem in his deduc-
ing which party policy is most congruent with his own view. But it is
only as these links are completed that the way is paved for partisan
motivation on an issue base.

Only 40 to 60 per cent *of the "informed" segment* of the population
(that is, the part that holds an opinion on an issue) perceive party
differences and hence can locate one or the other party as closer to their
"own" position. There is considerable variation in this figure from
issue to issue, just as there was with issue familiarity itself. Some of
the long-standing issues of the New and Fair Deal period show two
out of every three informed persons perceiving party differences; on
most of the foreign policy issues fewer than one out of every two persons think the parties differ appreciably. In either case, the discrepancy between those who hold attitudes and those who can relate the
content of these attitudes to differences in party position is substantial.
The lesson seems clear that even when "political" attitudes are held,
there is no guarantee that *partisan* implications are drawn.

What underlies this failure to perceive party differences on policies
of concern to the individual? Its roots are to be found in circum-

---

[1] This measurement of intensity differs radically from that employed in the
analysis of political attitudes in Chapters 2–4. There, intensity referred to the
repetition of references to an issue; here, intensity refers to the weakness or
strength of a single reference to the issue.

stances of the external world as well as in limitations of the individual. Where distinctions between the parties are academic, it would not be surprising if few people did succeed in a discrimination, however intense popular feelings on the issue might be. Nor can we always assume that people failing to perceive differences are less well informed than those who do, although this may be the general rule; they may simply be more "up to date" in their images of parties whose policies are indeed converging.

It cannot be denied that actual ambiguities in the positions of the parties must have some effect on views of party differentiation. But we feel that a large measure of the observed failure to perceive party differences by people holding opinions on an issue can be traced to the same personal limitations that keep many others from recognizing the issue at all. Knowledge of party position is an item of information, just as is knowledge of the initial issue. In many ways it is more subtle and more complex information. If a fair portion of the electorate fails to have standing cognitions of the issue, it is not surprising that a further portion has not absorbed the additional information concerning the parties. Some 15 to 30 per cent of the people who held opinions but failed to perceive party differences indicated in so many words that they did not know the parties' stands. The proportion of frank "don't know" answers is itself a token that failure to perceive differences can in many cases be traced to lack of information rather than actual perceptions that the parties hold the same position.

Table 7-3 permits a summary glance at the proportions of our sample who survive all three conditions for issue-oriented political behavior laid out at the start of this chapter—the expression of an opinion, the perception of what the government is doing, and the perception of relevant differences in party policy—on each issue. As we have observed, even these survivors need not be materially affected in their partisan choice by their issue beliefs; instead, they represent no more than a maximum pool within which the specified issues might have conceivable effect.

CONSENSUS ON ISSUE POSITIONS OF THE PARTIES

When we analyze further the party differences perceived on each issue by the quartile of the population that makes any discrimination at all, we find that there is only a limited degree of consensus as to *which* party advocates *which* policy. Thus we find some proponents of government activity in matters of health insurance who feel the Republican Party best represents their position, and some who feel the Demo-

Table 7-3. Perception of Partisan Implications of Own Issue Beliefs

Issue	Proportion of Respondents Who Perceive Party Differences on Issue, Having Fulfilled Prior Conditions
Foreign Policy	
Act tough toward Russia and China	36%
U.S. international involvement ("Stay Home")	32%
Friendliness toward other nations	32%
Economic aid to foreign countries	23%
Send soldiers abroad	22%
Give aid to neutral countries	18%
Domestic Policy	
Influence of big business in government	35%
Influence of unions in government	31%
Government guarantees of jobs	31%
Segregation of schools	31%
Cutting taxes	30%
Racial equality in jobs and housing	28%
Aid to education	27%
Insure medical care	24%
Firing of suspected Communists	23%
Leave electricity and housing to private industry	22%

crats are closest to this view. Others who fear government intervention similarly include people of opposite partisan perceptions.

Where there is a babel of perceptions about party positions on a prominent issue, the significance of the public mandate becomes inscrutable. This fact would be true even if all other sources of ambiguity, such as narrow margins of victory and high competition of issues for voter attention, were removed from consideration. We can imagine, for example, a hypothetical case in which a single issue motivates the march to the polls, and one party wins an overwhelming landslide of votes. If there was no prior consensus among the voters as to the respective party positions, there can be no clear issue outcome: the victorious party may have drawn support equally from both opinion camps.

We find clear evidence of some consensus about party position only for those issues that concern the familiar New Deal-Fair Deal controversies. Questions having to do with governmental underwriting of medical costs, aid to education, guaranteed employment, control of big business and labor unions, and federal housing and electric power production all revealed tendencies to link the Democratic Party with the New Deal position. On the other hand, questions having to do with desegregation, protection of Negro rights in jobs and housing, and dismissal of government workers accused of being Communists revealed no consistent party image. Similarly, there was no sign of consensus about party position on any of the items covering aspects of foreign policy.

Although agreement on party alignments on New Deal controversies was substantial, it was in no sense complete. Where it was strongest— on the item concerning private control of electric power and housing —about 75 per cent accepted the view that the Republicans were the advocates of laissez faire. Since 50 per cent would mark the lowest possible ebb of consensus and 100 per cent its maximum, we see that there was substantial contradiction in perceptions even here. For one or two other issues in the New Deal grouping that we have cited, the majority view was held by as few as 65 per cent.

It is likely that party identification plays an important role in reducing consensus over the issue alignments of the parties. It follows from our prior discussions that the strong partisan who lacks any real information permitting him to locate either party on a question of policy may find it relatively easy to presume that his chosen party is closer to his own belief regarding that policy than is the opposition. The fact that only a minority of the population seems concerned as to party position on any specific issue indicates that much of the opinion formation that goes on in the electorate occurs independent of party cues. This is likely to mean that people who identify as Democrats will arrive at much the same distribution of opinions as those who identify as Republicans. Hence if adherents of opposing views within each party presume that the party reflects their own beliefs, the parties appear to be all things to all people. We would find little congruence between member opinion and leadership policy, and little consensus on where the parties do stand, a picture that fits the data well. In a sense the fact of party loyalties actually serves to *reduce* consensus about party position.

At this level, then, we are forced to conclude that articulation between party program, party member opinion, and individual political decision is weak indeed. Naturally the subject is not exhausted by this analysis. It may well be argued that we have imposed a view of issues and policies that is unrealistically specific. Significant differences do exist in the public images of the parties. The public may well have broader perceptions of the policy roles that the parties are prepared to play, and articulation between issue concerns and partisanship may be clearer at this level.

It seems significant, for example, that almost twice as many people were able to fulfill all three of our conditions on foreign policy items that had to do with broad postures of the government toward other nations (acting "tough," being "friendly," or minding its own business) than were able to react to more specific programs concerning foreign aid and military assistance (Table 7-3). Similarly, although we found no consensus as to party position on these matters of foreign policy, when we ask which party the person believes will do a better job of keeping the country out of war, a much larger proportion perceives party differences, with a sizable majority of members of both parties naming the Republican Party as better able to preserve the peace.

It is important for our understanding of the political system that we attain some grasp of the level at which issue concerns affect mass participation in politics. If most of the policy items discussed in this chapter are so specific in character that only a small portion of the electorate can respond meaningfully to them, this is in itself an important fact.

chapter 8

Attitude Structure and the Problem of Ideology

The widespread lack of familiarity with prominent issues of public policy, along with confusion on party position that remains even among individuals familiar with an issue, attests to the frailties of the political translation process. This insensitivity to policy controversies seems particularly significant when laid against our data concerning the stability of party identification over time. If the political relevance or, more especially, the partisan relevance of "new" problems is seen but darkly or not at all, it is less surprising that party allegiances gain momentum over time and are rarely derailed by pressures arising outside the political order.

It might be argued that although the "man in the street" may have only a loose idea of what is going on in terms of specific policy, he has a firm sense of the global policy differences between the parties, and relates them with equal firmness to highly generalized values of his own. A hypothesis of this sort could be fitted nicely with findings concerning the stability of party identification over time. Leaders of each party are continually forced to take positions, and from time to time these specific decisions fail to square well with the broader philosophy that normally characterizes the party. But policy as it may be formulated in the most general dimensions of ideology seems fairly stable for a party or tandem of parties throughout long political eras. Parties of the "left" and "right" do not trade positions from election to election. Assuming stability in parallel values in individuals, it would follow that partisan preferences would be pursued for long periods of time.

This suggestion directs our attention to the clusters or "structures" of attitudes involving political issues. We shall scan our data for evidence of this attitude structure, first at the level of the specific policy matters considered in the preceding chapter and subsequently at a more abstract level of generalized political value. Since our several modes of procedure reflect some widely held presumptions as to what "attitude structure" is, it is important to make these notions clear at the outset.

"ATTITUDE STRUCTURES" AND IDEOLOGY

We speak of an "attitude structure" when two or more beliefs or opinions held by an individual are in some way or another functionally related. As a simple example, we might encounter a person who is opposed to government activity in the area of low-cost housing. If we question him further as to his attitudes toward government ownership of utilities, he might oppose intervention here as well, and go on to say that in general he dislikes the idea of government intrusion in economic areas where private industry has traditionally held sway. In such a case, we would feel that we had struck upon a cluster of attitudes that were functionally related, inasmuch as there seems to be interdependence between each opinion and the others. If this individual were to be persuaded that government intervention was generally desirable, we would expect attitudes toward both the housing problem and the utilities problem to change accordingly.

We may imagine a number of types of functional relationship binding attitudes together. There is, for example, a means-end relationship that often emerges clearly in attitude structures. A government activity thus may be favored because it is seen as a stepping stone to some broader goal. Or attitudes may be functionally related if they operate in the service of a similar need. There may be a sharply aggressive cast to all of an individual's foreign policy opinions that would lead us to suspect that out-group objects like foreign peoples and nations were targets for release of hostility.

One property of an attitude that is useful to recognize has to do with the specificity of the object that is evaluated. Affect may be aroused by objects as specific as a clause in a House bill or as general as the abstraction "freedom." Attitude structures are often thought of as hierarchies in which more specific attitudes interact with attitudes toward the more general class of objects in which the specific object is seen to belong.

At the very best, judgment on the presence or absence of a functional relationship between two or more attitudes demands some degree of inference on the part of the investigator. Although any specific person may show congruence of opinions "accidentally," it is generally supposed that correlations between attitudes that are visible in aggregates are reliable evidence of some structuring of the attitudes on the part of individual members.

Ideology. An ideology may be seen as a particularly elaborate, close-woven, and far-ranging structure of attitudes. By origin and usage its connotations are primarily political, although the scope of the structure is such that we expect an ideology to encompass content outside the political order as narrowly defined—social and economic relationships, and even matters of religion, education, and the like.

Any cognitive structure that subsumes content of wide scope and diversity must be capped by concepts of a high order of abstraction. The wider the range of objects so classified, the more remote and general the concept that is necessary to capture their similarity. Perhaps no abstraction has been used more frequently in the past century for political analysis than the concept of a liberal-conservative continuum —the "right" and the "left" of a political spectrum. The generality of this dimension makes it a powerful summary tool. Above the flux of specific domestic issues lie a number of broad controversies regarding the appropriate posture of the national government toward other sectors of the social order, such as the development of resources, industry, and trade; the church; the privileged and the underprivileged; relatively local political bodies; and the world community. Differences between liberal and conservative tend to focus upon the degree to which the government should assume interest, responsibility, and control over these sectors of endeavor.

The nature of the advocacy that is called liberal or conservative comes to depend, within the immediate context, upon what is and what is hoped for. The viewpoint termed conservative may thereby become that which is reluctant to disturb the existing order of relationships, whether they be laissez faire or interventionist. The liberal viewpoint sees room for improvement in the product of social and political process through change in these relationships.

The widespread use of a liberal-conservative distinction in political analysis leads us to focus attention upon it rather heavily in this and the following chapter. We shall first consider the evidence for structures of attitudes emerging from our items of relatively specific public policy. Then we shall attempt to improve our grasp of the meaning that may reasonably be attributed to these structures, by assessing their status as "ideology."

ATTITUDE STRUCTURES IN ISSUES OF PUBLIC POLICY

Analysis of the ten domestic issues and six foreign policy items explored in 1956 yields one set of opinions within each area that forms a satisfactory Guttman scale. Five domestic issues contributed to one scale, including the items on aid to education, medical care, employment guarantees, FEPC and Negro housing, and public versus private production of electricity and housing. In primary content these items all have to do with the desirability of governmental action in areas of social welfare. Therefore, although we intend to inquire further into the meaning of this structure, we shall label this the "social welfare" structure.

Similarly, four of the six foreign policy items showed relationships of a sort that qualified the set as a second attitude structure. The content shared across these issues and relatively absent in the two excluded items concerned the desirable degree of United States intervention in international affairs. At one extreme were persons who thought our government should not be concerned with problems in other parts of the world, should not give economic aid to poor countries, should not maintain overseas military installations to fight Communism, and should not offer aid to the so-called neutral nations. At the other end of the continuum were persons favoring American activity in all of these spheres.

There undoubtedly were other issues in 1956 which, had we attempted to measure them, could have qualified as parts of either the social welfare or the foreign structure. Neither of these sets of issues should be considered as more than a selection from the opinions that might be shaped by the same underlying attitude. On the other hand, the fact that the other attitudes that we had measured within each broad policy area failed to fit the major structures located gives us a sense of the boundaries for each structure and hence sets limitations on their meaning. From this viewpoint the data evince a rather slight degree of structure in the attitudes of the mass electorate.

It is important to recognize the degree to which our "normal" or *a priori* expectations in these matters are conditioned by sophisticated views of the parts that make up a coherent political ideology. Locked in this perspective, we may wonder at the low-income person who wants to see government services extended, yet agrees that "the government ought to cut taxes even if it means putting off some important things that need to be done." However, both responses may spring from the same motivation—a simple desire for improvement of one's economic lot. So long as the structure of political attitudes is loose, potential contradictions will not be confronted.

The fact that an issue reaction fails to fit into a larger organization of attitude that seems appropriate for it does not mean that the response is random or in any other sense "uncaused." The problem is rather that the structure imposed on the situation by the analyst turns out in such instances to be inadequate. It may be that the sources of responses to an issue are so diverse from individual to individual that all sense of patterning across an aggregate is lost. More often, clear roots may exist, but the analyst ignores them because they have no place in his preconceptions concerning "logical" or traditional ideological positions. His organizing dimensions simply depart from the modes of organization abroad in the general population.

The Interrelationship of Foreign and Domestic Policy Structures. Across our sample as a whole in 1956 there was no relationship between scale positions of individuals on the domestic and foreign attitudinal dimensions. An interventionist position in foreign affairs was as likely to be taken by a domestic conservative as by a domestic liberal, and the relative isolationist was as likely to favor social welfare activities in Washington as he was to oppose them. Whether this seems surprising depends once again on our preconceptions. In terms of elite behavior and party programs there has been some reason to associate parties of the "right" in domestic affairs with nationalism in foreign questions, as opposed to the frequent humanitarian internationalism of "leftist" parties. Yet it is difficult to find evidence for this configuration of attitudes in the general electorate of 1956, and we are forced to conclude once again that the typical American lacks a clearly patterned ideology of such breadth. He may feel strongly about a variety of individual issues, but there are severe limitations on our ability to predict his position in one issue area from his position in another.

Now that we have assessed some of the outer limits of structure visible in the electorate, it becomes important to focus more careful attention on the two major structures that are apparent. What is the nature of the commonality that underlies each of these structures? What political significance may be attributed to them? We may increase our understanding of these attitude patterns by analyzing some of their more important correlates.

THE SIGNIFICANCE OF ATTITUDE STRUCTURES ON POLICY ISSUES

Foreign Policy. Not only do the differences in activism-withdrawal fail to correlate with placement on the social welfare dimension; they fail as well to show a correlation with political partisanship in 1956. People who tended to give internationalist responses to the four foreign policy items were no more likely to express identification with the Democratic Party than with the Republican Party. This finding, when laid against other aspects of our data, is of great interest.

First, the absence of correlation between foreign policy position and partisanship seems to be of much the same cloth as the general confusion that we encountered in the preceding chapter as to the foreign policy alignments of the major parties. However, it appears to clash with other findings that we have presented. We noted in Chapter 2, for example, that in the Eisenhower elections the partisan balance of foreign policy concerns was of considerable benefit to the Republican cause. We must resolve the apparent contradiction by examining more closely the types of response that produce a sense of clear partisan pattern, as opposed to those that produce instead a sense of confusion in perceived partisan implications.

Partisan patterns on foreign concerns developed most clearly in 1956 where the issues were formulated at the simple and global level of getting into war or staying out of it. Such patterns faded out when the issue grounds were shifted to the more *specific* means of attaining the goal. People had feelings about the desirability of American engagement abroad that lent consistency and a sense of structure to their responses on items of this nature. But the "bridge" perceptions were lacking that would meaningfully link activist or withdrawal feelings to one of the parties. Hence the broad public mandate in 1956 could be taken to express, among many other things, a fear of getting into war, and an appreciation of the political *agents* thought best capable of avoiding war. But there was no visible mandate concerning the choice between intervention and isolation as a *means* toward peace. The victorious party drew no greater support from people of either policy persuasion.

The withdrawal-activism dimension of foreign policy attitudes did show some association with other dispositions toward politics, a fact that helps to round out our understanding of these opinions. Generally, internationalists were more likely to be politically informed and involved than were those favoring withdrawal from international commitments. The internationalist was more aware of differences in the policy commitments of the two major parties. He was also more likely to be interested in and familiar with a more extensive range of the policy questions that we probed than was his isolationist counterpart. The internationalist, too, tends to register a stronger sense of political efficacy than does the isolationist. People advocating withdrawal from foreign engagements are, by their own assessment, less effective participants in politics; the internationalist feels that he is in control of his political world and that it is responsive to his desires and acts.

The involvement and sense of effectiveness that characterize the internationalists undoubtedly have further political implications. In terms of the actual 1956 election, the mandate of the public on the activism-withdrawal question was rendered unclear by confusion over party lines. However, the rallying of more informed, involved, and active citizens to the internationalist position suggests that this persuasion is likely to be pressed more diligently outside of the immediate election situation than a census or unweighted poll of the national constituency would lead us to expect.

Domestic Policy. The items involved in the domestic issue structure reflect the social welfare controversies of the New Deal-Fair Deal era. They are, by and large, the questions that revealed the clearest consensus as to party differences in the preceding chapter. Therefore, it is not surprising that although foreign attitudes had lost their partisan element in 1956, position in the domestic issue structure remained clearly associated with partisan preference. Persons who favored social welfare activity by the federal government were likely to be identified with the Democratic Party. They perceived the Democratic Party to be closer than the Republican Party to their own position on other issues, and their voluntary references to domestic issues, within the system of proximal attitudes, were highly favorable to the Democratic cause or critical of the Republican.

The structure of opinions built around the problem of social welfare activity is of intense interest to us for reasons that go beyond its unique partisan implications, however. For this structure is one which has clearest relevance for traditional discussions of the "left" and the "right" in political ideology. Although we can hardly gainsay the significance of these core dimensions of modern ideology in the decision making of political elites, how important may we presume them to be at the level of mass political behavior?

Evidence as to the great momentum of long-standing party loyalties and the vicissitudes of the political translation process where specific matters are concerned have moved us toward the tentative conclusion that events outside the political order impinge only feebly upon the evolution of partisan decisions at the mass level. It would seem to follow that ideology of a sort that binds a broad range of human experience to dynamic evaluations of politics cannot be thought to be widespread in the American population.

This is, however, argument by indirection, and we can now confront the matter directly. We have isolated an attitude structure capturing the core ideological controversies of our epoch. The structure exists empirically, and, moreover, it shows relationships of substantial magnitude with partisan preference in the direction that would be predicted by notions of ideology. That is, people sort themselves into patterns of response that are coherent in terms of a liberal-conservative dimension; and people who choose liberal alternatives tend to identify with the more liberal, or "leftist," Democratic Party, whereas people choosing conservative alternatives tend more often to express loyalty to the conservative, "rightist" Republican Party. Furthermore, we find that people of lower status predominate both among those who rank as "liberal" in their social welfare attitudes and among the adherents of the "liberal" party. Citizens in higher strata tend to prefer the "conservative" alternatives to such questions, and give primary support to the conservative party.

It is common to leap from these bare facts to the conclusion that traditional ideological structures are important parts of the armory of attitudes generally used in political evaluation. For some predictions the social and political outcome is the same whether or not this assumption is warranted. In other cases, however, our expectations may be sorely betrayed if we are not more cautious in our view of ideology at a mass level. It is our contention that this assumption is frequently overdrawn. We shall attempt to demonstrate a number of other facts, equally real, which are inexplicable once this assumption is made. And we shall consider how the basic triangle of relationships laid out above can be generated with very little in the way of full-blown "ideology" in the motives and values of the actors involved.

First it is important to distinguish between behavior impelled by self-interest in a primitive and short-sighted sense, and the operation of self-interest within a structure of attitudes that might reasonably be labeled an "ideology." This discrimination may seem difficult, since it is customary to assume that perceived interest is the primary criterion whereby the individual locates an appropriate ideology. Thus ideology and self-interest become tightly linked in our minds.

We have no quarrel with the view that ideological position is largely determined by self-interest. But we do maintain that it matters whether self-interest proceeds in a simple and naked sense, or has indeed become imbedded in some broader ideological structure. We have suggested, for example, that the possession of ideology equips the individual to perceive the connectedness of many superficially diverse events and relate them to one another coherently. One important implication of such understanding is that the person is sensitized to the existence of "roundabout" routes that, despite a superficial detour, will better secure ultimate gratification.

Political action is, in itself, a roundabout route to the fulfillment of most forms of self-interest. From the point of view of a frontier farmer harassed by price cuts and discrimination in freight rates, the formation of a political organization to send a representative to a distant parliamentary body is a less clear means of remedying evils than burning the grain elevator. Even where it is perceived that the path to a goal is through politics, usually a variety of more and less direct paths are available. Frequently shorter paths are less effectual than the longer. One function of ideology is to maintain the perspective of time and roundabout routes that permit the most effective long-range political evaluations.

We may survey our domestic policy items more generally from this new vantage point. The responses that come to form a coherent "social welfare" structure lending credence to ideological assumptions are at the same time questions in which the path of self-interest for a lower-status person is quite clear, and they are scarcely more obscure for the individual of higher status. Several of the other items that might be comfortably located in a broad liberal or conservative ideology do not turn out to fit this key structure. In a rough way, we may distinguish two types. First, there are those in which some other dimension than the economic appears primary, or in which the number of steps necessary to link a policy choice to self-interest is multiplied and hence less clear. For a person who fears unemployment, a question concerning government guarantees of employment can be directly related to self-interest. But a question about the role of business in government can only be related to self-interest if one has an understanding of business interests and the advantages conferred by political power. The items of this type show little or no relationship with items in the social welfare structure. The second type, in which there is an actual conflict posed for lower-status persons between immediate financial interest and longer-range, indirect gains, is represented only by the tax item. And in this case alone the visible relationship with items of the social welfare scale runs in a direction perfectly contrary to our ideological expectations.

In sum, then, the pattern of responses to our domestic issues is best understood if we discard our notions of ideology and think rather in terms of primitive self-interest.[1] Of course, the basic triangle of rela-

---

[1] Lipset has pointed out that although lower-status groups favor "liberal" policies on matters of social welfare legislation, they tend at the same time to take antiliberal or intolerant positions on matters involving treatment of deviants or ethnic minorities. These empirical facts have contributed to Lipset's sense of dissatis-

tionships between status, issue "liberalism," and party is no more difficult to account for in these terms than it is when more full-fledged ideology is assumed. Indeed, the fact that these relationships are never overwhelming in magnitude is probably a good deal *more* comprehensible once we have scaled our assumptions down in this fashion. For the possibility of widespread confusion about political means and ends among the least informed seems easier to countenance if we recognize that the level of sophistication about such matters is generally rather low.

There are other points at which we may pit ideological expectations against simpler notions of self-interest. The fact that no mean proportion of lower-status people are Republican and high-status people are Democratic has always occasioned a good deal of comment. Whether we deal in terms of ideology or simpler interest concepts, these people are out of step, for they appear to espouse a political instrument counter to their interest. What forces permit them to maintain this apparent disequilibrium? Perhaps the most familiar explanation is an ideological one, for strongly ingrained ideology is one of the few motivating forces that can be seen to induce a person to act in terms of interest other than his own. The stereotype built up to account for the low-status Republican involves an origin in the tradition-bound individualism of rural America. For high-status Democrats, two types of ideological mechanisms receive attention. The person who has achieved status from modest beginnings may maintain his old ideology because of the deep impressions that past experiences of social inequity have made upon him. The aristocrat by birth, on the other hand, may be motivated to liberal ideals by what is essentially *noblesse oblige.*

There is no doubt that within midcentury America many persons fitting these descriptions could be located. But the question remains whether persons meeting such specifications loom at all large among the low-status Republicans and high-status Democrats to be found in a cross section of the electorate. It is our contention that they do not, but represent instead a deviant few who have attracted attention be-

---

faction with common assumptions concerning the configuration of beliefs treated generically as "liberalism." He argues for a distinction between "economic" and "noneconomic liberalism." See Seymour Martin Lipset, "Democracy and Working-Class Authoritarianism," *American Sociological Review,* XXIV (August 1959). We are most sympathetic with this critique. However, the data concerning opinions on taxes suggest that even the connotations of the term "economic liberalism" may be unrealistically broad. If these attitudes have internal coherence, they are expressions of self-interest, not "liberal ideologies."

cause of the pleasing manner in which they fill ideological preconceptions.

Several pieces of data may be brought to bear on the question. Figure 8-1 shows, for example, that low-status Republicans fall rather close to the radical extreme of the social welfare scale.[2] Their attitudes are not greatly different from those held by Democrats of equivalent status. With these findings in hand we are not likely to be impressed by the argument that these low-status people are kept within Republican ranks by their exceptionally conservative political ideologies.

Figure 8-1 suggests that the relationship between partisanship and social welfare attitudes noted previously is slightly stronger among persons of higher education levels. In the degree that higher-status Democrats depart from the attitudes of higher-status Republicans there is an indication that ideology of the sort postulated may be playing some role. However, this role appears weak at best. We would not be convinced, for example, that the higher-status liberal maintains his unusual position by any striking commitment to liberal causes. Higher-status Democrats are very substantially more conservative in their attitudes than either low-status Democrats *or* low-status Republicans. Differences in attitude attributable to party, although statistically significant, are thoroughly eclipsed by those differences correlated with status.[3]

If the ideological explanation fails to account for the low-status Republican and the high-status Democrat, what interpretation may be substituted? Figure 8-1 suggests again that we consider the problem in two parts. The strong attitude-status correlation that appears within each party grouping is now adequately accounted for in simple self-interest terms. The question then remains why people of low or high status with appropriate social welfare attitudes identify themselves with the "wrong" party. We must remember that a variety of other factors influence partisan choice. The importance of this fact increases as we scale down our assumptions about the role of ideological concerns in decisions by the broad electorate. For the sophisticated observer, the ramifications of some of these core domestic policy decisions are so broad that dimensions of attitude relating to them

[2] For reasons that will be apparent in the subsequent text, we use education as the criterion of status in this figure. However, other status criteria produce similar patterns.

[3] Although this is clear even on the basis of Fig. 8-1, the use of a single status criterion understates the full significance of the status dimension in predicting social welfare attitudes. For example, income as a second criterion makes a considerable independent contribution to the prediction of attitudes.

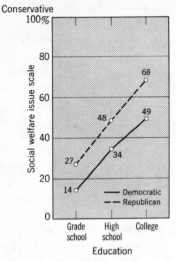

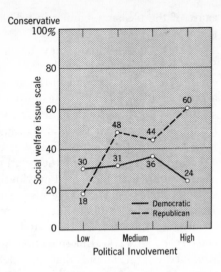

FIG. 8-1. Relation of education to social welfare attitudes, by party.

FIG. 8-2. Relation of political involvement to social welfare attitudes, by party.

deserve heavy weight in any political choice. But in the degree that the public lacks this ideological superstructure, the significance accorded such policy matters must be somewhat less. Consequently, other factors independent of these concerns, such as candidate attractiveness or long-standing party loyalty, increase in relative importance.

Furthermore, although people presented with certain policy alternatives can do a reasonable job of selecting responses that appear to further their self-interest, this fact is in itself no guarantee that they have ever sorted out how the parties stand on the matter. If the person has never been motivated to follow political affairs closely, we can well imagine that he may feel a bond with a party and may be able to discern self-interest in a set of policy propositions without having established a link between the party and its policy position.

This possibility is supported by Fig. 8-2, which shows that partisan differences on social welfare attitudes are indeed dependent on political involvement. Differences between adherents of the two parties are sharpest among the most highly involved; where involvement is low, there is no significant variation in social welfare attitude by party. Thus we conclude that one important factor in the choice of a party that is "wrong" in view of the individual's social welfare attitudes and status location is simple indifference and the lack of information thereby implied.

Generally, then, closer examination of some of the connections that have been assumed to exist on the basis of the original triangle of status, attitude, and party relationship reveals a variety of gaps. Although from time to time we catch glints of possible ideology operating, by and large the pattern of relationships that are statistically significant is explicable only in terms of a much more modest self-interest assumption. And even the simple self-interest assumption produces partisan relationships only where there is some degree of formal education and involvement in politics.

IDEOLOGY AND POLITICAL ELITES

Herbert McClosky has written as follows about the relationships between conservation and a range of specific political attitudes:

The correlation(s) between them tend, however, to be fairly low, suggesting that for the present, at least, many Americans divide in their party preferences, their support of candidates, their economic views, their stands on public issues, or their political self-identifications without reference to their beliefs in liberalism or conservatism. The latter have influence, of course, especially among some of the more articulate groups; for the general population, however, political divisions of the sort named appear to be more affected by group membership factors than by personality.[4]

These findings are clearly corroborated by our data on a national sample. There is no significant correlation between conservatism and party identification, for example, even with Southern respondents excluded. In short, if we focus upon the total range of individuals represented in the national electorate, we find almost no correlation between a general disposition that we would expect to be of prime political relevance and variation in issue attitudes or partisanship. However, we may locate subgroups in the population for which sophisticated expectations do receive some support. These islands of support become highly instructive in assessing the reasons for discontinuity elsewhere. For example, McClosky, before applying his scale to a cross section population, used it with leaders of both political parties. He found that it discriminated at a very satisfactory level between Republican and Democratic elites.[5] Now we can surmise that such party leadership must have differed radically from a "normal" population in a number of ways. First, such people certainly would rank as highly involved in politics. Second, we would suppose them to have a

---

[4] Herbert McClosky, "Conservatism and Personality," *American Political Science Review,* LII (March 1958), pp. 44–45.
[5] *Ibid.*

very abnormal command of political events and recent party history. Third, it is likely that they were disproportionately people of high education, for whom conceptual abstractions of the sort used in ideological thinking are relatively common coin.

These traits that distinguish political party elites are traits shared with the several "spectator" elites—journalistic and academic—who tend to apply concepts such as the liberal-conservative continuum to analyses of political motivations and events. The fact that theoretical expectations are borne out within party elites attests once again to the value of such concepts for the understanding of behavior in these circles. But party activists of this type represent such a tiny fraction of the electorate that they are too few to permit analysis even in a relatively large national sample. These data lead to the same conclusion as our preceding analyses: as we depart from the extreme combinations of involvement, background, and education represented by such elites, the significance of familiar ideological frames of reference drops off rapidly. It is not hard to see why the sophisticated observer is readily misled in his analytic constructions. He recognizes of course that individuals differ in the partisan or issue content of their political beliefs, for he sees these differences contested in the daily drama of politics at an elite level. But he falls prey to the assumption that the same basic frames of reference are shared by all citizens who take any interest in politics whatever.

We have suggested in Chapter 6 that most citizens tend to locate themselves in a political party at an early point in their adult life, and that this identification typically then gains strength throughout life. The party that wins favor appears to depend predominantly upon social transmission from the family or early reference groups. The critical initial decision appears to be taken most frequently under strong social influence early in life, when involvement in politics is at low ebb, and, presumably, political information is most scanty as well. Thus if involvement and background are preconditions for the establishment of meaningful links between basic values and party preference, then we must suppose that in the bulk of cases, the individual is committed to a party at a time when he is least likely to have the wherewithal to bring ideological considerations of this sort into play. Thereafter, the self-reinforcing aspects of a psychological identification progressively reduce the probability of change in partisan allegiance. If the crucial identifications were postponed until the individual had observed the parties for some time with the modest but more active involvement and fuller information of the middle-aged adult, we would expect that ultimate partisanship would show more convincing relationships with underlying values of this sort. Or if the psychological potency of party identification were weaker later in life, so that existing partisanship dictated less thoroughly the interpretation of political events, we might also expect more rearrangement of partisanship to achieve better fit with underlying values. In the absence of these conditions the impression of discontinuity between such values and partisanship remains almost complete.

chapter 9

The Formation of Issue Concepts and

Partisan Change

The popularity of the conservative-liberal distinction has been particularly notable in analyses of partisan change from election to election. If a liberal party wins an unusually strong popular vote, we are frequently informed that the public mandate is for a shift toward the left in governmental policy; if the party of the right gains new support, the public has become "cautious" or conservative about further political change. When the parties are loose coalitions of conservative and liberal wings, the meaning of the election outcome may be pursued at the level of legislative seats. Which wing within each of the parties showed the higher mortality rate in the balloting?

Any election may elicit diverse explanations, for change can hinge upon several crucial terms in the equation. If the Democratic Party is buried under a landslide of Republican votes, it may be argued that the electorate has become more conservative, that the Democratic Party has pushed too far to the left, that the Republican Party has moved in to capture votes of the "center," or any combination of the three.

Despite their differences, all these accounts depend on similar assumptions concerning the frames of reference used by the electorate to assess political events. Such accounts presume that some significant portion of the electorate (1) is sensitive to its own policy mood in terms of a left-right continuum; and (2) is sensitive as well to the shifting policy positions of both parties on the same continuum. The notion of the continuum is as crucial as the content here. The assumption is not simply that people consider one party to be "left" and the other "right" in a dichotomous sense. Instead, there is presumed to be some perception of distance separating the parties, and this distance can be discriminated as greater or lesser at differing points in time. Often it is presumed as well that people also have a sense of the distance of either party from a neutral point, a "middle of the road."

In view of the data we have presented these assumptions strain our credulity; yet, we cannot reject them out of hand. We have found some evidence to suggest that for a fraction of the American population these assumptions may be realistic. And the changes in the partisan vote division that attract these ideological descriptions rarely exceed a magnitude of 10 per cent of the active electorate. Thus it is conceivable that a balance of power may be held by a small minority of ideologues who are sensitive to shifts of the parties along a left-right continuum. Whether this view is valid is critical to an understanding of the issue meaning of partisan change.

If the liberal-conservative notion is not common, as we have maintained, the question remains as to what frames of reference for ordering issue concerns *do* enjoy more widespread use. Certainly the process of political evaluation is carried on by most citizens, and this process leads to more or less predictable organization of behavior. If ideology in a sophisticated sense is not widespread in the population, there must be surrogates for ideology that bring large aggregates to act *as though* propelled by ideological concerns. It is important to understand the character of these surrogates not only to satisfy intellectual curiosity, but also because the fact that they are surrogates rather than full-blown ideology may from time to time lead to crucial differences in behavior.

THE FORMATION OF POLITICAL CONCEPTS AT A MASS LEVEL

Smith, Bruner, and White, in their volume *Opinions and Personality*, report an intensive analysis of the political attitudes of ten relatively well-informed and intelligent subjects. Nine of the ten, on the basis of their performance in a standardized test, ranked within the top 10 per cent of the national population in intellectual capacity. Of the tenth, the authors write:

> *Many of the verbal coins used in the exchange of opinions were unfamiliar to him, so that we had to learn his views without relying on such standard pieces as "Socialism," "Liberalism," "veto" and "isolationism." . . . At a concrete level he functioned effectively, showing good common sense and practical judgment. It was in the realm of abstraction that his limitations were most marked. . . . He never read books, rarely listened to the radio, and did little more than scan such newspapers and magazines as came his way. Both his information and his opinions were arrived at almost wholly through channels of conversation.*[1]

[1] M. Brewster Smith, Jerome S. Bruner, and Robert W. White, *Opinions and Personality* (John Wiley and Sons, New York, 1956), p. 196.

Now "Sam Hodder," as this anonymous subject is called, was not a person of meager intelligence. He was *well above the average* in basic intellectual capacity, standing in the top 20 per cent of a cross-section population. But limited to a grade school education and subsequent life as a factory employee, events had not conspired to foster those habits of abstract concept formation taken for granted in intellectual strata of the society. Despite substantial innate capacity, then, even Sam Hodder did not in practice measure up to the expectations of political concept formation that often seem assumed for the bulk of the electorate.

We would imagine that if we asked Sam Hodder what he liked and disliked about the major parties, his predominant opinion would be that he liked the Democratic Party because "it is the party of the working man." If his political world was largely undifferentiated, he might have few perceptions beyond this. If there were further differentiation, he would perhaps indicate that the Republican Party had shown him it was actively against labor or the worker, or actively for big business, management, or one of the "natural" antagonists of the working man. He might be able, also, to document his impressions by reference to specific events or policy debates: the role of the parties in the Depression, or the championing of legislation such as Taft-Hartley or social security. His view of partisan politics might be more or less differentiated, but his evaluations would revolve around the perception that one of the parties took special pains to look after the day-to-day interests of a significant grouping in the population with which he identified.

This is not ideology in a programmatic sense. There is little comprehension here of the basic problems that lead to the need for political protection; nor is there any interest in "long-range plans" that would aim at resolution of these problems. In fact, there is little that requires abstract thinking at all. He is concerned with politics to the degree that he feels that political change might rob him and others like him of their jobs or of concrete benefits involving wages, working conditions, and the like. He has no conception of the modes whereby political power secures or protects interests—these are the concerns of group leadership, whether that leadership be of union or of party. Having perceived some correlation between group success and the emergence of concrete benefits, he is willing to put his faith in any leadership that has shown enough interest in his group to figure out what must be done to maintain its welfare. He partakes of ideology by endorsing a leadership that has ideology. He engages, so to speak, in an "ideology by proxy."

The difference between ideology and "ideology by proxy" is more than academic, for at points of political change the concepts employed by Sam Hodder in his evaluations make for critical differences in attitude and behavior. If the fact of change in goals should actually be brought to Sam's attention, he would lack any independent reference points from which to evaluate the matter. Leadership programs have helped him in the past. If leadership ideas have changed, it is probably for good reason; the people at the top are in a better position to know what must be done than he is. He will always be able to judge what are, for him, the "results." Hence under certain circumstances the total flavor of political events may come to depend on the level at which the many "followers" like Sam Hodder have been in the habit of conceptualizing their relevant experience.

Favorable or unfavorable reactions to the political parties or candidates often consist of beliefs that they are agents that will aid or ignore this or that grouping in the population. In some of our protocols these perceptions are connected tightly with other comments more clearly ideological in character. But often it is apparent under probing by the interviewer that the respondent does not fit these notions of group benefit into any broader or more abstract frame of reference.

However simple these conceptions of politics may appear, there are many people in the American electorate whose modes of conceptualizing the political world and its social or economic consequences are a good deal less complex still and who appear even more remote from the type of thinking presumed by "ideology." Some of these people are staunch adherents of one of the political parties, although they freely admit it is simply a matter of family tradition and they personally have no idea what the parties "stand for." Others ignore the parties despite direct questioning, and focus their political evaluations upon the personal characteristics of the current candidates themselves —their sincerity, their religious beliefs, their family life, their "popularity." And there are those who lack the interest or background to differentiate successfully between either the candidates or the parties.

It seems important to estimate the incidence of these various modes of conceptualizing issue controversy in a cross section of the adult population. Unfortunately, there are no simple yardsticks to measure the sophistication of a person's conceptualization. We cannot quantify the character of a person's political conceptions, even in the loose manner with which we measure the intensity of attitudes. We are interested in the presence or absence of certain abstractions that have to do with ideology; but we are also interested in the degree to which the individual's political world is differentiated and, most important, in the nature of the degree of "connectedness" between the elements that are successfully discriminated. In short, we are interested in the structure of thought that the individual applies to politics; and this interest forces us to deal in typologies and qualitative differences.

Toward this end we attempted to assign our 1956 respondents to various "levels" of conceptualization on the basis of their discursive responses in evaluating the good and bad points of the two parties and the two candidates, as described in Chapter 3. Despite the inevitable crudities of the categories employed, these levels seemed to provide a clear ordering in terms of conceptual sophistication. The expected ordering turned out to receive striking confirmation in other characteristics of the occupants at successive levels. We shall focus most of our attention upon four major levels.

The first of these (to be denoted Level A) embraces all respondents whose evaluations of the candidates and the parties have any suggestion of the abstract conception one would associate with ideology. We did not wish to be bound to familiar content in assessing this level of issue conceptualization. However, it rapidly became apparent that virtually all high-order abstractions used were familiar from current political commentary. Persons placed here talked in terms of the liberal-conservative continuum, or one of the narrower domains of abstract content involved in current ideological controversy: trends in the relationship between federal power and local autonomy, the fate of individual incentive under government "dole," and the like.

The second grouping (Level B) was reserved for persons whose issue comment revolved around fairly concrete and short-term group interest, or what we have already described in some detail as "ideology by proxy." In the next category (Level C) were persons engrossed in simplistic associations between the "goodness" and "badness" of the times and the identity of the party in power, or who appeared to have exhausted their view of the situation with mention of some rather isolated and specific issue. The final level (Level D) thereby contains individuals who evaluated the political objects without recourse to issues that might fairly be related to debates over domestic public policy. Excluded as true issue content, for example, were observations concerning mudslinging, charges of graft, comments on the personal attributes of the candidates, or references to their age, health, or past experience.

We were eager to avoid a number of potential pitfalls in a classification procedure of this order. We did not wish the assignment to be influenced by the partisan implication of the concepts employed. To the degree that the two parties tend to stress different ideological vocabularies, we desired to give each party vocabulary equal recognition. Similarly, the respondent who dislikes a party because it caters to the interests of special groups is employing concepts at the same level as the person who expresses gratitude for this interest, and should therefore receive the same classification. In short, we were not interested in the partisan product of the evaluation process, but rather in the character of the concepts that were playing a role in that process.

Secondly, we did not wish to confuse enthusiasm for quality of conception. A person who felt very strongly about a particular evaluation was not to be rated more highly than a person who used the same concepts for an offhand evaluation. To be sure, we would expect the individual who is intensely interested in politics to have arrived at different organizing concepts than the person who pays little attention to political events. But we need not think that a sense of pleasure or displeasure about a candidate or party that is fuzzy in focus and vague in source is intrinsically weak in its motivational significance for the individual. Particularly if the person lacks the capacity to organize what might seem more "telling" evaluative structures, these vague premonitions can be emotionally consuming.

DIFFERENCES IN POLITICAL CONCEPT-FORMATION: ILLUSTRATIONS FROM A CROSS-SECTION SAMPLE

Level A, Ideology and Near-Ideology. We shall consider two categories of respondents distinguished within Level A. The first was reserved for persons whose comments imply the kinds of conception of politics assumed by ideological interpretations of political behavior and political change. We shall refer to these individuals as "ideologues." The second category within Level A includes people who employ concepts of some ideological flavor but who, for one reason or another, do not apply them in a manner that seems to qualify them as "ideologues."

Some people clearly perceived a fundamental liberal-conservative continuum on which various of the political objects might be located and along which these objects might shift relative positions over time. These ideologies are not, from a sophisticated point of view, exceptional observers. Their commentary is neither profound, stimulating, nor creative. But they have absorbed some of the ideological abstractions of our day, and are able to put them to use in their political evaluations. In brief, they are the persons who fulfill most clearly the assumptions about political perceptions discussed at the beginning of the chapter.

The first interview drawn from this upper category within Level A is somewhat unusual in the degree of content pertaining to state politics, but otherwise is quite representative of the responses that received this classification. The respondent is a woman residing in the suburbs of Chicago.

(I'd like to ask you what you think are the good and bad points about the two parties. Is there anything in particular that you like about the Democratic Party?) No. *(Is there anything at all you like about the Democratic Party?)* No, nothing at all.

(Is there anything in particular that you don't like about the Democratic Party?) From being raised in a notoriously Republican section—a small town downstate—there were things I didn't like. There was family influence that way. *(What in particular was there you didn't like about the Democratic Party?)* Well, the Democratic Party tends to favor socialized medicine—and I'm being influenced in that because I came from a doctor's family.

(Is there anything in particular that you like about the Republican Party?) Well, I think they're more middle-of-the-road—more conservative. *(How do you mean, "conservative"?)* They are not so subject to radical change. *(Is there anything else in particular that you like about the Republican Party?)* Oh, I like their foreign policy—and the segregation business, that's a middle-of-the-road policy. You can't push it too fast. You can instigate things, but you have to let them take their course slowly. *(Is there anything else?)* I don't like Mr. Hodge. *(Is there anything else?)* The labor unions telling workers how to vote—they know which side their bread is buttered on so they have to vote the way they are told to!

(Is there anything in particular that you don't like about the Republican Party?) Mr. Hodge! *(Is there anything else?)* I can't think of anything.[2]

This respondent operates with a fairly clear sense of the liberal-conservative distinction and uses it to locate both the major parties and the more specific policy positions espoused. The second interview drawn to represent this category is somewhat weaker. The following remarks, transcribed from a woman in a small Ohio city, serve to illustrate the marginal inclusions in this category:

(Like about Democrats?)[3] Well, that depends on what you are thinking of—historically or here lately. I think they are supposed to be more inter-

---

[2] In order to preserve space, we shall omit reproduction of responses to the questions regarding the candidates, save where such responses add integrally to our understanding of the manner in which the respondent evaluates politics.

[3] The initial questions having to do with the parties and candidates are the same throughout. Once having quoted them in full, we shall abbreviate them in

ested in the small businessman and low tariffs. *(Is there anything in particular that you like about the Democratic Party?)* Nothing except it being a more liberal party, and I think of the Republicans as being more conservative and interested in big business.

(Dislike about Democrats?) I think extravagance, primarily. *(Is there anything else?)* Nothing that occurs to me offhand.

(Like about Republicans?) Well, I never thought so. I have been a Republican the last several years because of the personalities involved, I guess.

(Dislike about Republicans?) This again is traditional—just that they give too much support to big business and monopoly concerns. *(Any other things you don't like about the Republican Party?)* No.

In this case the concept of the liberal-conservative continuum appears to be relatively peripheral. The respondent feels that evaluations based on concepts of this order favor the Democratic Party, but by her own account the "personalities" have in recent years loomed larger in her voting decisions. However, these concepts *are* present, and although not impressively developed, are used in a manner that implies that the respondent is sensitive to changes over time in the location of political objects on the underlying continuum.

It is striking, then, that responses of only 2½ per cent of our cross-section sample warranted inclusion in this top category. Since people placed here are much more likely to take a fuller role in politics than are persons lower on the scale, they bulk somewhat larger in the active electorate. But these ideologies still represent no more than 3½ per cent of our actual voters in 1956. In view of the fact that the partisan division of the national vote for federal office often shifts by as much as 5 or 10 per cent within the biennial or quadrennial period, it is clear that this group alone could account for only a minor portion of such short-term change, either by switching party or by staying at home.

There is, however, a more substantial group of respondents who have some claim to ideological perception. We have segregated them from the upper layer of ideologues because we are somewhat less confident that they fulfill the assumptions that we are examining. These people displaying "near-ideology" consist of three general types.

The first type is most similar to the full "ideologue." Frequently these people employ the liberal-conservative distinction, but their use of these concepts has little of the dynamic or highly relativistic

this fashion, although further probing that was introduced under each "root" question will continue to be reproduced in full.

quality found in the ideologue. "Liberalism" or "conservatism" is a status attribute of a party: there is less sense here of a continuum embracing many shadings of position, with objects shifting inward toward the center or outward toward extremes over time. Others give no explicit recognition to the liberal-conservative distinction, but employ organizing concepts of a sufficiently high order of abstraction to cut some swath through areas of ideological controversy. An interview drawn to exemplify this type of "near-ideology" comes from a man in southern Ohio:

(Like about Democrats?) Yes, I like their platform. *(What is that?)* They're more inclined to help the working class of people, and that is the majority in our country. And I like the idea of stopping the hydrogen bomb tests. It would make for more friendly feelings toward other countries, and they would be more friendly to us. I think the Democratic Party wants peace as much as the Republican Party.

(Dislike about Democrats?) Yeah, there's a lot of things. One thing is they're too much for federal control of utilities. *(Is there anything else you don't like about the Democratic Party?)* Well, it seems they don't always run the best men there are for their offices. *(For example?)* There's several I could mention that don't have the best reputation in the world.

(Like about Republicans?) Well, they play up to individual rights, which is good. That's good—it makes a person feel more independent.
(Dislike about Republicans?) They believe in big industry, utilities, etc. *(Anything else you don't like?)* They've passed a lot of labor bills I don't approve of.

This respondent does not introduce the liberal-conservative distinction explicitly. This opening comment about Democratic interest in the working class is of the group-interest type that will form the broad criterion for Level B. But he also includes commentary about the problem of federal control over utilities and the value of individual rights. Both of these observations involve abstractions common to the ideological disputes of our era. The respondent's own position concerning the role of government toward utilities is left rather unclear: he resents tendencies of the Democrats toward federal control, yet appears to dislike the Republican position as well. Here as elsewhere, however, we restrict our attention to the nature of the concepts employed rather than become involved in judgments of the coherence of ideological positions. Another 2 per cent of our sample was considered to be of this type. These people constituted about 2½ per cent of our 1956 voters. Up to this point, then, we have accounted for about 4½ per cent of the total sample, and for slightly less than 6 per cent of our voters.

A second type of interview considered "near-ideology" included persons who used one or another of the labels common to ideological discussion, but in a context rather bare of supporting perceptions, so that we must take it on faith that the term had the normal connotations for the user. Generally the flavor of the context is not one to cast great doubt on the appropriateness of the meaning, but the lack of supporting material usually indicates that other simpler concepts are equally or more prominent in the individual's thinking about politics. The respondent drawn to exemplify the second type is a man from Texas:

> *(Like about Democrats?)* (After a long delay.) I think the Democrats are more concerned with all the people. *(How do you mean?)* They put out more liberal legislation for all the people.

> *(Dislike about Democrats?)* They have a sordid history over the past 20 years, though no worse than the Republican Administrations. *(How do you mean?)* Oh, things like deep freezes and corruption in government.

> *(Like about Republicans?)* No!

> *(Dislike about Republicans?)* Oh, they're more for a moneyed group.

Here the bulk of the content follows the lines of group benefit concepts that are generally classified at a lower level. Nevertheless, the term "liberal" is employed in a context of some reasonable meaning, and it is possible that fuller probing would have developed a more explicit indication of more abstract ideological conceptions. The second type of near-ideology adds another 3½ per cent of the sample to Level A, and another 5 per cent of our total of 1956 voters. Thus it is the largest group so far considered, although we have accounted for about 8 per cent of the sample up to this point.

The final type of interview classified as near-ideology within Level A was in one sense the inverse of the preceding type. Whereas respondents of the preceding type had absorbed labels but had difficulty bringing appropriate specific information to them, individuals here were laden with information but showed no tendency to distill such detail to a higher level of abstraction. We find among these people, as well as those of the preceding type, an increasing tendency to depend upon party and group concepts as organizing focuses for issue content, rather than ideological positions. Thus responses of these types are already merging with the concept usages of individuals in Level B.

The interview drawn to represent this final type of near-ideology was contributed by a man in southern California:

(Like about Democrats?) The Democratic Party is more for higher social security. They're more for old age pensions and better working conditions for the working man. They want a higher standard of living for all people, not just a few. The promises that are made by the Democrats are kept if at all possible. The facts are told to the American people.

(Dislike about Democrats?) It seems to me they could handle their campaign better. *(How do you mean?)* Well, for instance, they could do a little better job of selling to the public. They should try and quiet Truman down so he will not pull a boner as in the Democratic convention. *(Do you have any other dislikes for the Democratic Party?)* No.

(Like about Republicans?) Not one thing! *(In general, is there anything that you like about the Republican Party?)* No!

(Dislike about Republicans?) I dislike everything about the Republican Party. *(Could you explain what you mean?)* I was growing up at the time of the Hoover Administration. What a time I had, too. There was barely enough to eat. I don't think the Republicans wanted that, but they did nothing to stop it. Not until Roosevelt came along and made things start to happen. Now the Republican Party still stands for big business, at the expense of the farmer and the working man. Promises made are not kept—ask the poor farmer, if no one else.

Over the course of these remarks there are points at which summary constructs familiar in ideological discussion would be highly appropriate. However, the recital of specific measures supported by the Democrats is not generalized to such a level of abstraction. Instead, the "standard of living" is used to sum up the direction of party policy, and this matter is treated as a benefit linked to a group, albeit a large group, within the population. Similarly, a perception of Republican passivity in the face of the Depression is vividly contrasted in the subject's mind with initiatives taken by Roosevelt. Yet this is not seen as a special case of a general posture toward change. Rather, it is left as a concrete vignette, developed once again into a proposition about group interest.

We did not feel that any of the types of response discussed here as "near-ideology" provided satisfactory support for assumptions concerning ideological perceptions. We include them as part of Level A, however, for it is possible that some among them would, in other settings, so amplify their observations as to merit "ideologue" classification.

If the reader has been struck by this generosity of assignment, he should hold this fact in mind as we measure our progress across the electorate. For despite our attempts at generous estimates, we find that with all of the ideologues and near-ideologues of Level A cumulated we have only covered about 12 per cent of all subjects interviewed, and 15 per cent of our 1956 voters. In other words, about 85 per cent of the 1956 electorate brought simpler conceptual tools to bear on their issue concerns.

Level B, Group Benefits. In the last interviews to be cited from Level A, we noted an increasing tendency to evaluate the political objects in terms of their response to interests of visible groupings in the population. Such perceptions are the dominant themes characterizing Level B, and constitute what we have described earlier as "ideology by proxy."

Such relationships between political object and group can be appreciated at a simple and concrete level. A party or candidate is sympathetic with or hostile to the group. There is little comprehension of "long-range plans for social betterment," or of basic philosophies rooted in postures toward change or abstract conceptions of social and economic structure or causation. The party or candidate is simply endorsed as being "for" or "against" a group with which the subject is identified or as being above the selfish demands of groups within the population. Exactly *how* the candidate or party might see fit to implement or avoid group interests is a moot point, left unrelated to broader ideological concerns. But the party or candidate is "located" in some affective relationship toward a group or groups, and the individual metes out trust on this basis.

As was the case with Level A, several types might be distinguished within Level B. Some respondents tended to perceive politics in terms of a competition of these group interests, with the political parties arraying themselves in favor of one group and in opposition to another. However, many respondents did not develop the discussion of group benefit beyond the context of a single group, nor did they express a feeling that the party or candidate not seen as favorable was actively pursuing a threatening policy, either by ignoring or seeking to harm the group, or by supporting another group seen as a natural antagonist. In terms of numbers, Level B was fairly evenly split between these two types.

In addition to this content distinction, there was a considerable range in the quality of response within both types. For example, some of the people who paired the parties with opposing interest groups could bring little further content to the matter under probing. For analytic purposes, these rather shallow versions of the group benefit themes were separated from the normal run of responses of this sort.

People having relatively substantial perceptions of a competition of group interests make up the first category of any size that we have encountered. Fourteen per cent of our sample received this classification. Although the perception of group interest provides a tangible criterion for inclusion at this level, the reader is urged to compare the illustrative interviews drawn randomly from this group with those of the higher level in terms of the more general grasp of politics that is represented. These illustrative responses come from an Ohio farm woman:

(Like about Democrats?) I think they have always helped the farmers. To tell you the truth, I don't see how any farmer could vote for Mr. Eisenhower. *(Is there anything else you like about the Democratic Party?)* We have always had good times under their Administration. They are more for the working class of people. Any farmer would be a fool to vote for Eisenhower.

(Dislike about Democrats?) No, I can't say there is.

(Like about Republicans?) No.

(Dislike about Republicans?) About everything. *(What are you thinking of?)* They promise so much but they don't do anything. *(Anything else?)* I think the Republicans favor the richer folks. I never did think much of the Republicans for putting into office a military man.

(Now I'd like to ask you about the good and bad points of the two candidates for President. Is there anything in particular about Stevenson that might make you want to vote for him?) I think he is a *very* smart man. *(Is there anything else?)* I think he will do what he says, will help the farmer. We will have higher prices *(Anything else?)* No.

(Is there anything in particular about Stevenson that might make you want to vote against him?) No. But I have this against Stevenson, but I wouldn't vote against him. In the Illinois National Guards he had Negroes and Whites together. They ate and slept together. I don't like that. I think Negroes should have their own place. I don't see why they would want to mix.

(Is there anything in particular about Eisenhower that might make you want to vote for him?) No.

(Is there anything in particular about Eisenhower that might make you want to vote against him?) Yes. He favors Wall Street. I don't think he is physically able, and he will step aside and that Richard Nixon will be President. *(Anything else?)* To tell the truth, I never thought he knew

enough about politics to be a President. He is a military man. He takes too many vacations and I don't see how he can do the job.

One theme that appears here, the attention to specific "promises," deserves special comments. In the upper ranges, particularly among the full ideologues, references to promises made or broken are almost nonexistent. But as we depart from the upper level, references of this sort increase in frequency to the point at which they become almost the center of any attention paid to content with policy implication.[4] The political "promise," in the form retained by the respondent, has characteristics that contrast sharply with the sorts of concerns associated with ideology. Promises arise *de novo* with each campaign; they have minimal roots in either a party tradition or a long-range program. The tendency to focus upon these pledges as the issue core of politics seems to token narrow time perspectives, concrete modes of thought, and a tremendously oversimplified view of causality in social, economic, and political process.

With the interview involving perceptions of conflicting group interest added to those of Level A, we have now accounted for about one-quarter of our sample and slightly less than one-third of the voters. Another 17 per cent of the respondents talked of benefits accruing to a single group through the aid of a single party. The interview drawn to illustrate this type comes from a man in Texas:

(Like about Democrats?) Well, I don't know. I've just always before been a Democrat. My daddy before me always was. *(Can you name any good things that you like about the party?)* Well, no, I guess not.

(Dislike about Democrats?) I don't know of anything.

(Like about Republicans?) No.

(Dislike about Republicans?) Well, I just don't believe they are for the common people. *(Anything else that you don't like about the Republican Party?)* No, I don't think so.

(Like about Stevenson?) No, ma'am.

(Dislike about Stevenson?) Well, I wouldn't know hardly how to put that. I just don't hardly think he's the man for President.

(Like about Eisenhower?) Well, his past is all. *(Is there anything else that might make you want to vote for him?)* No.

---

[4] This is not true within Level D, of course, for subjects were classified here only if there was no reference to the sort of issue material made concrete in the campaign promise.

(Dislike about Eisenhower?) Nothing but the right man in the Democratic Party.

These interviews, chosen randomly from among the more capable responses falling in Level B, serve to represent the conflict-of-interest and the single-group interest responses. As we have suggested, some interviews of rather low calibre with group-benefit mentions were separated to form a lower category within Level B. By and large, the quality of responses here is close to what we shall later encounter in Level C, despite the group references. These poorer interviews of Level B, making up another 11 per cent of the sample, include responses similar to that of a New York City woman:

(Like about Democrats?) Well, my father is a Democrat and I'm one by inheritance sort of. I know nothing about politics but I like the Democratic Party because I know they are more for the poorer people.

(Dislike about Democrats?) Nope.

(Like about Republicans?) No, there isn't.

(Dislike about Republicans?) Yes. They are out to help the rich people.

(Like about Stevenson?) I heard him talk on TV, and he is a wonderful talker. I believe what he says and I think he will make a good President. I think he is capable and honest and I like him.

(Dislike about Stevenson?) No.

(Like about Eisenhower?) He is a fine man. A good military man, though, not a good President.

(Dislike about Eisenhower?) Yes, he was not a good President because he relied too much on his helpers. They led him. He didn't lead them.

As we complete our survey of the range of interviews included in Level B, it seems undeniable that we have moved to levels of conceptualization remote from those presumed by ideological interpretations of political behavior. Yet Levels A and B taken together account for little more than half of the total sample, and for only some 60 per cent of the 1956 respondents who voted.

Level C, the "Goodness" and "Badness" of the Times. The third level coincides closely with the third quartile of our sample. In some ways interviews classified here are most effectively defined in negative terms. On the one hand, these responses do not include perceptions of group interest, and they lack as well any sense of a structure of concepts that might be conceived to border on ideology. On the other hand, these interviews escape classification in Level D by virtue of some reference, however nebulous or fragmentary, to a subject of controversy over public policy.

The issue content of this sort tends to be sparse within each interview and heterogeneous from interview to interview. Nonetheless, it is subject to some characterization. The most prevalent type of response provides the denotation for this level. Typically, there is a perception of the economic state of the immediate family, which is an index of the "goodness" or "badness" of the times. The possibility that what happens to some may not happen to others in the same way seems too differentiated a view of society or politics to have much role in the evaluation process. And, of course, once the nature of the times is assessed, the leap to party culpability is simple and direct.

A second prominent type of response assigned to Level C involved the concrete detail that had issue relevance but appeared to stand as an isolated structure, an island of cognition in a sea of darkness. A prototype is the elderly woman economically dependent on her social security checks, who associates this aid appreciatively with the Democratic Party. Beyond this single policy item, however, she professes to know nothing whatever about politics, and is unable under probing to supply further content. Thus while Level C includes vague generalities about the times, it includes as well these isolated and specific issue perceptions.

Several characteristics not used as criteria for assignment had great incidence in these Level C interviews. There is a vastly increased tendency for the respondent to plead great ignorance of anything political. Now and again there is some apparent element of modesty underlying this confession; in the great majority of the cases, however, it is easy to see what the individual means. Furthermore, there seems to be an increasingly moral cast to evaluations at this level. Irritation and concern over matters of graft and campaign "mudslinging" are given frequent vent. Such observations are not absent from responses at higher levels; but in Levels C and D they come to form the main thrust of the individual's perceptions with monotonous regularity. An impressive proportion of individuals at these lower levels roundly condemns both parties for "running each other down so." These people seem genuinely depressed by any cross-party criticism of policy and platform. When a person has just watched or listened to some of the campaign speeches, these reactions often remain much more salient than the content of the criticism itself.

Let us present some sample interviews from Level C. While we limit ourselves to two illustrations, these illustrations stand for about one-quarter of our interviews. Hence responses of this sort outnumber all those of Level A by more than 2 to 1, and they outnumber responses of the top ideological category by a ratio approaching 10 to 1. The first interview comes from a woman in New York City:

(Like about Democrats?) What was in all the papers last week? Stevenson will see to it that they stop testing the bomb and I'm in favor of that. I don't want them to explode any more of those bombs. *(Is there anything that you like about the Democratic Party?)* I don't know anything about the party, really. I just want them to stop testing the bomb.

(Dislike about Democrats?) I don't know much about the parties. *(Is there anything you don't like about the Democratic Party?)* No—I don't know much about the whole thing.

(Like about Republicans?) My husband's job is better. (Laughed.) *(How do you mean?)* Well, his investments in stocks are up. They go up when the Republicans are in. My husband is a furrier and when people get money they buy furs.

(Dislike about Republicans?) No. *(Is there anything at all you don't like about the Republican Party?)* No—I don't know that much about the parties.

(Like about Stevenson?) As I mentioned before, he's saying stop testing the bomb because it can cause so much damage. My husband says that's such a minor point, but I don't think so.

(Dislike about Stevenson?) Nothing, nothing at all.

(Like about Eisenhower?) No, nothing in particular. *(Is there anything at all?)* No.

(Dislike about Eisenhower?) That he might die and Nixon would be President and I don't care for Nixon. He might not have his four-year term. There's a lot said about the other sickness that he had—not the heart attack.

The second interview comes from a woman in Louisville:

(Like about Democrats?) Well, I really don't know enough about politics to speak. I never did have no dealings with it. I thought politics was more for men anyway. *(Well, is there anything you like about the Democratic Party?)* I like the good wages my husband makes. *(It is the Republicans who are in now.)* I know, and it's sort of begun to tighten up since the Republicans got in. *(Is there anything else you like about the Democratic Party?)* No.

(Dislike about Democrats?) No, I couldn't think of a thing.

(Like about Republicans?) Well, truthfully, the Republican Party just doesn't interest me at all. *(There isn't anything you like about it?)* No— I just am not particularly interested in either one.

(Dislike about Republicans?) I just don't know. It's immaterial to me about the Republican Party. I never thought enough about them to get interested in them.

(Like about Stevenson?) Well, I'll tell you, I haven't read enough about either one of the candidates to know anything about them at all. *(Is there anything about Stevenson that might make you want to vote for him?)* None other than that he's a Democrat.

(Dislike about Stevenson?) No.

(Like about Eisenhower?) No.

(Dislike about Eisenhower?) Well, just that he's a Republican.

Level D, Absence of Issue Content. The remaining quarter of the sample failed to comment upon any issues of political debate in their responses to the unstructured questions. While vote turnout is relatively low within this group, these people still account for 17 per cent of our voters in 1956, and hence by themselves outnumber our ideologues in the active electorate by a 5–1 ratio.

To the degree that occupants of Level D have perceptions of the parties at all, they are bound up in moralistic themes like mudslinging and chicanery. More often the parties are poorly discriminated, and comment is devoted almost entirely to the personal characteristics of the candidates—their popularity, their sincerity, their religious practice, or home life.

Initially our interest in the upper ranges of response was such that we planned no differentiation of types within Level D. It became apparent in the classification process that three broad types were emerging clearly. The first group consisted of party-oriented people. These were persons whose only conscious connection to the political process seemed to lie in a potent sense of membership within a party. They tended by and large to pay little attention to the candidates, and their presence in Level D indicates that they were unable to suggest how their party differed in its stands from the opposing party. The second type stood in sharp contrast in its preoccupations. These people had little information about or patience with the parties. The prevailing theme was "parties don't make any difference. It's the man who counts." Once again, the fact of location in Level D signifies that there were no issue implications in the subsequent perceptions of the candidates. These perceptions had to do almost exclusively with comparisons of looks, sincerity, popularity, religious practice, and family life.

The third type comprises the individuals who were unable to say anything about politics at all, save to explain why they found it difficult to pay any attention to it. This set of respondents was not, however, completely inactive politically, as about one quarter of them, for one reason or another, managed to vote in 1956.

Since Level D comprised one quarter of the sample it was feasible to return to the interviews and subdivide respondents into these types. The distribution that emerged within Level D was as follows:

	Proportion of Level D
Simple party orientation	⅕
Simple candidate orientation	⅖
No political perceptions	⅕
Unclassified (mixed types)	⅕

Let us turn to samples of these major types. A woman from California was drawn from the party-oriented individuals in Level D.

(Like about Democrats?) I'm a Democrat. *(Is there anything you like about the Democratic Party?)* I don't know.

(Dislike about Democrats?) I'm a Democrat, that's all I know. My husband's dead now—he was a Democrat. *(Is there anything you don't like about the party?)* I don't know.

(Like about Republicans?) I don't know.

(Dislike about Republicans?) I don't know.

(Like about Stevenson?) Stevenson is a good Democrat. *(Is there anything else about him that might make you want to vote for him?)* No, nothing.

(Dislike about Stevenson?) I don't know. *(Is there anything about him that might make you want to vote against him?)* No.

(Like about Eisenhower?) I don't know. *(Is there anything about Eisenhower that might make you want to vote for him?)* I don't know.

(Dislike about Eisenhower?) I don't know. *(Is there anything about him that might make you want to vote against him?)* No.

An illustration of the candidate type within Level D comes from a Massachusetts man.

(Like about Democrats?) I haven't heard too much. I don't get any great likes or dislikes.

(Dislike about Democrats?) I hate the darned backbiting.

(Like about Republicans?) No.

(Dislike about Republicans?) No.

(Like about Stevenson?) No, I don't like him at all.

(Dislike about Stevenson?) I have no use for Stevenson whatsoever. I had enough of him at the last election. I don't like the cut-throat business— condemn another man and then shake hands with him five minutes later.

(Like about Eisenhower?) As a man I like Eisenhower better. Not particularly for the job of President, but he is not so apt to cut your throat.

(Dislike about Eisenhower?) No.

The interviews that had virtually nothing to say may be rapidly disposed of. The illustration drawn came from a woman in Missouri:

(Like about Democrats?) No—I don't know as there is.

(Dislike about Democrats?) No.

(Like about Republicans?) No, it's the same way I am about the other party.

(Dislike about Republicans?) No. Parties are all about the same to me.

(Like about Stevenson?) No, I don't think so.

(Dislike about Stevenson?) No.

(Like about Eisenhower?) I really don't care which man is best or otherwise. I don't know about either one of the men enough to give an opinion.

(Dislike about Eisenhower?) No.

We have now accounted for our total sample. This profile of an electorate is not calculated to increase our confidence in interpretations of elections that presume widespread ideological concerns in the adult population. To be sure, we have been able to assess only those aspects of political conceptualization that are revealed in conscious verbal materials. It might be argued for example that in tranquil times when no need for innovative leadership is felt, the poorly educated might find such leadership disturbing without being able to say exactly why. Such ineffable sentiment might, for the inarticulate, come to focus on reactions to personal attributes of the candidate. This is a possibility, yet one which we are not inclined to credit highly. If there were strong links between elements of the

Table 9-1. Summary of the Distribution of the Total Sample and of 1956 Voters in Levels of Conceptualization

	Proportion of Total Sample	Proportion of Voters
A. Ideology		
I. Ideology	2½%	3½%
II. Near-ideology	9	12
B. Group Benefits		
I. Perception of conflict	14	16
Single-group interest	17	18
II. Shallow group benefit responses	11	11
C. Nature of the times	24	22
D. No issue content		
I. Party orientation	4	3½
II. Candidate orientation	9	7
III. No content	5	3
IV. Unclassified	4½	4
	100%	100%

"deeper self" and reactions to ideological position that do bypass conscious concept formation and evaluation, we might have expected a stronger association between our measurement of conservatism and partisan decisions. Many of the people who reacted with dismay to the possibility of change suggested by the scale items undoubtedly failed to think of themselves, at a conscious level, as "conservative," if for no other reason than the fact the concept is not part of their cognitive tool chest.

But the fact remains that both the structured approach and the analysis of free answers lead to precisely the same conclusions: the concepts important to ideological analysis are useful only for that small segment of the population that is equipped to approach political decisions at a rarefied level.

chapter 10
Election Laws, Political Systems, and the Voter

The political world to which the voter responds is composed of more than the actors and events that mark the competition for his support. It includes as well the formal rules and informal norms that circumscribe his participation. One need only consider the electoral laws of the several states or the tenor of political activity where serious interparty competition is lacking to be convinced that the American political system, although bound together by many nationwide features, embraces a variety of political subcommunities. Each of these communities is a pervasive medium within which behavior must occur. And each leaves some characteristic impress on that behavior.

We cannot conclude our examination of the political context of the voting act without a closer recognition of these facts. Up to this point we have been primarily concerned with an interplay between remote events of national politics and individual constructions of political reality that result. Such national events may be conveyed to all corners of the nation by our media of mass communication. Yet these events are interpreted by groups of individuals in local settings—cities, counties, states, and regions—and these settings differ in their characteristics as political communities. Without empirical evidence we would have little basis to predict whether the effects of these "system" factors on individual behavior would be strong or weak relative to others. But even the discovery of moderate effects could shed important light on the nature of the American political process as a whole.

Taken together, the legal limits on political participation and the rules governing the conduct of partisan politics constitute an important aspect of the individual's political environment that bears directly upon our analysis of electoral behavior. The immediate political environment varies, furthermore, not only in terms of electoral codes but in terms of intangible political atmosphere as well. At times, subtle community sentiment becomes embodied in more formal regulations, just as formal regulations act to guide the development of community sentiment. However, other aspects of the political atmosphere also mark the community. Although analysis of the formal regulations governing the franchise provides a first level of description of political communities across the nation, any account would be incomplete without recognition of at least the gross differences in party system that occur from area to area.

If these components of voters' political environment are familiar, our treatment of them departs somewhat from customary modes of analysis. In keeping with our dual interest in political preference and political participation, we have organized electoral regulations into two mutually exclusive sets of rules, the one concerned with the regulation of *participation* and the other concerned with political *partisanship*. With one or two exceptions we will not consider the unique implications of any particular item included in either set. Instead, by considering simultaneously all regulations that relate to the partisanship of voters we will, for example, establish a range of conditions relevant to partisan behavior. We can then rank the residents of the various states according to whether the sets of electoral laws and regulations under which they live make partisan behavior easier or harder for them. At one extreme we can locate persons whose partisanship is reinforced through registration tests of party loyalty or through closed primaries; at the other extreme are voters who are never called upon to give any demonstration of party allegiance. The specific items on which our summary measure of the facilitation of partisanship is based include the following: type of primary election —open, closed, or blanket; arrangement of primary ballot—separate tickets, consolidated ballot, etc.; party tests for voting in primary; existence of nonpartisan primary; form of general election ballot and provision for presidential primary.

We shall treat the regulation of suffrage in a similar fashion. In general, we shall not isolate the poll tax or the literacy test and examine their correlates in political behavior. We shall consider all state regulations governing suffrage and organize them to provide an overall measure of the formal facilitation or inhibition of political participation within a state. The regulations governing participation vary between the major regions. Consequently, in the North we base our summary measure of vote facilitation on the following: required length of United States citizenship, residence requirements in state, county, and voting district, and presence of a literacy test for voting. In the South the components of the measure include age, residence requirement in state and county, and poll tax requirement for voting.

THE FORMAL FACILITATION OF PARTISANSHIP

We would suppose that election laws relevant to partisanship would have their greatest significance for the development of the loyalties represented in our measure of party identification. The data confirm such expectations. Although almost all segments of the population appear to respond meaningfully to questions about party loyalty, the character of these allegiances varies in conjunction with laws having to do with partisanship. Voters governed by rules most likely to promote partisanship are most likely to be strong party identifiers (40 per cent) and least likely to classify themselves as Independents (22 per cent). Conversely, the voters in states that provide minimal encouragement of partisanship are significantly more often self-classified Independents (34 per cent) and less often strongly identified with a party (34 per cent).

In extending our comments on the significance of this association two important points must be made. First, although there is a relationship between extent of party identification and the election laws governing the residents of the states outside of the "Border" tier and the Solid South, there is no such relationship within the remaining fifteen states. Most Southern States are clustered at the extreme of partisan facilitation relative to electoral requirements outside that region. More important still, it is likely that the unique monopoly enjoyed by the Democratic party throughout the South alters the impact of many factors that might otherwise be associated with independence in the partisan competition for allegiance.

Secondly, we must proceed with caution in treating the causal implication of the relationship as it emerges outside the South. The nature of the election laws comprising our measure of partisan facilitation is such that we would expect a person to be "forced" to a declaration or choice of party only as a part of the act of voting, and usually the act of voting in a primary election. The closed primary, the oath of party loyalty, the casting of a straight party vote and the others might be expected to have little meaning for the persistent nonvoter who has seldom if ever come into contact with them. We find, however, that people who seldom if ever vote show the same substantial differences in their strength of party identification under differing state laws as do citizens who never miss an election. Hence the causal sequence from election laws to partisan attachments cannot be as simple as it may first appear.

Even politically inactive persons rarely exposed to the usual political stimulation of the mass media or local campaign events may by social mechanisms have some contact with the political life of their communities. The informal "opinion leader" may serve as one such social agent, conveying the relevant political sentiment to a more or less passive audience. In addition to the information carried by the self-selected opinion leader, a broad variety of political information is undoubtedly transmitted in the more structured setting of the group. Many primary and secondary groups perpetuate political standards or norms and convey these to their members. In some instances this transfer may be a matter of deliberate group policy, as with the political education committees of the labor unions and the political activities of many large industrial organizations. In other instances standards may be transmitted more subtly, as in the case of religious groups, many civic and service clubs, and such broad secondary groupings as are constituted by Negroes or farmers. The group may well join the informal opinion leader in transmitting cues about political partisanship to the less involved members of the community.

In the absence of historical or longitudinal analysis, such an explanation of the causal link between election laws and the partisanship of citizens would at least satisfy the logical demands of available data. It would also suggest that election laws are significant elements of our political system and not merely the esoteric interests of election officials and manipulative politicians. Similarly, it helps document the contention that our national party system is built in some degree on the unique system of each of the member states.

Ballot Form and Ticket Splitting. There are, of course, specific institutional forms that are quite unambiguously related to voting behavior, whatever the specific nature of the political subculture. One of these, which contributed as well to our summary measure of the formal facilitation of partisanship, is the general election ballot. Whatever relationships we find between the political motivations of voters and the way they mark their ballots, the form of the ballot itself has an influence on the proportion of straight and split tickets cast. This becomes evident when we divide our sample of the national electorate into those voting in states with the single choice type of straight-ticket voting and those in which a straight ticket requires more than one mark on the ballot.

In 1956, of the Eisenhower voters in single-choice states, fifty-nine per cent voted a straight ticket; in multiple-choice states, forty-eight per cent; of the 1956 Stevenson voters in single-choice states, sixty-nine per cent voted a straight ticket; in multiple-choice states, sixty per cent. Since the distribution of party identifiers in the two types of states did not differ we conclude that the sheer ease of voting a straight ticket facilitated this type of behavior. The role played by the form of the general election ballot thus provides a more specific illustration of the formal facilitation or inhibition of partisanship in political behavior.

FORMAL RESTRICTIONS ON VOTING

The second set of formal or legal factors that we shall consider includes those related to suffrage. The most significant definitions of eligibility to vote were made in times past through constitutional amendment. By comparison, the present-day legal qualifications set by each state are of small consequence. Nevertheless, in some states a combination of election codes and extralegal practices has led to the effective disfranchisement of many citizens. In the South the proportion of citizens who have never voted (see Table 10-1) is clearly associated

Table 10-1. Relation of State Restrictions on Voting to Past Frequency of Voting, by Region

Frequency of Past Voting	Laws Governing Suffrage, North			Laws Governing Suffrage, South	
	Restrictive	Moderate	Permissive	Restrictive	Moderate
Voted in all elections	52%	48%	49%	21%	30%
Voted in most elections	20	23	23	17	17
Voted in some elections	11	15	16	21	20
Have never voted	17	14	12	41	33
	100%	100%	100%	100%	100%
Number of cases	691	942	724	410	528

with state-imposed restrictions on voting. Moreover, among those *who have voted* in some previous presidential elections, the residents of the more restrictive states have voted less regularly in those elections for which they were eligible. Under such restrictive legislation, therefore, there are not only more citizens who never vote, but proportionately more of the persons who have voted are irregular, in-and-out voters. In the North these associations between institutional restrictions on voting and the act of voting are so small that they may be regarded as inconsequential.

These empirical findings are illuminated by our consideration of differences in regional political systems. The difference in regularity of voting in the South fits the concept of a community concerned about the extent of political participation. In the more restrictive states the institutional forms maintain a larger pool of citizens who never vote, and the presumed sentiment of the political community does not stimulate the regular performance of civic duty by those who do establish their voting eligibility. In the North, on the other hand, legal forms in some states disfranchise some potential voters—but those who do vote are apparently quite unaffected by any local impediment to their appearance at the polls.

Restriction of suffrage in the South has in recent years been directed primarily at limiting the political activity of the Negro. Table 10-2

Table 10-2. Relation of State Restrictions on Voting to Past Frequency of Voting, by Race (South Only)

| Frequency of Past Voting | Negro | | White | |
| | Law Governing Suffrage | | | |
	Restrictive	Moderate	Restrictive	Moderate
Voted in all elections	3%	10%	26%	34%
Voted in most elections	0	10	22	19
Voted in some elections	12	20	24	19
Have never voted	85	60	28	28
	100%	100%	100%	100%
Number of cases	95	89	315	439
Proportion of totals	(52%)	(48%)	(42%)	(58%)

provides our most general description of Negro and White voting. The high rate of persistent nonvoting among Negroes is the most obvious message of the table. In comparing differences in nonvoting among both Whites and Negroes we also observe evidence of considerably greater relationship between legal restrictions and nonvoting among Negroes. We assume that the greater impact of restrictive electoral laws on Negroes is, in part at least, a function of the relatively low motivational levels among Negroes. This does not fully explain the racial differences in voting behavior, however, as we discover when we add a third dimension to our analysis, the racial composition of county populations.

In Table 10-3 we have subdivided each of the population groups in

Table 10-3. Relation of State Restrictions on Voting to Past Frequency of Voting, by Race within Density of Negro Population (South Only)

	Per Cent Non-White in County			
	Under 30 Per Cent		*Over 30 Per Cent*	
Frequency of Past Voting	Suffrage Laws Restrictive	Suffrage Laws Moderate	Suffrage Laws Restrictive	Suffrage Laws Moderate
White				
Voted in all elections	26%	34%	27%	33%
Voted in most elections	21	17	27	28
Voted in some elections	25	20	21	15
Have never voted	28	29	25	24
	100%	100%	100%	100%
Number of cases	230	372	85	67
Proportion of totals	(38%)	(62%)	(56%)	(44%)
Negro				
Voted in all elections	(23%)[a]	16%	0%	3%
Voted in most elections	(0)	14	0	5
Voted in some elections	(38)	16	7	25
Have never voted	(39)	54	93	67
	(100%)	100%	100%	100%
Number of cases	(13)	49	82	40
Proportion of totals	(21%)	(79%)	(67%)	(33%)

[a] Figures in this column are given in parentheses because of the small number of cases.

Table 10-2, separating residents of counties with populations that are less than 30 per cent Negro from those in counties where more than 30 per cent of the people are Negroes. In this table we may note three significant facts. First, most Negroes living in heavily Negro counties do not vote—regardless of the stringency or leniency of state laws (only 2 per cent classify themselves as relatively consistent voters). Second, Negroes living in counties with a smaller proportion of Negroes in the population vote more often than do other Negroes living in the same states under the same laws but in counties with larger Negro populations. And third, the variability in the turnout of the Southern Negro is not fully accounted for by differences in state legislation; the racial composition of the county is also a contributing factor. Where White dominance is numerically more extreme, there is apparently less community resistance to Negro voting.

A number of major conclusions are suggested by this analysis: (1) it is the informal, extralegal barriers—not state legislation—that account for much of the variability in the turnout of the Southern Negro; (2) greatest regularity in voting among Whites is reported most often in heavily Negro counties and, in particular, in those counties where voters are not greatly hampered by state-imposed limitations on voting; and (3) the institutional pattern relating legal regulations to individual behaviors persists in all four major categories formed by combinations of race and racial composition of counties. Our earlier generalization concerning the significance of participation in the political system of the South has not been vitiated by the analysis of racial differences in voting behavior. Instead, this analysis suggests two distinct dimensions to be found in the structure of Southern politics— one centered on the position of the Negro, the other concerned with the absence of stable party competition. In both instances the question of political participation is central. In the case of Negro voting, the local institutions outside the formal rules and regulations are clearly significant. But in all areas, even where this problem is most acute, we find the patterned reflection of a system of one-party politics.

The interplay between formal rules and individual behaviors among Negroes and Whites outside the South adds a further dimension to our understanding of the situation. There are very sharp differences in the vote participation of Whites and Negroes in the North. Again, there is no apparent relationship between the formal rules and individual behavior for the 95 per cent of the population that is White. Under restrictive legislation some 75 per cent report participation in all or most elections; 72 per cent of the Northern Whites who enjoy *more permissive* electoral codes report a comparable frequency of voting. The same comparison for Northern Negroes, however, discloses significant differences: under restrictive legislation only 30 per cent report fairly regular voting in the past, whereas 54 per cent of the Negroes governed by more permissive laws report regular voting.

The effect is not so great at the other end of the scale, where 35 per cent of those under restrictive legislation report that they have never voted, as compared to 22 per cent of those under more moderate legislation.

It would seem that insofar as the process of political disfranchisement of Negroes is concerned, the selective impact of legal codes is felt in both the North and the South, and in the South this effect is amplified by the selective application of informal extralegal sanctions. The rate of Negro participation in the Northern elections is, of course, much higher than under nominally equivalent conditions in the South. Indeed, Northern Negroes governed by the more permissive regulations participate at a higher rate than do three of the four categories of Southern Whites we have examined. Nevertheless, Negroes in the North not only participate in politics substantially less than their White neighbors but also appear to be more seriously handicapped by the legal restrictions on the franchise in their districts.

CONDITIONS OF INSTITUTIONAL EFFECTIVENESS

Thus far in this chapter we have introduced a number of observations on the interrelations of institutions and political systems. We are now in a position to clarify more directly the behavioral effects of the interplay between situation or context terms and the attitudes central to our analysis.

Proper juxtaposition of institution, attitude, and behavioral variables leads repeatedly to the conclusion that *formal political institutions have their greatest impact on behavior when the attitudes relevant to that behavior are least intense.* In terms of the suffrage problem, for example, this means that the magnitude of the effects of legal restrictions on voting depends on the degree to which the individual voter is motivated to vote. If his motivation is high, formal facilitation or inhibition of his behavior is relatively ineffective; if his motivation is low, his actual performance may be greatly affected by the same legal forms.

To demonstrate this proposition let us first consider the role of voting restrictions in the South as strength of motivation to vote varies.[1] Among those Southerners highly motivated to vote who live under the more permissive laws regulating suffrage, 12 per cent

---

[1] Motivation level is measured here by the range of political attitudes possessed by the voter. Involvement in all six major political attitudes indicates maximum motivation.

have never voted; under the more restrictive codes, 18 per cent. Among those who have voted, 57 per cent in the first situation have voted in every election, whereas 52 per cent of the less advantaged report a comparable record of participation.

When motivation to vote is low, the pattern is quite different. There is, of course, a generally lower level of past participation; less than one in five has voted in every election and almost half have never voted. The important data, however, concern the differences to be found when we compare persons residing where institutional barriers are weaker with their counterparts in restrictive states. First, the level of persistent nonvoting goes up from 32 per cent to 51 per cent, an increase of 19 per cent. Among the highly motivated the comparable absolute difference was 6 per cent. Similarly, among actual *voters* with low motivation levels, 23 per cent operating under more permissive rules report never missing an election, whereas only one in ten who was confronted with the greater barriers to voting reports never missing an election. Again, this difference of 13 per cent is to be compared to a difference of only 5 per cent among highly motivated voters. Both absolute and relative differences in participation, associated with formal facilitation and inhibition of participation, are visibly greater for citizens with low levels of motivation.

Another demonstration of the same general proposition may be observed among the nation's voters using single-choice and multiple-choice ballots in the general election. The impact of the form of the ballot on straight- and split-ticket voting varies with the motivation of the voter. In view of the fact that a high level of partisan motivation leads to straight-ticket voting, we would predict that other factors such as the ballot form will have their greatest influence on such voting in the absence of partisan motivations. This prediction holds true. The data may be summarized as follows:

Among strong party identifiers, a single-choice ballot
    increased straight-ticket voting by   0%
Among weak identifiers it increased it by   27%
Among Independents it increased it by   60%
Among weak identifiers whose vote conflicted with
    their identification it increased it by   60%

In each of the situations just reviewed we have observed substantial evidence that the formal political institutions in question had their greatest impact on political behavior when the attitudes relevant to that behavior were weak. This proposition is of considerable importance to the study of political institutions. The role of the institution, whatever the specific political system dictates that it be, is not of uniform importance to all citizens. The political involvement of some overrides or at least mitigates the influence of the institution. Programs of institutional change, whether sponsored in a spirit of civic reform or in the interest of narrower goals, are of less consequence for such citizens. The need for change is less pressing—as the highly involved citizen surmounts the formal obstacles to his personal goals —and the consequence of change will therefore be less dramatic. Alteration of those institutions that have greatest relevance for the casual or marginal voter will, on the other hand, probably have maximum impact by virtue of their pronounced influence on the relatively uninvolved participant. The easing of registration requirements, for example, might increase voting rates among the uninvolved citizens, but probably would not greatly affect the behavior of intense partisans.

★ ★ ★ ★ SECTION IV

THE SOCIAL AND ECONOMIC CONTEXT

Prior party attachments form, as we have seen, the great watershed for public reaction to current political events. With the examination of this phenomenon in Section III it was natural to ask what conditions lead to the formation of partisan allegiances *initially*. The instrumental character of the political system would suggest that if we trace a party commitment deep enough into the past, we must sooner or later encounter recognizable "beginnings," and that these beginnings are likely to involve pressures arising outside the political order as narrowly defined. True as this may be, such a tracing leads with surprising frequency to events lying years or even generations behind us, in such remote circumstances as a ravaged Georgia plantation or a job for a bewildered Boston immigrant. Such roots of current choice provide a strange commentary on the view of the democratic process as a periodic reevaluation of contemporary events.

It is not our intention, however, to leave the matter in such restricted form. The causal priorities assigned in the course of our argument are a judicious reflection of the total cast of the data that we have analyzed over the years. None of our ensuing observations should be construed as contesting this emphasis; many further facts will come to light that tend rather to underscore it. Yet it has been presented only as an emphasis, and not as a "simple and sovereign" principle of political behavior.

Already, as our materials have been developed, we have noted a constant if "premature" intrusion of nonpolitical causes and intervening mechanisms in our account. We have remarked upon the widespread perceptions of group interest that appear in citizen evaluations. We have considered visible biases in individual response that appear to rest on diffuse sentiment communicated by primary groups within the political community. We have also encountered some of the reverberations touched off in the political order by grosser events

—most notably, disasters like war and depression—that envelop the society.

Over the ensuing chapters we shall approach some of the prominent social and economic elements in the causal nexus more directly. We need not restrict our attention to the role that such nonpolitical factors play in initial party choice, for it is apparent that many of these determinants and intervening mechanisms contribute to the course of events up to the time of the act itself, even for the long-term partisan. Knowledge of social processes may add much to our understanding of the fact that party allegiances not only remain stable but grow stronger over time. The ambiguity of the merits of political objects and events is such that people are dependent upon "social reality" to support and justify their political opinions. When primary groups engage in political discussion and are homogeneous in basic member viewpoints, the attitudes of the individual must be continually reinforced as he sees similar opinions echoed in the social group.

Although the fact of membership in a politically alert primary group is of no help to an understanding of the partisan direction of an individual's vote, it does suggest that he is likely to hold a more stable party preference over time. By the same token, such primary-group mechanisms are of obvious import in maintaining the patterns of distinctive political behavior long associated with many sociologically defined groupings in the electorate.

We shall find it of value to distinguish between those patterns associated with self-conscious groups, such as racial or ethnic communities, and those groups that emerge from certain formal categories, such as the age cohort of people over 60 years old or such as women. In Chapter 11 we shall propose a system of variables that seems critical for the operation of group influence in the case of the self-conscious group. Treatment of the far more diverse mechanisms that create patterns in the opposite type of social entity—the simple sociological category—is postponed until Chapter 15.

The intervening chapters deal with social phenomena that are intermediate between these poles or with economic phenomena that we must consider in the light of their effects upon the political process. Social class provides a natural point of convergence between the social and the economic problem in politics. Its status as a self-conscious group or mere analytic category has often been debated. We shall find it useful in Chapter 12 to conceive that this status varies markedly over time in response to economic conditions, and to evaluate its political implications in these terms. Several conceptual threads developed in the chapters on group influence, social class, and economic antecedents are drawn together in a discussion of agrarian voting in Chapter 13.

Having considered several aspects of group behavior, we turn in Chapter 14 to an analysis of change wrought in personal dispositions when the individual shifts his social and political milieu. Although primary stress is laid here upon geographic movement from one partisan climate to another, we shall also find it enlightening to consider some of the effects of analogous change resulting from individual mobility in the social hierarchy.

chapter 11
Membership in Social Groupings

During each political campaign we hear comment about the "Catholic vote," the "Negro vote," the "labor vote," and so on. Unlike the political parties, these groups stand at one remove from the political order. Their reason for existence is not expressly political. The labor union exists to force management to provide more liberally for the worker; the Catholic church exists for religious worship. But members of these groups appear to think and behave politically in distinctive ways. We assume that these distinctive patterns are produced, in one fashion or another, by influence from the group.

THE PROBLEM OF GROUP INFLUENCE

Groups have influence because we tend to think of them as wholes, and come to respond positively or negatively to them in that form. In this sense, even people who are not members of a group may be influenced by the position that a group takes in politics. Groups can become reference points for the formation of attitudes and decisions about behavior; we speak then of *positive* and *negative reference groups*. People who are actually members of the group are likely to have a more differentiated image of it. But there remains a sense of norms and values attributed to a generalized "group": these are the expectations concerning appropriate behavior for the "loyal" Catholic or union member. It is the group standards that are psychologically real and are responsible for influence when it occurs.

In this chapter we are concerned with the apparent political influence exerted among major, nationwide groupings such as the labor unions, Negroes, Catholics, and Jews. This is not the only level at which political influence dependent on social contact may be examined. Much influence is exerted in smaller, face-to-face "primary" groups such as families, circles of friends, and the like. In fact, there is some evidence to suggest that when primary-group influences run counter to secondary-group political standards, the more intimate contacts may more often than not carry the day.[1] Nonetheless, although many of the mechanisms of influence may be the same in both cases, the study of secondary-group effects has its own unique fruits. It is probably accurate to assume that influence ramifies through primary groups at the grass roots of the nation in a manner fairly constant for both parties. The success or failure of influence at a face-to-face level is not likely to account for the gross trends of the sort constituted by secondary-group voting. If every man managed to influence his wife to vote as he does, we would have no more than a "multiplier" effect on both sides of the political fence. In contrast, successful influence by secondary groups can cause a large-scale, unidirectional shift in the partisan division of the national vote. We are interested in understanding the conditions under which these group pressures are more or less successful.

When we discussed the political parties, it seemed reasonable to speak in terms of a "psychological group," in part because the boundaries of the parties are so poorly delimited by the fact of official membership. In secondary membership groups like labor unions, these formal group boundaries are quite clear. We do not have to ask our informants whether they "consider" they belong to one or another groups; membership is a factual matter. But as we examine these groups more closely, it turns out that the concept of group identification and psychological membership remains extremely valuable. Individuals, all of whom are nominal group members, vary in *degree* of membership, in a psychological sense; and this variation provides us with an excellent tool for breaking apart a voting "bloc," like the American Negro community, in order to understand the workings of influence within the secondary group.

The significance of group identification in all social groupings provides us with a foundation for a more general model of group influence in politics. The scheme would tell us what dimensions of the situation were important for measurement, and how these measures should be combined once they were taken. Appropriate measurements based on such a scheme would allow us to anticipate the direction and degree of the influence that the grouping would wield in the specific situation.

In this chapter we treat membership in social groupings by sketching

---

[1] Norman Kaplan, "Reference Group Theory and Voting Behavior," (unpublished doctoral dissertation, Columbia University, 1955).

the outlines for a general model of this sort. The specific currents observed in the Negro vote in the 1956 election become, in this light, substance of a case study to lay against the more abstract elements called for by the scheme. Likewise, the distinctive behavior of union members toward the objects of politics becomes a special case of the broad phenomenon of group influence.

THE ELEMENTS OF THE MODEL

A model for group influence should perform two distinct services:

1. Increase our understanding of deviation from group political standards by individual members. If the group exerts influence on its membership, and these individuals are members, how and why do they resist?

2. Increase our understanding of the waxing and waning of distinctive political behavior on the part of certain social groupings in the population. What specific conditions govern this variation in group political "strength"?

The same system of variables can handle both problems, for the problems are closely related. If we can specify the conditions under which an individual fails to be influenced by his group, then it is likely that the decline of group potency in politics will result from the extension of these conditions to an increasing proportion of the membership.

At the simplest level, there is a triangle of elements involved in the situation: (1) the individual, (2) the group, and (3) the world of political objects. This triangle suggests three different relationships among these elements: (a) the relationship of the individual to the group; (b) the relationship of the group to the political world; and (c) the relationship of the individual to the political world. These three relationships determine the types of variables that we take into account. A full model will call for measurements that adequately capture the important dimensions of each relationship, if we are to understand the way in which the individual will respond to politics *given the presence of a group that is real in the sense that it can exert a greater or lesser influence on his behavior.*

The relationship of the individual to the world of politics represents a combination of group and nongroup forces. The group forces in the field are predictable as a function of two "background" terms; the relationship of the individual to the group and the relationship of the group to the world of politics. The nongroup forces are, of course, independent of either of these terms. An analysis of the social origins of political motives therefore involves (1) the manner in which the two background terms interact to produce group forces; and (2) the manner in which group forces interact with other forces in the immediate field of political attitudes.

Two important implications are suggested by a logical exercise of this sort. On one hand, we must arrive at some means of sorting the group forces in which we are interested from nongroup forces, within the total field that characterizes the relationship of the individual to the world of politics. But if we pay little systematic attention to the total relationship of the individual to the political world in elaborating this portion of the model, we must not forget that these nongroup forces exist. In fact, this is a first-level answer to the problem of member deviation from group political standards. Group members do not make political decisions in a psychological field limited to group forces, any more than nonmembers make decisions in a vacuum. The current objects of orientation in the political world are available to everybody and, if perceived, have characteristics that can be distorted only within limits.

Our immediate concern lies with the strength of group-generated forces. We wish to understand the conditions under which that strength varies, over time, from individual to individual and from group to group. For this task we can conceptually ignore other forces in the field, which derive from the relation of the individual to politics, *group considerations aside*. But we must remember that these forces exist and contribute to the final attitudes and behavior.

ESTABLISHING THE FACT OF GROUP INFLUENCE

The immediate problem is to find ways to estimate the strength of group forces on the individual. With other forces present in the field, it is easy to mistake their effects for the effects of group influence.

First, it is important to think in terms of the *distinctiveness* of group behavior, rather than its absolute nature. For example, a majority of Catholics in our 1956 sample voted Republican. Traditionally, there has been a Democratic norm among Catholics. Does this finding mean that the norm has died away, or that the group now has new, pro-Republican standards? It means neither. The Catholic Republican vote moved only slightly above the 50 per cent mark, when the nation as a whole was voting 57 per cent Republican. The group force was weak and nongroup forces pushing toward a Republican vote were strong; the nongroup forces were dominant enough to pull a majority of Catholics into the Republican camp, but the presence of group forces in a Democratic direction remains detectible, *relative to the behavior of nongroup members.*

With vote distinctiveness as a criterion, Table 11-1 summarizes the behavior of several key secondary membership groups with traditional Democratic voting norms over a period of three presidential elections. Several aspects of the table are striking. First we find that there is considerable variation in *degree* of distinctiveness, from election to election and from group to group. We also find that each group

Table 11-1. The Distinctiveness of Voting Behavior among Several Social Groupings with Democratic Norms, 1948–1956[a]

	1948	1952	1956
Members of union households[b]	+35.8	+19.8	+18.1
Union members	...[c]	+24.9	+21.4
Catholics	+16.2	+12.8	+7.1
Negroes	...[d]	+41.2	+24.7
Non-South	...[d]	+50.8	+33.1
South	...[d]	+17.6	−1.1
Jews	...[d]	+31.9	+40.8

[a] The entry in each cell represents the deviation in per cent Democratic of the two-party vote division from the comparable per cent among the residual, nonmember portion of the total sample. A positive deviation indicates that the group vote was more Democratic; a negative deviation indicates that the group was more Republican than the residual nongroup.

[b] "Members of union households" includes both union members, where interviews were conducted with the member himself, and other nonunion individuals living in a household that contained a union member. In most cases, the nonmember is the wife of a member.

[c] Members and nonmembers were not separated within our sample of union households in 1948.

[d] Due to the reduced size of the 1948 sample and the small proportion of Negroes and Jews in the parent population, insufficient cases are available for presentation.

seems to vary within a characteristic range. Catholics tend to be least distinctive throughout; the labor unions fall in a middle range. Negroes, despite a sharp drop in distinctiveness between 1952 and 1956, remain on the high side along with Jewish voters.

Nevertheless, there is room for dissatisfaction with distinctiveness, cast in this form, as a working measure of influence. The fact of membership in secondary groupings of the type we are considering locates the person in a peculiar position in social structure, which *in itself* ensures a distinctive pattern of life experience. For example, Negroes have been kept in the lower levels of the nation's status structure; they tend to predominate in the least desirable occupations, receive the lowest pay, are least well educated, and so on. Their high birth rate means that young people are more numerous among Negroes than among other elements in the population. In the North, they tend to reside in metropolitan areas; in the South, in small towns and rural areas. All of these distinctive characteristics have a potential effect on their reactions to politics; and this would be true *even if the group did not exist as an entity cognized by its members.* Northern Negroes as a group made a massive shift of allegiance from the Republican to the Democratic Party during the 1930's. Was this group cohesiveness in response to an Administration interested in the welfare of the Negro community, or was it simply the independent reaction of a set of individuals to economic pressures, part and parcel of the nationwide establishment of Democratic dominance at the lower status levels? In the one case, we would speak of group influence; in the other, we would turn to considerations of social class and economic deprivation.

Of course, we cannot ignore the fact that group influence is in part contingent upon the life situations of the membership. But the important point remains that group influence *is* an additional element in the picture; shared membership provides a focus and direction for behavior that is lacking among nongroup members who happen to be placed in the same life situation. Therefore, it is important to distinguish between the patterns of behavior that develop from the life situations of group members, without reference to the group *qua* group, and the residual distinctiveness that may be traced directly to the fact of group membership.

Hence we must contrast behaviors of group members not simply with those of the remainder of the population, but with the restricted part of that population that shares the peculiar life situations of group members. We want to isolate a "control" group of nonmembers that matches the "test" group of members on all important aspects of life situation save the fact of membership.

With life situation controlled, our estimate of group distinctiveness should be materially improved. Table 11-2 summarizes this new estimate for our groups in the context of the 1956 election. If we compare the figures for vote distinctiveness with those in Table 11-1, we find that much of the picture has remained the same. Catholic distinctiveness has almost disappeared, and the estimate of Jewish distinctiveness has risen slightly. But the major change has been a substantial reduction in the estimate of distinctiveness of the non-Southern Negro vote. This group remains significantly Democratic; but taking into account its extremely low status, its relative youth, and its Southern origins leaves it less Democratic than might appear at first glance.[2]

With such controls, we have more nearly reduced the relationship between the individual and the world of politics to its group-relevant aspects. In effect, we have arrived at an improved estimate of the strength of group forces in the total field at the time of the voting act. The estimate is not perfect and depends on an aggregation of cases; we cannot say that any specific group member is more swayed by the

Table 11-2. Distinctiveness of Presidential Vote among Certain Groups, with Life Situation Controlled, 1956[a]

	1956 Presidential Vote
Members of union households	+17.1
Union members	+20.4
Catholics	+2.9
Negroes	
Non-South	+11.6
South	+15.4
Jews	+45.4

[a] The entry in each cell represents a deviation in per cent Democratic of the two-party vote within the test group from a comparable per cent computed for control groups matched with the test groups for a variety of conditions of life situation.

group than any other, although we get the clear impression that some groups exert more effective influence than others. We must now turn to other elements in the model to account for this variation in influence.

[2] The application of the Southern-origin factor to Negroes represents one point at which we lack sufficient information to exercise controls prudently. As the matter stands, the distinctiveness of the Negro group may be underestimated in Table 11-2.

THE RELATIONSHIP OF THE INDIVIDUAL TO THE GROUP

The first variables to be considered must define the way in which the individual relates himself to the group. We would like to measure aspects of the individual-group relationship that are meaningful for the relationship of *any* individual to *any* group, whether or not that group ever expends effort in political affairs.

Let us think of the group as a psychological reality that exerts greater or lesser attractive force upon its members. Whatever the nominal membership status of the individual, there is room for a great deal of variation in the degree of psychological membership that characterizes the relationship. Just as party identification measures the sense of personal attachment to a political party, so a measure of group identification will indicate the closeness or *"we* feeling" that an individual senses with regard to his membership group.

We have measured group identification by asking members of various politically significant groups the following questions:

Would you say that you feel pretty close to (e.g.) Negroes in general or that you don't feel much closer to them than you do to other kinds of people?

How much interest would you say you have in how (e.g.) Negroes as a whole are getting along in this country? Do you have a good deal of interest in it, some interest, or not much interest at all?

From responses to these items an index of group identification was prepared. The first hypothesis that the model suggests is as follows: *the higher the identification of the individual with the group, the higher the probability that he will think and behave in ways which distinguish members of his group from nonmembers.*

Actually hypotheses much like this have found supporting evidence in other empirical work on voting behavior. Therefore, we are not surprised to find that if we take all members of groups that vote distinctively Democratic, the people who are highly identified with these groups vote even more distinctively Democratic than members who are less highly identified. The least identified third voted 43 per cent Democratic, a figure not very different from the vote proportion in the population as a whole. Medium identifiers, however, voted 56 per cent Democratic; and those most highly identified with these groups voted 69 per cent Democratic. In general, then, the hypothesis receives clear support, and strength of group identification deserves a place as a variable in our model.

Secondary groups that are not primarily political take little interest in some issues, and in these cases group members do not hold attitudes that differ significantly from those of nonmember control groups nor do high identifiers differ from more peripheral members. But as a general rule, whenever a group holds distinctive beliefs about some issue, then within the group a differentiation appears between members according to the strength of their group identification.

This combination of facts argues most conclusively that we are dealing here with a true group-influence phenomenon. To ascertain that influence exists is but a first step, however. We are also interested in assessing the relative strength of influence exerted by various groups and the conditions under which this strength increases or decreases. We find considerable variation in the degree of disparity in presidential vote between strong and weak identifiers within various groups. Table 11-3 summarizes this variation. If we compare these

Table 11-3. Vote Division Within Four Test Groups,
According to Strength of Group Identification, 1956[a]

	Highly Identi- fied	Weakly Identi- fied	Discrepancy
Members of union households	64	36	+28
Catholics	51	39	+11
Negroes			
Non-South	72	63	+9
South	...[b]	...[b]	...[b]
Jews	83	55	+28

[a] The entries in the first two columns represent the per cent Democratic of the two-party vote division. The final column summarizes the differences between percentages in the first two, a plus indicating that high identifiers in the group voted more strongly Democratic.

[b] Southern Negro voters in the sample are too few for further subdivision.

figures with those in Table 11-2, we find some interesting similarities in the rank ordering of the groups. Vote distinctiveness *within the group* bears some relation to distinctiveness between the group and a control group matched for life situation, as we would expect if both were taken to reflect strength of group political influence. But there are differences, also: high identifiers are more distinct in the union case and less distinct in the Negro case than Table 11-2 would lead us to expect. Most Negroes are highly identified with their group; therefore the total group is more clearly Democratic than it might appear if the proportion of high and low identifiers within the Negro group was closer to that found within the union group. But part of the discrepancy results from other factors to be added to the model shortly.

Group identifications help to answer the two primary questions with which a theory of group influence must deal. At the individual level, we may sort out a set of nominal members who are most likely to deviate from the group position under nongroup forces. They are the people who do not strongly identify with the group, who are psychologically peripheral to it.

A similar proposition can be formulated at the group level. Some groups boast memberships intensely loyal to group purposes and interests. Others have trouble maintaining member identifications. We shall call a group enjoying high member identification a *cohesive group*.[3] Group cohesiveness is one determinant of the influence which a group can wield over its membership.

If a group has generated distinctive political attitudes and behavior among its members, this distinctiveness will fade if group cohesiveness

Table 11-4. Relation of Group Cohesiveness to Group Identification, 1956

Cohesiveness	Mean Identification Score[a]	Group
High	2.5	Southern Negro
	2.2	Non-Southern Negro
	2.2	Jewish
Low	1.8	Union member
	1.6	Catholic
	1.6	Member, union household

[a] The response to the two identification questions (see p. 168) are scored such that a maximum value on the index is 3.0, when the most positive response is made to both items. The corresponding minimum value is 0.0, when the most negative response is made to both items. About 61 per cent of Southern Negroes responded positively toward the group on both items; the corresponding proportion among Catholics was 28 per cent.

is destroyed. Cohesiveness itself must depend on a number of factors according to the type of group and the setting involved. Within the

3 Dorwin P. Cartwright and Alvin Zander, *Group Dynamics: Research and Theory* (Row, Peterson and Co., Evanston, Ill., 1953), Part II, pp. 71–134.

large and far-flung social groupings under discussion in this chapter, a prime determinant may simply be the degree to which group members feel set apart from other people by virtue of social barriers. If we set up a mean identification score as a simple index of cohesiveness for each group, the resulting array (see Table 11-4) seems to support this hypothesis.

THE RELATIONSHIP OF THE GROUP TO THE WORLD OF POLITICS

If the relationship between individual and group is summarized by the concept of identification, attempts to deal with the relationship of the group to the world of politics focus upon a vaguer concept of *proximity*. All of our secondary membership groups except the political party have their basic existence outside of the political order. At this point it becomes important to specify this distance from the world of politics more precisely.

If we analyze our intuitions concerning proximity, we find that they depend upon the frequency with which we have seen the group *qua* group associated intimately with objects that are clearly political—issues, candidates, and parties. We would think, for example, of lobbying activity, political pronouncements, and candidates who publicize the fact of membership in that group. We would consider what we know of the primary goals of the group, and their apparent relevance to politics. The perceived relationship between the group and the world of politics has substantial grounding in objective events, constituted largely by the actions of group leaders. But we could not expect that all individuals, or even all group members, would perceive the relationship of the group to politics in precisely the same manner. Thus we shall think of proximity as a subjective dimension, a tendency to associate group and politics at a psychological level.

Where proximity has partisan significance we would hypothesize that: *as proximity between the group and the world of politics increases, the political distinctiveness of the group will increase.*

Or, at the individual level: *as perception of proximity between the group and the world of politics becomes clearer, the susceptibility of the individual member to group influence in political affairs increases.*

The concept of proximity will have to undergo further refinement before these hypotheses have full meaning. We must specify a good deal more precisely the dimensions that are involved in our general sense of proximity, and attempt to measure them more objectively.

We have suggested that perceptions of proximity between one's group and the world of politics rest upon associations that have been built up between the group and the political objects. How do these links become established? In some cases, the associations are directly given, as when the political candidate is a highly visible member of the group. The link is, so to speak, "built into" the object of orientation itself. We shall discuss phenomena of this sort under the general heading of *group salience* in politics. More often, however, the establishment of associations between the group and politics depends on conscious effort by elements within the group to propagate certain standards of member behavior. This *transmission of standards* is a communication process, and its effectiveness depends on the clarity with which the standard is transmitted and the insistence that accompanies it.

But the perceived proximity of the group to the world of politics depends on more than the perception of a group standard at a point in time. While the successful transmission of a group standard in a particular situation may increase the member's sense of proximity, we would propose that the effect of any particular standard, once received, will vary according to the individual's generalized, pre-existing sense of proximity between group and politics. In part, then, proximity is dependent upon reception of past standards; in part, too, it is dependent on the individual's sense of the *fitness* of group activity in politics. Underlying values that deny the group a legitimate role in the political world act as barriers to reduce the sense of proximity, however clearly standards may be received.

What we have roughly labeled proximity, then, has a number of dimensions that demand independent treatment, and we shall discuss several of these. Throughout, we encounter evidence that the perceived relationship of the group to politics, like the relationship of the individual to the group, bears directly upon the strength of group forces in the field at the time of political decision.

The Transmission of Group Political Standards. Whatever the process of communication that alerts the member to a partisan group standard, we can think of group norms as forces, having a given direction and varying degrees of strength. The standard prescribes support of one party, candidate, or issue position, and forbids support of the other. And these prescriptions are propagated with varying amounts of urgency or intensity.

There are two conditions in which group standards may lack sufficient clarity to permit influence. The end result of each is the same—a lack of distinctiveness in the aggregate group vote—but the differences are of considerable theoretical interest. In one case, the usual channel for communication of such norms is silent as to a particular standard, or emits it very weakly. For example, within international unions where standards were most clear according to the content analysis of preelection editions of official journals, the vote division among members in our sample was 67 per cent Democratic. This fell to 55 per cent, then to 51 per cent, and finally to 44 per cent where standards were least clear. These differences occurred even though the proportion of high identifiers from category to category varied over a range of only 3 per cent, so that we cannot explain the variation in vote by differences in group cohesiveness.

In the other case, conflicting standards are conveyed to the membership. When standards conflict, there are several possible outcomes. At one extreme, we might find that no single member became aware of the conflict in standards, but that various sets of members felt pressures in opposing directions. Here is the point at which analysis of influence at the individual level becomes more accurate than that at a group level. For in such a situation, even if every member responded to influence, the aggregate outcome might lead the observer to believe that no influence had occurred at all.

At the other extreme, all members may be aware of a conflict in standards. To some degree, the group force is cancelled out: even if the member is concerned with respectability in the eyes of the group, he can pick the standard that would best suit his desires independent of group considerations and act accordingly without feeling guilt. If, however, the situation is ripe for influence—if the individual is motivated to conform to the group—it is unlikely that events will work out in just this way. A conflict in group standards usually occurs as a result of decentralization of leadership. Few large and far-flung groups can long maintain a leadership with monolithic control over group standards. Among the secondary membership groups this is especially true. But if an unwieldy group tends to develop its subgroups with their conflicting standards, the general model still applies. Although awareness of different standards among other elements of the total group may relax group pressures to some degree, the individual is likely to feel most strongly the forces from the subgroup with which he is most strongly identified.

Conflicting Standards: A Case Study. We have found the Negro community to be the most cohesive of the groups we have surveyed. Furthermore, Negroes, as we shall see, are almost unanimous in their belief that the group has a right to further its ends by political activity. Several of the necessary conditions for influence are fulfilled. In 1952, there was a good deal of solidarity among Negro leaders in their endorsement of the Democratic presidential ticket. And the Negro vote itself in 1952 was very distinctively Democratic.

In 1956, however, Negro leaders were much less enthusiastic about the Democratic Party, owing in part to the role of Southern Democratic legislators in blocking civil rights legislation and in part to Republican sympathy with Negro aspirations. The National Association for Advancement of Colored People adopted a posture of watchful waiting, with occasional executive threats of a Republican endorsement. The two senior United States Congressmen from the Negro community gave clear public support to opposing candidates for the presidency: Adam Clayton Powell in New York City endorsed Eisenhower, whereas William L. Dawson of Chicago supported Stevenson.

This conflict in standards was reflected in the perceptions of Negroes in our sample. When asked how they thought Negroes around the country would vote in the 1956 election, responses had shifted sharply away from the near Democratic unanimity that the same question elicited in 1952. Furthermore, the conflict was most clearly perceived at the level of the leadership. Almost as many Negroes saw the leadership voting Republican as Democratic in 1956. The distinctiveness of the Negro vote fell off sharply.

We hypothesized that when a secondary group fragments into subgroups propagating standards that conflict, much the same influence process goes on, with identification focused on the appropriate subgroup rather than the total group. In Chicago, where Dawson had stood firm for the Democrats, there was an overall decline of 5 per cent in the Democratic presidential vote, by comparison with 1952. Within the city, three of the most clearly Negro wards declined 4 per cent, 4 per cent, and 9 per cent—close to the city average. In New York City, the picture was different. In the heavily colored New York Assembly Districts 11 and 12, which included much of Powell's constituency, the Democratic presidential vote fell about 15 per cent. And this occurred despite a fraction of a per cent increase in the Stevenson vote in New York County as a whole. The effect of conflicting standards is to reduce the distinctiveness of the total group vote; but where we can isolate subgroups, we find evidence of influence.

The Political Salience of the Group. In some situations, the need for active propagation of group standards is at a minimum, because the standard is self-evident. This is the case when important political objects of orientation embody group cues, so that the course of behavior characteristic of a "good" group member cannot be held in doubt. Fundamentally, this situation is no more than a special case of the transmission of clear and strong standards. But it deserves separate treatment because it implies a simpler and less fallible communication process and because it involves a stratagem dear to the hearts of political tacticians. This dimension is one component of the model that is especially subject to short-term variation, since salience usually depends on the most transient objects of political orientation: the candidates and the issues.

Political salience of the group is high, for example, when a candidate for the election is recognized as a member of the group. Attracting the votes of members of a particular group by nominating a candidate who is a group member is, of course, a time-worn strategy in the art of political maneuver. Frequent executive appointment of group members to high posts is of the same order, although perhaps less potent in creating salience. It is our thesis that the success of the maneuver among group members depends upon the values of other variables in the total model. High salience alone does not create a unanimous group response.

The political salience of the group can also be increased by a coincidence between group goals and current political issues. The degree of salience that accrues with regard to issues in any particular situation is some joint function of the importance of the issue in the campaign and the importance of the goal to the group. One of the central issues of the 1948 campaign was the Taft-Hartley Act, which union leadership felt threatened vital aspects of the movement. To the degree that these elements communicated to the rank and file, the labor union ought to have been particularly salient for members voting in the election. Since that time, civil rights controversies have tended to increase the political salience of Negro membership.

Salience: A Case Study. The behavior of Catholic voters toward Catholic candidates for the United States Congress allows us to examine the salience phenomenon. We recall that in Table 11-2 the presidential vote among Catholics in 1956 was barely more Democratic than that among a Catholic control group (a margin of 3 per cent). We find a much more distinctive vote if we shift the scene to those congressional races in which a Catholic candidate was pitted against a non-Catholic (Table 11-5). Furthermore, Catholic voters are quite willing to cross party lines to support a candidate of the same creed. Thus if we decompose Table 11-5 we find that where the Catholic candidate is a Democrat, Catholics vote over 10 per cent more Democratic than

Table 11-5. Political Salience: The Vote of Catholics for Catholic Congressional Candidates in Races Involving Non-Catholics, 1956[a]

| | Catholic Identification | | |
	High	Low	Total Group
Catholic voters	63%	59%	61%
	(43)	(51)	(94)
Catholic control	...	...	49%
			(76)

[a] The per cent entry refers to the proportion of the indicated group voting for the Catholic candidate in the split-religion congressional race. The figure in parentheses indicates the number of cases involved in each proportion.

their control group; but where the Catholic candidate is Republican, Catholics vote over 10 per cent more *Republican* than their controls.

By sacrificing a large proportion of our cases, we can refine the data in a manner that sharpens these relationships further. Obviously, the theory underlying the salience hypotheses demands that the voter recognize the candidate as a group member if salience effects are to emerge. If we restrict our attention to those voters (one-third of the

Table 11-6. Group Salience: The Vote of Catholics for Catholic Candidates Whose Names Can Be Recalled, in Races Involving Non-Catholics, 1956[a]

| | Catholic Identification | | |
	High	Low	Total Group
U. S. House of Representatives			
Catholic voters	85%	69%	77%
	(13)	(13)	(26)
Catholic control	...	...	51%
			(25)
U. S. Senate			
Catholic voters	86%	57%	70%
	(22)	(28)	(50)
Catholic control	...	...	49%
			(47)

[a] The per cent entry refers to the proportion of the indicated group who voted for the Catholic candidate in the split-religion congressional or senatorial race. The figure in each parenthesis indicates the number of cases involved in each proportion.

total) who can refer to their congressional choices by name after the election, we should clear away some individuals for whom we could little expect salience to be operative.

Although the cases for analysis are few, Table 11-6 shows a group vote much more distinctive yet than that in Table 11-5. And the inadequate number of cases is offset somewhat by the fact that similar results are to be found when we look for the same patterns within the 1956 U. S. senatorial races in which Catholics were involved. These similarities emerge even though the Catholic voters appearing in both segments of the table are few indeed.

There is, therefore, substantial evidence that the salience of a group membership, created by group cues in the political object, intensifies group forces in the member's psychological field at the time of the vote decision. On the other hand, we should note that the sharpening of findings from Table 11-5 to Table 11-6 indicates that lack of attention to candidates for House and Senate may make severe inroads upon the vote increment which the aspirant can reap from salience effects.

The Legitimacy of Group Political Activity. However strong the group identification, and however firm the association between group and political objects, the member may resist the intrusion of "non-political" groups upon the political scene. There are cultural values bound up with beliefs about democracy and the individual that inveigh against such activity. The sophisticated view of democracy as a competition between interest groups does not have great popular currency. Voting, whether at the mass or the legislative level, is morally a matter of individual judgment and conscience; recognition of group obligation and interests is thoroughly taboo to some Americans.

We asked members of various groups whether they felt it was "all right" for organizations representing the group to support legislative proposals and candidates for office. The responses to these questions showed a fairly strong relationship with the group identification variable. The more highly identified a group member, the more likely he was to grant the group a right to engage in political activity. Within each level of group identification, however, members of the two religious groups—Catholics and Jews—show much greater reluctance to accept the legitimacy statements than either of the two more secular groupings—Negroes and union members. Also, with identification controlled, there is somewhat less readiness to grant legitimacy among older people. This fact would conform with the impressions that popular values opposing frank interest-group politics represent an older America.

The Backgrounds of Group Identifications. We have indicated some of the sources of feelings about legitimacy. It is natural to inquire as well concerning the roots of group identification. Why do some group members identify with the group, whereas others fail to?

This is a difficult problem, and our evidence to date is fragmentary. But we can draw a few general conclusions about major determinants of identification. There are numerous groups, of course, that are created for the purpose of political and ideological persuasion, such as the National Economic Council or the American Civil Liberties Union. Members are recruited and come to identify with the group on the basis of pre-existing beliefs and sympathies. Here the case for influence is much less clear, except as group activity serves to reinforce and guide member efforts. But in most groups formed along occupational, ethnic, or religious lines membership is more likely to determine attitudes than are attitudes to determine membership.

There is little doubt of this fact in the groups we have watched most closely. Except in some semiorganized areas of the South, even membership in the labor union is effectively involuntary. If labor union members vote distinctively, we cannot say that only workers with certain attitudes join the union; rather, we must concede that influence exists. But if membership is involuntary, identification is not. How can we be sure that high union identification plays a formative role in the development of political attitudes?

There is a clear and substantial relationship between strength of union identification and length of membership in the union. The longer an individual has belonged to the union, the more likely he is to identify strongly with it, and we can find no other causative factors that begin to approach this relationship in strength. A relationship between age and union identification has been observed before, but it was never clear whether the relationship existed because of simple contact with the union over time, or because the unusual "barricades" generation of the 1930's would currently constitute the bulk of older union members. Our data show clearly that older men who have recently joined the union have weak identification with it, whereas younger men aged 25 and 30 who have belonged to the union for longer periods show stronger identifications with it. In fact, if we control length of union membership, we find that the relationship between age and union identification is somewhat negative. The later in life a person joins a union, the less completely he will be identified with it given any particular length of membership. His identification will still increase with length of membership, but the level will not be quite as strong as it would be for a person who had joined when younger.

This cluster of findings is of considerable theoretical significance. In the first place, it makes it difficult to maintain that identification with the union results as a rule from existing political attitudes similar to those represented by the union. Instead, we get a sense of an acculturation process—slow and cumulative influence over a period of time, with identification as the key intervening factor. It appears that a potent force in the growth of group identifications is simple contact and familiarity, just as an immigrant comes to identify with the new country and accept its customs as time passes. Furthermore, like the immigrant, identifications never become as strongly rooted if the initiate is no longer young.

These findings are important from another point of view as well. For the pattern of relationships between age, length of membership, and strength of identification is precisely the same as we found where the group involved is the political party. That is, party identification appears to grow stronger with age; but the critical variable, instead of being age, is length of psychological membership in the party. With length of membership controlled, age is negatively related to party identification, just as it is in the union case.

Those few persons who have been union members for long periods of time yet who have remained unidentified are less likely to vote Democratic than any of the other union subgroups isolated. Not only are they much more Republican in their vote than union members generally; they are even more Republican than the control group matched with union members on aspects of life situation (33 per cent Democratic vote among those who have been members 15 years or more, as opposed to 36 per cent for the control group). Thus lack of identification among long-standing members of the union may have actively negative implications not present among new members who are not yet strongly identified.

We find no such clear relation between age and group identification among Catholics, Negroes, or Jews. Age, in these groups, logically coincides with "length of membership." There is some faint increase in identification among older Catholics, and an equally faint decrease in identification among older Negroes. We would expect these differences to appear if Catholic cohesiveness is waning and if the current civil rights ferment is beginning to sharpen cohesiveness among Negroes. But these tendencies are very weak, and there is no trend visible at all in the Jewish situation. We must conclude that no reliable relationship is present.

The contrast in the development of identification between these groups and the union or party is sharp. We are led to consider differences in the characteristics of the several groups that might account for such variation. It is obvious that the individual takes on serious membership in a union or in the psychological group represented by a political party later in life than is the case with the other groups. The individual grows up within the atmosphere of a religious or ethnic group in a much more inclusive sense than with either the party or the union.

Thus, different patterns of identification may be traced to basic differences in types of groups. But it is possible to suggest a more general proposition to cover all cases: instead of considering age or even the absolute length of time of group membership as the proper independent variable, let us employ the *proportion of the individual's life* spent as a member. Recast in this fashion, the presence of the strong positive relationship between length of membership and identification, the negative relationship between age and identification with length of membership constant, and the fact that certain ascribed groups show no variation with age would all be predicted by a single independent variable. If there is no relationship between "length of membership" and identification among Catholics, Jews, and Negroes, it is because members of these groups have held membership for 100 per cent of their lives, and variation in their identification must be explained with other factors. We arrive at the general proposition that one fundamental determinant of group identifications is the proportion of one's life spent in close (psychological) contact with the group.

SECONDARY GROUPS, THE POLITICAL PARTY,
AND THE INFLUENCE PROCESS

If the political party, and psychological membership in it, fit a more general model for social memberships and political influence, it is equally clear that the party has a peculiar location in the space that the model encompasses. We have laid out with some care what seem to be the components of the relationship between any group and the world of politics. This effort was necessary because the secondary groups with which we dealt were not at base political, and this fact turns out to be a crucial limitation in the political influence they can wield. Now if we were to fill in the values that the scheme requires for prediction, we would find that in the case of the party, proximity is at an upper limit, for the party has a central position in the world of politics. In all major elections, its salience is absolutely high: one candidate is always a group member, the prime group goal is political victory, and all controversial issues represent subordinate goals that the group has assumed. The legitimacy of its activity in politics goes without question, for the major parties at least, and the communication of their standards is perfect. Therefore, we would expect that the political influence of psychological membership in a party would be extremely potent, relative to other secondary memberships. If we take distinctiveness of political attitudes and behavior as a criterion, this proposition cannot be questioned.

We are most directly interested, at this point, in suggesting the processes by which nonpolitical membership groups come to have a certain amount of political influence. Thus far we have paid little attention to the fact that these processes have duration over time. The political influence of secondary memberships, as witnessed in the distinctiveness of a group vote, is not necessarily a product of the immediate situation. The labor union need not indoctrinate its membership anew at each election. If the labor vote was distinctive in 1956, there is no need to presume that this distinctiveness represents only the political action of the union during the 1956 campaign. Influence, when successful, has enduring effects, and in this sense the distinctiveness of a group vote at any point in time represents cumulative influence. We hypothesize that the political party plays a crucial role in the durability of this influence.

When a political candidate is a member of one's group, or when the issues of politics bear directly upon goals important to the group, membership in that group becomes salient in the individual's orientation to politics. In these instances, the need for political translation, for communication of specific standards regarding proper group behavior, is slight. But under normal circumstances, when salience is not high, the group, if it is to have influence, must lend the observed world political meaning in terms relevant to the group.

Now issues and candidates are transient political objects; the entity that endures is the party. If group influence leads the identified member to take on identification with the party, then little renewal of influence is needed. The individual has, as it were, acceded to a self-steering mechanism, that will keep him politically "safe" from the point of view of group standards. He will respond to new stimuli as a party member and code them properly. As time passes, his identification with the party will increase of its own accord, because the individual will find that event after event demonstrates—in nongroup matters as well as group matters now—the rectitude of his own party and the obnoxiousness of its opponent.

If there were no parties, but only a flux of candidates and issues, it does not follow that there would be no political influence exerted by other membership groups. The psychological economy of the individual demands parties as an organizing principle, and if bereft of this, there might be much more straightforward dependence on other groups for guidance. In situations of this sort, secondary groups with quite apolitical origins have in fact come to function as political parties.[4] But where parties exist, influence from nonpolitical secondary groups is likely to have a good deal of continuity.

Given the flux of objects like candidates and issues, group influence is likely to be most effective when meaningful contact is established between the group and the party, for parties subsume candidates and issues and, more important, endure over time. However, this proposition is true only if we define influence in a very particular way, that is, as cumulative over time. An individual led to a Democratic orientation by a group membership in 1930 may still be registering a manifestation of that influence in 1956.

But for the practical politician who wants to know how many votes a group leader can "deliver" to one party or the other in a specific election, influence may have a rather different meaning. Here we encounter a paradox. If party identification is a trustworthy bridge from group identification to "proper" political behavior, it is also a structure which, once laid down, is not readily moved. Thus the mechanisms that are best calculated to build a reliably distinctive group vote are at the same time mechanisms that tend to undermine the maneuverability of the group in politics.

When political events cause a group leadership to switch official support to the opposing party, the strong party loyalties that it has helped to create and reinforce may be reversed only with great difficulty.[5] We can imagine that these loyalties, even when direct crea-

---

[4] As an example, see Key's treatment of factionalism in the South. Secondary groups constitute one type of nucleus for the factions that compete for political power in a one-party system. V. O. Key, *Southern Politics in State and Nation* (Alfred Knopf, New York, 1950), pp. 52–57.

[5] It is interesting to note that for large-scale, secondary groups at the national level, these switches are rare and tend to be limited to rebellious factions. Many aspects of political process seem to converge toward maintenance of these continuities. Factors such as the dependence of the party on group support and the loyalties and interpersonal commitments built up between group leaders and the party enhance the temptation to work for reform within the chosen party when

tions of group influence, gain some functional autonomy as they grow stronger. They come to have a force of their own, rather than remaining dependent on forces from the nonpolitical secondary group. And, since the political party can exert unusually intense influence on political motives, this force may turn out to be stronger than any counter-force that the nonpolitical group can bring to bear *in politics* at a later date. It would follow from the general outlines of our theory that when such reversals of group standards occur, the new influence will have most effect among the youngest group members.

The political party may be treated, then, as a special case of a more general group-influence phenomenon. The party may be located within our model, and values on appropriate dimensions may be calculated for the party member at any point in time. The nature of the group, so located, ensures the power of its influence within the world of politics. But of great significance also is the role of the party as a bridge between other social groupings and that political world. The influence of other secondary groups in politics comes to have more enduring effects as loyalties directed toward them may be transferred to abiding political loyalties.

---

things go awry. These facts make treatment of influence in its cumulative sense the more meaningful.

★ *chapter 12*

The Role of Social Class

Of all the social groupings into which electorates may be divided, it is likely that the *social class* has drawn the most consistent attention from students of mass political behavior. In the first place, the notion of social class provides an inclusive analytic concept. A "lower" class comes to have meaning because there is an "upper" class that serves as its foil; hence, analyses of social class come to deal with the total social structure at once.

Likewise, the concept of class is sufficiently general to permit wide application. Every nation has its minorities, but it is not always clear how specific subgroups, differing in composition and goals, may be compared from nation to nation. As for the social class, however, current evidence in sociology indicates that all societies are stratified into "upper" and "lower" layers as a result of unequal distribution of values and honors. In various times and places the characteristics of these layers have varied superficially, but the concept of class reduces such historical diversity to a set of minimum common elements, a reduction that is indispensable if we aspire to more powerful theory.

Class phenomena attract broad interest, too, because they represent a junction between the social, the economic, and the political order. The class, a social phenomenon, is yet defined in economic terms; and if class membership is conceived to have motivational significance, then the motives engaged are presumed to be economic. It is because of this economic aspect, furthermore, that the social class becomes linked with political strife. Political power signifies some potential for control of the economic system. If stratification arises from unequal distribution of rewards, there is likely to be competition between the classes for control of the allocation process.

Competition between upper- and lower-status groups appears to have been an element of some importance in political matters since the birth of the American republic. The precise nature of this role,

184

however, is subject to scholarly debate, and our resources of data, particularly for the currents of mass behavior in the earlier elections, are meager or nonexistent. But we know that at the time our political system was designed, influential minds found in the "different sentiments and views" of the various classes "the most common and durable source of faction."[1] We know furthermore that the emergence of Jacksonian democracy—whatever its popular base—frightened gentlemen of the upper strata as a triumph of "mobocracy." And more recently, in the rise of trade unions and in the class-saturated political alignments formed in the wake of the Great Depression of the 1930's, the recurrent importance of social class in American politics is well documented.

We treat the social class apart from other social phenomena to some degree because of its popularity and its transitional position between the purely social and the purely economic. The most important consideration dictating separate treatment, however, lies in the nature of the social class itself. For whatever popularity the concept enjoys, its intellectual status has remained controversial, even among sociologists. Nobody wishes to deny the reality of differences in status and privilege within the large social unit; yet the meaning that can be attributed these distinctions by the investigator is constantly subject to dispute. A large portion of social theory seems to presume that the social class is a self-conscious group striving toward recognized goals. This assumption is challenged by theorists who feel it tends to reify what is usually no more than an analytic construct imposed on the situation by the investigator. Status differences exist, and these differences are related to differences in attitudes and behavior. They do not, however, assure us that the social class has reality as a group, or that class "members" come to behave distinctively because they take the class as a reference point in decisions about behavior.

Thus the argument comes to rest on the nature of the class as a group. It is our thesis that the "group" reality of the social class is variable. Under certain circumstances, it is not difficult to conceptualize the social class as a "group." Under other circumstances, it is hard to see it as more than a vague demographic aggregate, arbitrarily marked off for purposes of analysis. When and to the degree that the social class is a group, we shall find our theory of the preceding chapter quite applicable to it. But as the variable nature of the social class is one of its most intriguing characteristics, it requires separate discussion as a special and marginal case of the group phenomenon.

[1] *The Federalist, No. X.*

THE SOCIAL CLASS AS POLITICAL GROUP

The social class *per se* rarely becomes formalized as an organization. There is no official class leadership and no official class policy. Despite an absence of formal organization, leadership, or even informally accredited spokesmen, however, the social class may have reality as a group in the minds of many people. When the citizen being interviewed tells the investigator that he favors the Democratic Party "because it is the party of the common man, not the party of the big shots," it seems clear that he sees the society as divided into at least two camps representing conflicting interests, and that he feels he shares the interests of one of these camps. It is in this sense that the social class may have psychological reality as a group.

Identification: A "Subjective Reality" of Groups. The social class transcends the simple "demographic aggregate" to the degree that individuals in the population identify with a social class. When there is a *"we* feeling" directed toward other members of the class grouping as a whole, rather than purely toward other union members or other businessmen, then the class may influence behavior in the sense of our previous discussion of group influence.

Stratification refers to the differentiation of the population as a result of the unequal distribution of social values and honors. The product of stratification is a set of *social strata.* The social class, on the other hand, refers to a grouping of people who feel a sense of identification and shared interest as a result of membership in a common stratum of the society. The psychological unity tokens a degree of functional cohesiveness that the term *stratum* does not connote. Thus at base the psychological circumstances of identification determine whether a class exists. Social strata, the molds in which social classes may form, seem present in all societies. But the class itself emerges and disappears over a period of time. An adequate approach to the problem of social class in politics involves consideration of the conditions under which a sense of class identification develops in the social stratum.

STATUS POLARIZATION

However helpful the distinction between "stratum" and "class," it should not mislead us into thinking that a society may properly be described in such "either-or" terms. It is desirable to think of different states of a society as differences in degree, rather than in kind, between such "ideal types" or qualitative stages. We shall attempt to approach the problem quantitatively rather than qualitatively. We shall refer to the condition of active discord between social strata as *status polarization*. We shall think of this polarization entirely as a matter of degree; a society may be more or less polarized, at any point in time. We cannot specify a degree of polarization beyond which a stratum becomes a class; the simple dichotomy is inadequate to express differences along the underlying continuum of polarization which we posit. But when the status groups of a society are sharply polarized, we shall assume that the entities that past theorists have labeled "classes" are present; and when a society is "depolarized," we shall presume that the concept of social strata is more appropriate.

Status polarization, then, refers to the degree to which upper and lower status groups in a society have taken up mutually antagonistic value positions. Polarization is by definition a group-level concept. A single element cannot polarize; the term has meaning only as a description of concurrent motion of two or more elements—in our case, status groups. We can say in a general way that *variation in the status polarization of a society reflects variation in the intensity and extent of class identification among its members.* When polarization is high, most of the citizenry must have perceived a conflict of interests between strata and have taken on class identifications with fair intensity. When polarization is low, either few people are identifying, or extant identifications are weak, or both.

Since polarization is bound up with divergences in values and interests, the concept is linked not only with status groups but with specific areas of conflict as well. We will find it useful to think of the degree of polarization as varying, not only over time, but from sphere to sphere within a social system as well. Under certain conditions, for example, there may be more status polarization visible in the economic sphere than in the political sphere. Generally speaking, we may hypothesize that polarization emerges first in connection with economic values, and that beyond a certain degree of intensity it will spread to other areas. As it becomes manifest in values less immediately bound up with economic interest, a more salient and generalized antagonism exists between class groups.

Finally, it is important to consider that the course of events depends not simply upon the intensity that polarization attains in sensitive spheres of the social system; it is also important to ascertain how constituent class identifications are distributed in the population. Polarization may become so intense within subgroups of a society that violence occurs, even when the vast bulk of the society is indifferent to the interests at stake. For the purposes of understanding the broad flow of events, then, we shall consider first the degree of polarization within the bounds of the larger society. A theory of the social context of political behavior must undertake to specify (1) the conditions in the total society that serve to thrust status polarization into the political order; and (2) the conditions that act to increase or limit polarization within that order.

DETERMINING SOCIAL CLASS

The ambiguous nature of the class as a group poses important problems. Who "really" belongs to which class? In the groups discussed in the preceding chapter we had little difficulty separating nominal members of the group from nonmembers. Similarly, in a caste society the location of an individual in the hierarchy of strata is quite clear. But in the United States and other modern democracies, the persistent or extreme formalization of social differences is absent. The distance that once separated serf from master has been filled in with a variety of roles and occupations that defy simple class assignment. Furthermore, there are strong American cultural values that inveigh against recognition of class differences. No other group that we have considered is begrudged the very reality of its existence in this manner.

These ambiguities have implications in two directions. First, if numerous individuals in the society are located in positions that are relatively indeterminate with respect to class lines, must we not expect a considerable attenuation of the role that class can play in political behavior? Secondly, if status is frequently ambiguous, how do we assign individuals to a social class for purposes of analysis? The first problem is an empirical matter; the second is methodological.

The two common solutions to the problem of assigning individuals to status groupings reflect some of the controversies over class phenomena that we have discussed. On the one hand, there are those whom Richard Centers[2] has called the "objectivists," who define class operationally according to some objective criterion like income, occupation, or education. This practice distinguishes what we have called social strata.

The opposing "subjectivists" look for evidence of psychological iden-

[2] Richard Centers, *The Psychology of Social Classes* (Princeton University Press, Princeton, N. J., 1949).

tification with a particular class as a criterion of membership. Centers, as an exponent of the subjectivist view, devised a relatively satisfactory method of getting individuals to locate their own position in class terms.[3] He asked a national sample in 1945: "If you were asked to use one of these four names for your social class, which would you say you belonged in: the middle class, lower class, working class, or upper class?" Analysis revealed that the responses gave meaningful insights into patterns of behavior. With regard to political variables, for example, people who chose to designate themselves as working class were more frequently Democratic in their voting and party affiliation and chose more "radical" alternatives on a number of issue questions dealing with the role of government in the economy. Middleclass identifiers were more likely to be Republican and "conservative" in their politico-economic attitudes.

The study also showed that although occupation appeared to be the primary determinant of subjective class, identification of this sort was not always congruent with objective role in the social structure. For example, about one quarter of the people interviewed were either blue-collar workers who identified with the middle class, or white-collar people identifying with the working class. Nor was there any tendency for people who "misidentified" in this way to claim a higher status; in fact, members of the white-collar stratum designated themselves as "working class" more frequently than manual laborers chose the "middle class."

But the simple fact of choice between alternative class names posed by an interviewer may be only a pale shadow of the concept of "identification" that we have linked with status polarization and the development of a class group from a stratum. Only 2 per cent of Centers' sample responded that they did not know what class they were in or said that they did not believe in social classes. It does not necessarily follow that 98 per cent of Americans are "class conscious," except in a restricted sense of the term.

Class Consciousness, Class Identification and Self-Assignment. One demonstration of the weakness of the Centers question as a means of assessing class consciousness comes from our own data. In asking the Centers question in 1956 we preceded it with this query.

There's quite a bit of talk these days about different social classes. Most people say they belong either to the middle class or to the working class. Do you ever think of yourself as being in one of these classes?

---

[3] See the account of early studies in *ibid.*, Chapter IV.

Respondents who replied affirmatively were then asked "Which one?," whereas those who responded negatively were asked which class they would choose if they had to make a choice. About 4 per cent of the sample indicated that they usually thought of themselves as belonging in some other class, like an upper or lower class, or that they did not know to which class they belonged. But one out of every three respondents indicated that he never thought of himself as being in one of the classes mentioned, yet was subsequently willing to choose one of the class names.

This in itself is no conclusive finding; we might simply be encountering evasiveness. But we find further that people confessing awareness of their social class actually think and behave differently on political matters than do those individuals who say initially that they are unaware. For example, within the aware group in 1956, working-class identifiers tended to divide their presidential vote 14 per cent more Democratic than did middle-class identifiers. Among the "unaware" group, however, this class-related difference nearly fades from sight: the unaware working class are only 2 per cent more Democratic than the unaware middle class. It is hard to consider that these unaware individuals participate in any "consciousness of class." Yet they comprise one-third of the national population.

The distinction in voting behavior between the aware and the unaware gives results conceptually parallel to those in Chapter 11, where a full identification variable was present. That is, where we feel there can be no identification—among the unaware—there is no significant tendency to behave in group-relevant ways. Among the aware, such a tendency is present. Thus the class is another case of a social grouping that may be fitted to the model for group influence proposed in the preceding chapter.

Our Operational Treatment of Class. As tools for the ensuing discussion, we shall determine the class membership of the individual in part by his subjective location in the status hierarchy, as modified with the "awareness" distinction. We also have at our disposal a full battery of objective indicators of class, such as occupation, education, and income. Of the objective criteria, occupation tends to predict political attitudes and voting most efficiently, and we shall generally turn to it when we wish a measure of this type. Subjective class by itself shows relationships with political attitudes and behavior that are of about the same magnitude as those that emerge when occupation alone is used. The addition of the "awareness" variant to the subjective measure, as shown previously, makes the predictive value of the subjective measure stronger than that of occupation.

We shall also need a set of operations to measure the political manifestations of status polarization. For this purpose we shall employ coefficients of correlation that represent the *strength* of relationship between class indicators and political attitudes or behavior. The size of such coefficients will increase as lines of class cleavage swing more and more closely into alignment with broad divisions of political opinion. In a state of complete political depolarization, knowledge of a person's social status tells us nothing about his political attitudes or behavior. In other words, there is no relationship (i.e., zero correlation coefficient) between status and the political variables. Whatever compound of past experience and current attitudes is leading to aggregate differences in political partisanship, it is likely to be independent of the concurrent fact of social stratification. The role of social class is at its lowest ebb. In the state of perfect polarization, to know a person's class is to know his political ideals and allegiances, automatically and without margin for error (1.00 correlation coefficient). The social classes have become solidary and mutually antagonistic. The correlation coefficient, reflecting such differences in the state of the group, provides us with a convenient metric for graphing trends.

SHORT-TERM FLUCTUATION IN STATUS POLARIZATION

The extensive modern literature on social class and political behavior has shown persistently that individuals of higher status (subjectively or objectively) tend to give "conservative" responses on questions of economic policy and tend as well to vote Republican; individuals of lower status tend to respond more "radically" and vote Democratic. This simple finding has assured us that social class has some bearing on the way in which the individual behaves politically. It has also served theorists as evidence of the importance of the economic motive in political behavior. But there is much that it does not tell us. In the first place, it is a static generalization. It does not allow us to anticipate variation in class voting from election to election. It casts no light upon the waxing and waning of class-based political discord. Secondly, the relationships on which the generalization is based are quite modest ones. If it is evidence of an economic motive in political behavior, we might wonder why it is so weak, rather than marvel that it appears at all.

We find marked short-term variation in the clarity of status voting in this country over the past score of years. If we take some measure of status—any of the common indicators will do—and examine the strength of relationship between this measure and the vote for President, using national survey data collected over the four past presidential elections, we find that the relationship has been positive over this time. That is, lower-status groups have continually favored the Democratic Party, and higher-status the Republican Party; but at some times this fact is quite prominent and at other times the association is almost trivial. Instead of a static disposition toward leftist or rightist voting according to one's class, the role of social class in political behavior is a dynamic one. It is this phenomenon we have chosen to conceptualize as status polarization; and our aim is to specify conditions under which it fluctuates.

The fact that status polarization of the vote has varied so widely in only a dozen years might suggest that it is unduly influenced by superficial aspects of the immediate political situation, such as the pairing of two competing personalities in a given presidential race or the campaign themes chosen for emphasis in a certain year by the parties. A variety of supporting data lend assurance that this is not the case. While the trend line of coefficients for the presidential vote from 1944 through 1956 covers a considerable range, it does not oscillate wildly. Instead, it declines from 1948 in an orderly and almost linear fashion. The 1952 observation (0.25) falls very close to the midpoint of the range defined by the 1948 (0.44) and 1956 (0.12) observations.

Moreover, comparable coefficients for the congressional vote in 1952 (0.26), 1954 (0.20), and 1956 (0.10) show precisely the same orderly downward trend. The 1954 observation is of particular interest here, in addition to the fact that it represents an independent sampling of the adult population. It might be argued that the 1952 or 1956 points fall as they do because of the candidacy of Eisenhower or Stevenson. Yet in 1954 neither name was on the ballot, and the observation for that election takes its proper place in the declining polarization trend. Furthermore, since congressional races involve a plethora of candidate pairings, it is hard to attribute this variation in polarization to peculiar candidate pairings.

Finally, we encounter evidence of precisely the same trend in status polarization over this period when we depart from matters of parties and elections entirely. For example, we may relate status not simply to one or another partisan choice, but to economic issue responses of the kind that contributed to the "social welfare" attitude scale in Chapter 8. Typically, lower-status persons tend to select "liberal" alternatives, whereas those of higher status give "conservative" responses. But the clarity of such class differences varies over time also. Unfortunately, we do not have a standard battery of issue items applied to the population periodically since 1944. Nevertheless, highly comparable questions posed in 1945 and 1956 show a depolarization quite like that of the vote over the same period.[4]

Evidence of this order leads to the conclusion that the broad lines of change in vote polarization are rooted in events that transcend the immediate circumstances of any particular election. Even if such fluctuations depended entirely on events within the political order, they would be of interest. But the fact that they seem to reflect broader conditions in the society adds greatly to their fascination. At a minimum, we would suppose that change of this scope must depend on a configuration of social and economic events, with their psychological derivatives; and, where we observe signs of polarization in the electoral process, additional factors arising from the political system must condition the phenomenon as well.

THE CONDITIONS OF STATUS POLARIZATION: KEY PSYCHOLOGICAL TERMS

We may distinguish two major dimensions of variability at a psychological level that provide crucial insight into the polarization phenomenon. Ultimately, we may trace these differences to broader social, economic, and political conditions; at the outset, however, they have interest as more than "intervening states."

Class Awareness and Identification. In our theoretical discussion we have suggested the importance of clear class identifications in the development of status polarization. We have also shown that the third of the population unaware of its class makes no contribution to the status polarization of the vote and hence, by default, serves to depress it. The same contrasts between the aware and the unaware seem to emerge wherever class differences are visible in partisanship or economic attitudes. Thus, for example, people who associate them-

---

[4] The polarization coefficient (calculated in both cases for White males, using occupation status) was 0.37 in 1945; in 1956 it was 0.17. Downward trends of very similar slope were found for three other questions having to do with government welfare activity and the role of government in areas traditionally restricted to private enterprise. See Philip E. Converse, "The Shifting Role of Class in Political Attitudes and Behavior," *Readings in Social Psychology,* Eleanor Maccoby, Theodore Newcomb, and Eugene Hartley, ed., 3rd edition (Henry Holt and Co., New York, 1958), pp. 388–399.

selves with the "working class" and are aware of this location are 19 per cent more Democratic in their party identification than the aware "middle class"; the comparable difference among unaware people is 10 per cent. Similarly, on an issue attitude like the question of government guarantees of full employment, the aware working-class people give 22 per cent more frequent "liberal" responses than the middle-class aware; among the unaware this class difference fades to 14 per cent. The fact that there is some residual class differentiation of attitudes and behavior among the unaware may be readily traced to social influence in primary groups, where attitudes "appropriate" to the individual's class may be taken on without recognition of their class relevance.

It follows that signs of status polarization in a society are limited by the proportion of the population unaware of their social class. If we can determine the conditions under which persons come to think of themselves as class members, we should arrive at clues that will help us reconstruct some of the sources of variation in polarization over time. It is harder to specify these conditions than might be imagined. Awareness of class, like the various group identifications of Chapter 11, shows little tendency to vary systematically with common sociological divisions of the population. Men and women, the educated and the uneducated, the various occupational strata, and the major ethnic and racial subdivisions of the population all show about the same two thirds rate of "awareness" that characterizes the nation as a whole.

Nevertheless, there are two points at which class awareness does show revealing variation. One involves differences in awareness across age grades in the population, and the other involves the rural-urban continuum. The first leads to consideration of past economic history, whereas the second sheds light upon the role of broader social patterns in the polarization phenomenon. We shall consider the evidence for each later in the chapter.

Levels of Conceptualization. We have observed that correlations between status and political behavior are normally rather low. Discussions in earlier chapters create the suspicion that this is not primarily because people are disinterested in their social class location but because they fail to translate class interest into political terms. In some cases this may spring from confusion over relevant alternatives; more often it probably reflects ignorance of the fact that political alternatives are relevant at all, even among those "aware" of their social class.

If these surmises are correct we would expect that signs of class voting would be clearest among the most sophisticated and would tend to diminish as we proceed to those whose view of politics is simpler or more fragmentary. Indeed, persons whom we classified as ideologues or near-ideologues who were at the same time aware of their social class contributed very disproportionately to the slight degree of status polarization that characterized the 1956 election. At other levels class voting is barely visible save as we "purify" our groups by removing those persons unaware of their social class. Once again we see that the people who organize their political behavior in the manner often assumed by sophisticated investigators are those who are most similar to such analysts in political concept formation. The familiar picture of the democratic process as a clearing house for conflict of class interest becomes increasingly inappropriate as we move to layers of the electorate more remote from the informed observer. If the role of social class in mass political behavior is less potent than we are frequently led to believe, these discrepancies in sophistication appear to be largely responsible. If we wish to deal with social class in its traditional garb in politics, we are dealing with a fairly restricted and sophisticated portion of the population.

Earlier we showed that this kind of sophistication was strongly dependent upon education and political involvement. The education component is fixed early in life and remains constant. Hence it does not seem helpful in accounting for fluctuations in polarization. Rather, the fact that there are poorly educated persons in all societies poses a fundamental limiting condition on status polarization in politics. But political involvement is more responsive to external conditions. Of course it can be doubted that isolated bursts of political enthusiasm on the part of the individual provide much real sophistication. Yet, we may imagine that some events external to the political order can drive persons to an enduring interest in politics.

It is feasible to examine differences in class voting within degrees of political involvement. The more involved the individual is in politics, the more likely he is to cast his vote according to class lines. In this case we have the benefit of comparable data for the 1952 election, which provide some insight as to what goes on when polarization varies over time. Differences in the class behavior of the involved were much sharper relative to the uninvolved at the high levels of polarization in 1952 than we find them to be in 1956. The suggestion is that the decline in polarization between 1952 and 1956 sprang from changes in behavior among the more sophisticated. In a time of depolarization, the behavior of the involved voter becomes less and less distinct from that of the apathetic, *with respect to the class axis.* This statement does not mean that the sophisticated lose interest in politics when class interests are not clearly perceived. Other axes of political dispute may engage the attention of the politically alert. The relationship between involvement and class voting may simply be a special case of a more general phenomenon: whatever the current major dimensions of political conflict, they are reflected less clearly where involvement is lower.

We have seen that individuals highly involved in 1956 had shifted their attention from the class dimension in some degree since 1952. We can imagine that elections may be sharply contested when status polarization is absent. Conversely, and for much the same reasons, elections may show high levels of status polarization in conjunction with low overall levels of voter interest. The 1948 election, marking a low point in vote turnout for its era, is a case in point. An examination of aggregate statistics suggests that turnout dropped off most radically in those areas where we typically observe little or no status polarization: in the South the decrement in the vote was very marked, and it was disproportionate in rural areas of the North as well. Not all of the decline, however, can be accounted for in this manner; it remains visible even in the large Northern industrial states where polarization tends to focus. It is as though most of the forces that propelled citizens to the polls in 1944 and 1952—including dramatic personalities and the whole quadrant of foreign issues—had dropped from sight, leaving only one force, the increasing polarization of socioeconomic attitudes, active in an opposing direction. Where these attitudes had some significance, the decline in turnout was not large; but where they enjoyed little leverage, the failure of the citizenry to participate became striking. If we were to ignore the dependence of involvement on other sources as well as socio-economic concern, these aspects of the 1948 election would remain incomprehensible.

In short, when external conditions warrant, status polarization occurs in politics primarily among those who are sophisticated and for whom class position is salient. We have introduced these two intervening psychological dimensions separately because as an empirical matter they are independent of one another. That is, knowledge of a respondent's level of conceptualization of politics does not help us predict whether he will report awareness of his class location. At all levels of conceptualization the probability of class voting increases if there is some sensitivity to social class location, although these differences are not large save among the sophisticated. But political sophistication and class awareness vary independently.

With these facts in mind, we may turn to some of the broader external conditions that enhance and inhibit the development of status polarization in the political system. Both class awareness and the involvement component of sophistication will provide useful clues to the impact of these conditions as we proceed.

THE ECONOMIC BACKGROUND OF STATUS POLARIZATION

In view of the economic axis of class feeling we would readily assume that status polarization should increase in time of depression and decrease in periods of prosperity. The most striking feature of the polarization trend in the recent past has been the steady and rapid depolarization between 1948 and 1956. This decline occurred in a postwar period when the nation was enjoying a striking ascent to prosperity and a consequent release from the pressing economic concerns that had characterized the Depression. Therefore, the basic outlines of variation in polarization fit our preconceptions of changes in the economic state of the union.

Although class awareness shows little variation across most sociological divisions of the electorate, there are differences in the proportion who express awareness as a function of age. These differences are far from striking in their magnitude but are nonetheless intriguing. When we deal with age we cannot be sure that patterns that make historical sense are not due instead to the phenomena of the life cycle. Across a fair portion of the age continuum we find rising awareness with increasing years, but there is a large drop after 60. Perhaps awareness builds up through the active working lives of people in a particular age grade, to fade out rapidly after retirement. But there are significant irregularities here that seem to betray the overlay of historical events. The age group in which awareness is most prevalent includes those individuals who were in their twenties and thirties during the depths of the Great Depression, a generation long assumed to have been strongly affected by economic events. Although people who were over 60 in 1956 also experienced the Depression, they tended more often to be vocationally established, and may have resisted some of the new definitions of social reality in class terms that appealed to a younger age cohort.

This interpretation is bolstered by the fact that this "Depression generation" is also prominent in its status voting. People falling in this cohort contributed disproportionately to the high levels of vote polarization recorded in the 1948 and 1952 elections. But by 1956, these orientations had become scarcely visible. We cannot say that the decline in polarization between 1948 and 1956 depended entirely on changing patterns of behavior within this group. Status voting falls away within other age strata as well. But it is this portion of the electorate that showed the greatest relative depolarization and that best illustrates the fading of the effects of the Depression.

We may also trace out the progressive obliteration of past disaster by surveying changes in the proximal attitudes of this "Depression generation" from election to election. We have pointed out elsewhere that a concern over issues of domestic policy is a striking accompaniment of status voting.[5] In 1952, respondents of the critical age category reacted to the election in terms of domestic issues with a frequency significantly greater than that of any other age cohort. By 1956, however, these persons were no more likely to bring up domestic issues in their spontaneous evaluations of the political scene than were people of other ages. There was a major decline in references to prosperity and depression between 1952 and 1956; it appears the rate of decline was highest within this critical group. It is in this sense that involved people who had contributed to high levels of polarization in 1948 and 1952 increasingly turned their attention to other axes of political dispute by 1956. What we may be observing are the declining effects of the Great Depression of the 1930's rather than other economic perturbations that have occurred in the interim.

The postwar period surveyed here had its high prosperity marred by two economic troughs, in 1949 and 1953–1954. The second of these two disturbances is more interesting from the point of view of our data, as it very nearly coincided with the 1954 congressional election. Although recovery was apparent by the time voters went to the polls in November of that year, much of the campaign had been conducted under the threat of serious collapse, a situation exploited by Democrats attempting to regain control of Congress. Yet the polarization coefficient referring to the congressional vote in this election seems to suggest that polarization was declining steadily throughout this period. Pending the slow accumulation of further data, then, we conclude that although economic distress is a prime mover in enhancing the role of social class in politics, it must constitute a severe and prolonged trauma before its effects are felt.

The Role of War in Status Polarization. We have linked the decline of status polarization in politics between 1948 and 1956 to increasing prosperity and fading memories of the Great Depression of the 1930's.

[5] Converse, *Ibid.*

But the economic state of the nation cannot be seen to determine the level of polarization completely. If the progress of polarization after 1936 involved only the receding spectre of depression, we should expect it to show a constant decline within our recorded history. Between 1944 and 1948 the general trend of the economy was upward, and the Depression was more remote by four years. Yet the polarization of the presidential vote shows an increase between these elections. How may we account for this discrepancy?

If we compare the behavior of voters whose concern over domestic issues outweighs their interest in foreign policy with those for whom the reverse is true, it is clear that higher rates of status voting attach to the domestic issue group. Among voters concerned primarily with foreign issues, such tendencies are almost invisible.[6]

It appears plausible therefore that much of the discrepancy could be understood in terms of an interplay between war and depression. Polarization tendencies carrying over from the Great Depression may have been dampened as a result of the national crisis posed by the Second World War, rebounding upward after that conflict was concluded. The temporary lull in foreign threat from 1945 to 1950, along with the outbreak of "postponed" strikes in major industries, the struggle in Congress to place legislative controls on the activities of labor unions, and the development of first anxieties over an "inevitable" postwar depression, all must have contributed to a rise in the relative salience of domestic issues that had lain dormant during the war. After the 1948 peak of polarization, however, the renewal of the threat of global war and the outbreak of hostilities in Korea may have acted, in concert with increasing prosperity, to depress the level of status polarization once again.

POLITICAL MANIFESTATIONS OF STATUS POLARIZATION

Economic attitudes of class relevance were showing much the same increase and decline of polarization in the period from 1944 to 1956 that were registered in partisan choice at the presidential and congressional level in this period. Hence we contend that the primary lines of fluctuation in polarization in this era had to do with events in the economic rather than the political order. Nonetheless, it would be unwise to assume that the trend of status polarization in politics has remained unmodified by the context of parties and candidates within which voters have arrived at political decision. In fact, we

[6] *Ibid.*

can isolate a number of circumstances of these years that would appear, on theoretical grounds, to have facilitated the prevailing direction of polarization change.

The Role of the Candidates. We have presented data that suggest that the major lines of change in vote polarization from 1944 to 1956 were not dependent upon the personalities of the five presidential candidates in this era. Nonetheless, two observations may be made concerning the role of candidates in the political polarization phenomenon. First, since the personalities associated with these four elections have been types that, in a *post hoc* vein, lead us to expect in each instance the specific change in polarization that has actually been observed, we cannot disengage the candidates from the polarization phenomenon. It may be that each pairing of candidates during this period has facilitated the existing motion of polarization, so that the magnitude of variation was larger than otherwise might have occurred. That is, had Eisenhower run for the presidency in 1948, there might have been a crest of polarization, but one somewhat less marked than that which the Dewey-Truman contest evoked. Conversely, had Truman run in 1952, the decline in polarization of the presidential vote might have been less sharp.

Secondly, it is hard even conceptually to disassociate the man from the times. Each pairing of presidential candidates seemed to fit the tenor of its times. Yet to what degree are the salient features of these personalities a direct product of the times in which they operated? Roosevelt the wartime leader presented a different image from the Roosevelt who lashed out at "economic royalists." Clearly these changes depended less on the man than upon external events well beyond his control. Harry Truman was not responsible for the timing of the Taft-Hartley Act; if Eisenhower had run in 1948 could he have maintained the same class neutrality with this issue prominent? On the other hand, Truman was delighted to make the most of the Taft-Hartley furor, and another man might have kept it from becoming such a focal point for the campaign. In short, we cannot hope to determine here whether the times make the man, or the man the times. We suspect that a good deal of the aura of each election, and the connotations that have come to surround the protagonists of each race, have been determined by the context in which they were destined to operate. But we would not gainsay the capacity of these personalities to muffle or amplify the class divisions of the moment.

The Role of the Political Parties. The role of the parties in modifying the level of status polarization in politics may be analyzed from a number of vantage points. But we may immediately propose that unless the parties differentiate themselves in matters of policy relevant to class interest, we have little reason to expect partisan preference to reflect whatever polarization exists in other spheres of the social system.

In reality, both a perceptual and an institutional condition must be fulfilled for partisan behavior to manifest status polarization. The class-oriented voter, to act in accord with his class position, must perceive that differences exist between the parties that are relevant to class interests. Individuals who fail to arrive at such perceptions are much less likely to engage in class voting. However attentive the class-oriented voter may be, the differences that he *can* perceive are limited by the divergence that actually exists between the positions of competing parties.

There are some important circumstances in which party differentiation on class matters is not likely to be clear. Circumstances may arise in which status polarization outside the political order is inadequately reflected in matters of political partisanship. This pattern of events is most likely to characterize a period of rising polarization in a political system bound to traditional parties. If status polarization continues to mount, we would expect either that (1) new parties will break through institutional barriers, or that (2) events will force the existing parties to a clearer class alignment.

It would be ill-advised, however, to dwell upon the lag in party policies without noting as well the lag that is evident in the public response to the parties. There is reason to believe that in a system of long-standing parties it is the rare exception that any large proportion of the public departs from the existing parties in search of new policy positions. Usually calamity that is sufficient to make any broad segment of the public demand new answers is at the same time sufficient to stimulate change in the policies of even traditional "patronage" parties. And under such circumstances, enduring loyalties to the existing parties tend to maintain the traditional system.

The Role of Party Identification. For the period of declining polarization that we have observed we can trace out the conserving influence of party identification. The individual's identification with his party comes to have a force autonomous of the events which established the initial loyalty. Thus a person drawn to the Democratic Party on economic grounds during the 1930's is likely to retain this allegiance after economic problems have become less salient. When status polarization is declining, its manifestation in current voting behavior should be less marked than that witnessed by distributions of party identification between classes.

We have been measuring party identification only since 1952, a fact that leaves a limited time series for comparison. But numerous pieces of evidence support our deductions. For example, among non-Southern voters, polarization of the vote fell from 0.29 to 0.13 between 1952 and 1956; the polarization of party identification over the same period declined from 0.28 to 0.21.[7] Thus the relationship between status and party identification varied in the same direction as that between status and vote, but less sharply, supporting the hypothesis.

When forces act to change partisan alignments in the electorate the bonds of party allegiance constitute an inertia that is only slowly overcome. If this statement is true, then we would expect inertia to be marked among those who identify most strongly. In the face of pressure toward political change, Independents and weak identifiers will succumb most readily. Therefore, the marks of the past should be most visible among strong party identifiers. With regard to class, we have developed the thesis that status voting patterns established in the 1930's have been eroding since that time. Status voting should then be most prevalent among the strongly identified and least clear for people toward the "independent" end of the identification continuum. This configuration of relationships emerges handsomely from our 1952 materials and appears substantially intact in 1956 as well. In this era, the probability of status voting was much higher among strong partisans than among weak or independent people.

One further datum is relevant at this point. The South, as so frequently happens in political analysis, presents class patterns that are often anomalies. Generally speaking, polarization is lower in the South than in other regions of the nation; many of the materials presented in this chapter for the entire nation show sharper patterns when the South is excluded from consideration. Between 1952 and 1956, however, when levels were declining elsewhere, there was an actual increase in polarization in the South, from a coefficient not much above zero to a point of clear significance in 1956.[8] Coupled with this rise, we find status voting more prevalent among *weak* party

---

[7] It should be pointed out that some portion of this change is accounted for not by individuals shifting their party allegiance but by normal turnover of personnel in the electorate due to mortality in the older cohorts and new voters of the younger generation.

[8] This trend may reflect growing industrialization and urbanization in the South, processes that are likely in the long run to blur traditional differences in political behavior generally.

identifiers than among strong in the South in 1952, and a residual difference, no longer strong enough for statistical significance, in the same direction in 1956. In other words, patterns characterizing the regions outside the South in a period of rapid depolarization are reversed in the South, where there seems instead to be a mild increase in polarization.

This pattern of findings in the South is of particular interest as it lends weight to our interpretation of the association between status voting and strength of party identification. With polarization rising in the South, status voting within identification categories shows a gradient the reverse of that which we find where polarization is declining. This fact supports the "lag" interpretation. At the same time in the South there is no reversal of the relationship between involvement and status voting: in both 1952 and 1956 Southerners who voted most according to class lines were the most involved. Hence different interpretations of the type given for the two patterns seem warranted.

We feel confident, then, in viewing party identification as a conserving influence in mass political behavior. This influence is particularly clear when changes in polarization outside the political order create forces toward change within that order. When polarization is receding and no major conflicts of another nature arise to realign the parties on a different axis, the strength of party allegiances may maintain polarization in political partisanship above that which we would otherwise predict.

STATUS POLARIZATION AND SOCIAL STRUCTURE

Broad features of social structure have a bearing on the *potential* for status polarization. We can locate several properties of the American social system that appear to condition the polarization potential of the nation in this way.

Urbanization. Although class awareness shows little tendency to follow common sociological divisions of the population, one such correlate emerges with some clarity. Contact with modern urban life increases the likelihood of class awareness. The level of awareness is highest in the central cities of large metropolitan areas and declines steadily through smaller cities to a low among people living in sparsely settled areas. It is particularly low among people in farm occupations. Furthermore, the probability that an individual thinks of himself as a class member shows some variation according to the amount of his life that he has spent in urban areas where ideas of social class are abroad.

Among people who reside in large metropolises, those who have lived in such urban concentrations all of their lives are more likely to be aware of class than metropolitan people who grew up on farms.

Hence class awareness may well be determined in part by some "proportion of life in contact" formula of the type suggested for group identification in Chapter 11. These findings fit common assumptions that the migration of populations to urban areas tends to stimulate perceptions of social class, and it follows that urbanization is likely to increase the potential for status polarization in a society.

Class Identification and the Problem of Status Ambiguity. If a class location is ambiguous, we would expect less clarity in class-relevant behavior and, as a consequence, a reduced potential of the social group for status polarization.

In discussing operational definitions of class and status we noted that some students use objective criteria, whereas others depend upon the subject's self-assignment. Of the several objective indices of status, occupation tends to generate the strongest relationships with political variables, and up to this point we have often used it as a measure of status. But a substantial proportion of individuals assign themselves to a class other than that to which they would be assigned by the sociologist employing occupation as a criterion. Blue-collar workers of varying skill can and do identify with the middle class, whereas white-collar persons frequently identify with the "working" class. It is these people "misidentifying" across class lines who are symptomatic of status ambiguity in the culture.[9] Therefore it is among this group we must look for evidence of political behavior that is, from a class point of view, indeterminate.

Such behavior is readily demonstrable, as data compiled by Richard Centers have shown. Figure 12-1 compares the prevalence of recognizable class voting among individuals whose subjective class matches their occupation with class voting found among misidentifiers. This comparison is drawn separately within the three levels of political involvement employed previously. In each case, it is clear that most of the evidence for class voting within each group is contributed by voters whose class identification is congruent with occupation. As expected, tendencies toward class voting are indistinct among misidentifiers. Blue-collar workers who say they are middle class do not

---

[9] We shall use occupation as our objective criterion of "misidentification." We use the term "misidentification" only with some hesitation. We do not intend to imply that the misidentifier is either dishonest or suffers distorted perceptions. At the outset, the term need be no more than a denotation of an analytic category.

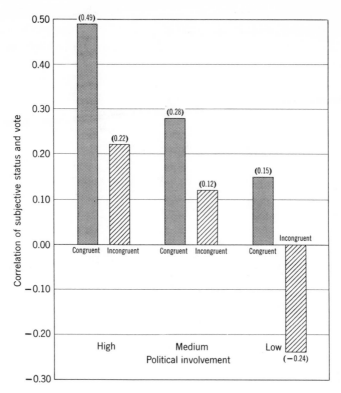

FIG. 12-1. *Status voting; political involvement and types of class identification, 1952. The solid bars include persons whose subjective class location is congruent with occupation, that is, blue-collar people choosing the "working class" and white-collar people of "middle class" identification. The shaded bars include blue-collar workers identifying with the "middle class" and white-collar, "working-class" individuals.*

vote in a manner that is very distinct from that of white-collar, working-class identifiers.

Our initial presumption is that class voting is blurred among misidentifiers because such persons behave under cross-pressures. The individual has reason to identify with one class, but the occupational milieu in which he operates from day to day consists primarily of members of the "opposing" class. The class with which he sympathizes has one set of political norms, but his active social group, to the degree it is class-oriented, has opposing norms.

The addition of the involvement distinction communicates further information. If misidentifiers behave under cross-pressures, then the pressure that tends to carry the day varies systematically according to degree of involvement in the political process (Fig. 12-1). We find that while the involved misidentifier more often than not follows his class identification in preference to his occupational milieu, the situation is reversed among the most apathetic third of the population. Differences in behavior lead us to suspect that either of two conditions obtains among the politically apathetic: (1) the choice of a class location is relatively meaningless in itself; or (2) this choice is not endowed with any of its traditional political meaning. In either case the behavioral result is the same: the pressure stemming from class identification is weak relative to that stemming from the actual social group, and partisan choice, to the degree that it shows traces of class influence at all, reflects occupation primarily.[10]

Earlier we introduced a method for determining whether or not the field of proximal attitudes is actually conflicted where sociological cross-pressures are suspected. If we apply this technique to test the hypothesis that behind the indeterminate class behavior of misidentifiers lies actual conflict in political attitudes, we find that where there is some political involvement, class misidentification is associated with greater inconsistency of the field of proximal attitudes. But where involvement is low, there is no significant difference between congruent persons and those who misidentify in choice of social class location. Therefore, the assumption seems warranted that among politically involved types the relatively indeterminate class behavior of misidentifiers is linked with actual psychological conflict.

Class misidentification leads to cross-pressures and thereby restrains the level of polarization in a society. It follows that the more frequent class misidentification is within a society, the lower is the potential of that society for status polarization. If the proportion of misidentifiers is an important datum in assessing the polarization potential of a society, then any characteristics of the social structure that promote misidentification serve at the same time to limit that potential. On the basis of current data it is possible to suggest a number of such characteristics.

First, it appears that the degree of misidentification in a society depends on the way in which its population is distributed along a status continuum. If we analyze the proportion of misidentifiers within

---

[10] Although the negative correlation among the misidentifying apathetic is not strong, a similar correlation of almost the same magnitude emerges when the same table is drawn from 1956 data. The 1956 graph duplicates the 1952 findings, although all coefficients are lower, reflecting the overall decline in status polarization of the vote.

successive groups along any of our objective status dimensions, we find that the rate of misidentification is low at the extremes (about 15 or 20 per cent) and rises symmetrically to a peak (approaching 50 per cent) at the center of the continuum. In other words, the closer an individual is located to a hypothetical dividing line between the two major classes by virtue of his objective situation, the more likely he is to locate himself psychologically on the other side of that line.

The caste society, with its sharply delineated strata, would have relatively few if any marginal people of ambiguous status. As we move from the caste extreme toward societies without gulfs defining status layers, however, the proportion of the population that occupies marginal locations increases. We would presume that as a result, the rate of misidentification increases as well, and the potential of the society for status polarization is consequently reduced. The United States, with its relatively swollen ranks of intermediate statuses—highly skilled labor and clerical workers—falls toward the extreme of the continuum. Other things equal—including the important elements of expectation and aspiration—it would seem that the United States has less potential for polarization than nations with other types of status structure.

We may also link the rate of social mobility in a society with the nature of its polarization potential. We find that when proximity to a hypothetical dividing line between classes is held constant, misidentification is more likely where the individual has, in times past, had some kind of contact with the opposing class milieu. For example, within each category of white-collar occupations, individuals of lower educational background are more likely to identify with the working class than are comparable people of high education. Similarly, blue-collar people of relatively high education are more likely to identify with the middle class. These situations are symptoms of mobility: a person's educational background, whatever his current status position, tends to reflect the status of his father's occupation. When education appears discrepant with current occupation, it is usually the case that the individual's current status differs from that of the family in which he was reared. When upward or downward mobility of this sort occurs, we tend to find what we classify as misidentification, and signs of conflict in political behavior where class is concerned.

Within societies in which movement of individuals upward or downward in the status hierarchy is rare, the possibility of misidentification arising from this source is minimized, and the potential of the society for status polarization is consequently increased. At the other extreme, the "open-class" society characterized by a high rate of social mobility maintains some ceiling on polarization potential by keeping its members' class identification, as it were, "off balance."

CLASS INTERESTS AND SOCIAL GROUPINGS

If we are to understand the finer grain of political events, it becomes important to assess not only the degree of status polarization that characterizes the society as a whole, but also the *distribution* of class interest in the population. There may be only a small portion of the population infused with class feeling; yet if these few are organized into cohesive groups, their activity may become disproportionately significant.

We have treated the union as a cohesive interest group with certain mechanisms for member influence. We assume that influence is exerted through the business community in much the same way. We are interested here not in the mode of influence but in the content of that influence as it relates to social class and politics.

Class awareness is somewhat higher among union members than among nonunion members of the same status level. Political involvement runs much stronger among union members than among comparable nonunion people. As far as business is concerned we find no unusual report of class awareness. But businessmen at all levels of income are much more strongly involved in politics than their status or educational background would lead us to expect. This unusual heightening of involvement among union members in the lower half of the status hierarchy and the business community in the upper reaches is of a piece with our earlier findings concerning political involvement and class voting, for these groups show strong status polarization in their political behavior as well. This combination of circumstances lends support to our assumption that perception of an economic stake in politics leads to involvement, rather than the reverse. People do not as a rule come to choose business or unionized occupations in order to implement prior political involvement. Rather, the exceptional involvement seems to rise from the occupational situation and its intrinsic conflict of economic interest.

Another striking demonstration of the way in which the labor union contributes to maintenance of polarization is its apparent effect on the class identifications of its membership. Union members are in general more likely to maintain their identifications with the working class than are other people of similar occupation status. Furthermore, this tendency toward "proper" class identification increases as a function of identification with the union. And when union members are involved, "misidentification" fails to appear in some of the peculiar combinations of life situations where we have come to expect it. For example, all other data suggest that workers of lower status who receive unusually high wages should also show a higher rate of misidentification with the middle class than is true of low-income, low-occupation types. Instead, this group shows only a slight increase in misidentification. But we find at the same time that this group contains a surprising proportion of union members: the labor union clearly brings its membership financial rewards not available to others of the same occupational status. When we examine *nonunion* people in this situation separately, we *do* find the expected large proportion of misidentifiers; but *union members* receiving wages normally associated with higher occupation strata *maintain their identification with the working class*. The labor union is dedicated to the promotion of such wage mobility; it must exert further influence on the membership to avoid dissolving its support in the process. Maintenance of appropriate class identification despite mobility is one challenge that the labor movement appears to meet.

Thus we find that groups somewhat more formal than the social class can, when class interests are incorporated as group goals, serve to heighten status polarization. Since the labor and management groupings are current points of heightened class sensitivity within the total society, they bear particularly close attention. At the same time we should not underestimate the significance of a polarization measure that encompasses the total society and thereby places such contestants in proper social perspective. The larger, more indifferent portion of the community serves to hold expression of tension within socially acceptable bounds. Summary measures of polarization in the total society ignore pockets of ferment in the social structure. Further information as to the distribution of class concerns in the social structure is necessary in order to understand more localized events. Nonetheless, such summary measures do reflect as well the restraining forces constituted by the majority of peripherally involved. Thus yeast and leaven are represented in proportions that are dictated by the total social scene. It is likely that such an assessment best anticipates the direction of large-scale social and political events.

chapter 13
Agrarian Political Behavior

Although the American farm population has formed a dwindling portion of the electorate over most of our nation's history, the peculiar problems of the farmer, his frequent dependence upon government, and his overrepresentation in most of our legislatures have maintained lively interest in his political responses. The "farm vote" is an entity that has meaning for the politician, journalist, and lay observer alike, and, among the reputed bloc votes, it holds fascination as one of the most unpredictable. In the national elections since 1948, the two-party vote division among farmers outside the South has fluctuated more sharply than it has within any of the other major occupation groupings or, for that matter, within any of the groups considered as voting blocs in Chapter 11.

The uncertainty shrouding the farm vote, however, is but one aspect of a larger syndrome of rural political behavior that has perplexed scholars. The term "farm revolt" itself reflects the long period in America's history in which massive and often violent protests were launched from rural areas against a system that brought economic hardship. With the Civil War aside, farm unrest was the primary source of political disturbance in America throughout the nineteenth century. The farmer reacts to economic pressure with political protest; yet the response has an explosive quality—great force without duration—which is unique.

The common threads that seem to exist in the behaviors of rural populations have never been adequately understood within any familiar theory of social or political process. It is striking that the same "reasonable" expectations of analysts have been betrayed so many times by rural groupings in virtually the same way. This observation suggests a tactic: we will handicap ourselves if we become restricted either to theories of group influence or to theories of social class before we have plumbed the problem that the political behavior of the farmer poses. Later we shall find it profitable to return to frames of reference suggested by both class- and group-influence conceptions. But let us first assess directly those prime peculiarities of rural political response, as we see them in our current samples, which evoke other times and settings.

CHARACTERISTICS OF FARM POLITICAL BEHAVIOR

Variability. We have indicated that one dominant feature of the political behavior of farmers is its variability. This variability is visible in aggregate statistics recording gross change in vote division within rural areas; it is visible as well in the vote division among farmers in our sequence of samples since 1948. When the partisan vote division is unstable in an area, we are likely to assume that inhabitants are crossing party lines with impunity from election to election. But the same effect may be produced if the area contains many irregular voters who drift into and out of the active ranks selectively along party lines in various elections. It follows quite directly, of course, that where partisan choice is fluid *and* turnout is irregular at the same time, the potential variability becomes even more extreme.

Recall data from our farm respondents concerning past political behavior permits us to analyze these two sources of variability for individuals over time. We ask how frequently the individual has voted in past presidential elections. Some have voted in all; others, though eligible, have failed to participate in any. The residual group is the source of turnout variability, at least with regard to presidential elections, and the prevalence of these sporadic voters in a population grouping provides a measure of this source of variation. A parallel question concerning regularity of vote for a single party reveals variability in partisanship over time.

Table 13-1 contrasts both types of variability for farmers and major occupation groupings within urban centers, outside the South. We see that the farmer shows greater variability in both senses than does the urban resident. We find also that within the urban sample, gradients of increasing variability tend to follow status lines. But of great significance is the fact that these gradients run in *opposing* directions. Variability in party voting increases among higher-status urban occupations; variability in turnout is greatest at lowest-status levels. Thus one source of variability characterizes each status extreme. The farmer, however, lies near the more variable pole on both dimensions; variability on one is not offset by stability on the other. The coming together of both types of variability defines rather dra-

Table 13-1. Variability of Political Behavior for Farm and Urban Occupation Groupings[a]

			Urban				
	Farmer	Rural Non-farm	Prof.	Bus.	Cler.	Skilled and Semi-skilled	Un-skilled	Urban Total
Turnout variability (Proportion who have voted in some past presidential elections, not in others.)	46%	43%	27%	28%	41%	43%	43%	39%
	(205)	(382)	(121)	(226)	(174)	(488)	(87)	(1277)
Partisan variability (Proportion who have voted for different parties for President in past elections.)	45%	38%	44%	40%	41%	36%	30%	37%
	(190)	(346)	(118)	(220)	(171)	(444)	(81)	(1214)

[a] Data are restricted to individuals over 28 years of age who have grown up and currently reside outside the South. The number of cases involved in each proportion is entered in parentheses; results are accumulated for both the 1952 and 1956 samples. "Rural Nonfarm" includes respondents living in places of 2,500 or less who do not reside in farm households. "Urban" categories thus include all towns and cities over 2,500 population. The "Urban Total" figure is greater than the sum of cases in urban occupation categories because of additional cases left unclassified in these terms. The case numbers in the "Partisan Variability" row are less than those in the "Turnout Variability" row because respondents who have never voted are excluded from the base.

matically the peculiar style of farm participation in the political process.

If the farmer fails to vote as a party regular from election to election, he also fails to vote as a party regular in marking any given ballot; he is more likely to split his ticket between the parties than is his urban counterpart, or than other persons living in sparsely settled areas who are not engaged in farming.

What conditions underlie such variability? Numerous hypotheses spring to mind that have rather prosaic implications. For example, if the farmer fails to vote in some presidential elections, need this reflect anything more significant than the fact that he lives in areas more remote from the polls and must depend on less reliable forms of transportation? Similarly, a phenomenon like split-ticket voting might symbolize a greater probability that the voter in the rural community has had some personal contact with one or another candidate on the slate, a fact that suffices to override party loyalty.

In the first case, it would be unreasonable to argue that distance from the polls is not a factor in the irregularity of farm voting. Clearly it must be. Yet such a mechanical explanation does not cope with all known facts. It does not explain, for example, why urban residents of early farm origin continue to turn out more irregularly than natives of urban centers. Similarly, the hypothesis concerning candidate familiarity and ticket splitting may have some grain of truth, yet it is quite inadequate to account for all aspects of our data. For example, we find that the individual of farm origin who has moved to the city continues to split his ticket there, in contrast with his totally urban counterpart.

In short, some relatively mechanical facts of the farmer's life situation may contribute to peculiarities observed in his political behavior, but a large part of this peculiarity must reside in a state of mind, a total posture toward the ongoing political process that survives changes in external aspects of his life situation. Thus the American farmer even in the 1950's showed himself to be sporadic in his voting and inconstant in his partisan attachments. The upshot of these characteristics for aggregate statistics from election to election is, of course, a peculiar fluidity in the partisan vote division. It is important to ascertain from our data what underlies these patterns of behavior.

THE MOTIVATIONAL ROOTS OF VARIABLE POLITICAL BEHAVIOR

We have seen that in the urban status hierarchy, variability in turnout and partisanship tended to shift in opposite directions along the status continuum. That is, lower-status people were more likely to flow in and out of the active electorate, but in so doing were more apt to abide by the same party preference over a period of time. The combination of high variability in both regards was unique for the farmer. Yet we know from material in preceding chapters that this combination *for individuals* is not particularly extraordinary. The syndrome is familiar and, in a motivational sense, quite comprehensible. Let us review its essentials.

Partisan Variability. The partisan fluidity of farm behavior suggests immediately that the affective bond between the farmer and the political party of his choosing is unusually weak. And we do find that strength of party identification is lower among farmers outside the South than among either blue-collar or white-collar urban types. Furthermore, this difference between farm and city is a difference between poles of a continuum, in a temporal sense as well as a spatial sense. The semirural people—those living in villages and sparsely settled areas, but not on active farms—have identifications of an intermediate strength between the poles defined by the farm on one hand and the city on the other. Similarly, although the differences are not large, we get the sense again that people with life experience limited to the farm and those who have always lived in urban centers pose the sharpest contrasts: individuals of mixed experience fall between these poles.[1] These gradients were apparent in our assessment of comparative behavior; they are present again as we compare motivational differences.

Political Involvement. It has been hypothesized that since most farmers tend to be exposed to economic pressures that demand government action, they will show unusual involvement in political affairs.[2] At an elite level, the power and vigor of the "farm lobby" even in modern industrial democracies offers striking evidence for this contention. But if we think in terms of the farmer at the *mass* level,

---

[1] It is at this point that our data for Southern farmers diverge most radically from those characterizing areas outside the South. Southern farmers show a stronger sense of identification with their party (almost always Democratic) than do Southerners living in urban areas. Fifty-nine per cent of these farmers in 1956 professed strong party identification. Furthermore, urban residents of farm origin are more strongly identified than urban residents of urban background. We take this situation to be rather unusual, a product of the long-standing one-party system.

[2] Seymour Lipset *et al.*, "The Psychology of Voting: An Analysis of Political Behavior," *Handbook of Social Psychology*, Gardner Lindzey, ed. (Addison-Wesley Publishing Co., Cambridge, Mass., 1954), II, p. 1129.

as is our aim, the expectation of high political involvement does not follow. Materials in earlier chapters have led us to associate variable political behavior and weak party ties with low levels of involvement.

Farmers are no exception to the rule: instead, they seem to epitomize it. Of course we would expect rural people in the South to be rather remote from national political wars, as our data on political involvement clearly show them to be. Outside the South as well, however, the farmer—and particularly the farmer who spends full time working his farm—professes remarkably little interest in the election campaign or concern over its outcome. In 1952, for example, when political interest was high but there were no strong economic pressures peculiar either to farm or city, the non-Southern farmer expressed much less active sense of political involvement than any urban occupation stratum save the small bottom layer of unskilled laborers. If rural vote turnout statistics are a satisfactory guide, this involvement had probably been lower still, although selective along party lines, in 1948. By 1956, however, the distribution of economic pressures had shifted between farm and city. The industrial sector of the economy was in good health; but the farmer had suffered five years of declining prices and rising costs, and the fall election was billed as another "farm revolt."

Data for 1956 show a mild decline in involvement of about the same magnitude within each of the major urban occupation strata. Rural nonfarm people showed a decline in involvement between 1952 and 1956 as well, although somewhat less marked. The level of involvement among non-Southern farmers remained constant between the two years. This stability against a backdrop of declining interest elsewhere in the broader electorate betokens some source of motivation peculiar to the farm that arose in 1956; we presume this source to lie in the heightened economic pressures that had built up since the preceding election. Worry about the economic future was, at the time of the 1956 election, most severe in agricultural areas. But more striking than the fact of higher *relative* farm involvement in 1956 is the fact that even under this degree of pressure, the level that this involvement attains remains modest. For this "exercised" segment of the 1956 electorate *still failed to register political interest equivalent to that of the skilled worker in the urban status hierarchy.* Whatever vigorous political activity marks the "farm lobby" at an elite level, we get the impression that its mass base is thin indeed.

We know enough about political involvement to push the matter back a step in the causal sequence. For matching the urban-rural gradient of political involvement is another having to do with amount of formal education. Educational attainment falls off as we move from urban to rural areas, and among rural people even outside the South, average education of farmers is lowest. There is ample evidence that these two characteristics—involvement and education—are functionally related. Here, too, the direction of causality seems unequivocal. Thus one source of rural indifference to politics may reasonably be located in the low levels of education that characterize these areas.

But education alone is not sufficient to account for observed differences in involvement between the farmer and people of urban background. For example, we noted that the political involvement of non-Southern farmers under the "base-line" conditions of 1952 was roughly a match for the narrow bottom stratum of urban unskilled workers. Yet if we isolate those unskilled workers from other urban types, we find an average education inferior even to that of the farmer. In other words, if we control education, farm political involvement for a year like 1952 does not even compare favorably with the most *déclassé* 10 per cent of the urban social structure.

Earlier we rejected physical remoteness as a simple "mechanical" explanation that would account *in toto* for farm irregularity in turnout. In a much less mechanical sense, this remoteness may be of considerable causal significance in understanding low farm political involvement. The full-time farmer has been much less firmly bound up with the flow of national events than any other group in the society. He has tended to work alone in an occupation which, save for the winter months, has left little leisure to attend to the world beyond the horizon. Interest grows from roots of information, and a continuing flow of information nourishes abiding interest. Even today the farmer may be less constantly exposed to political information than the urban resident; and certainly his exposure three or four decades ago can have borne no comparison to the flow of information available in urban areas. We know that interest in politics, like partisanship, is readily transmitted within the family from generation to generation. The current American farmer may bear the signs not only of some lingering remoteness from national politics, but apathy inherited from preceding eras in which the political communication system was much less developed.

Organizational Membership and Involvement. Members of farm organizations (among non-Southern farmers) tend to be more politically involved than nonmembers, and this difference is not well accounted for by discrepancies in education. Furthermore, within the set of farm organization members, political involvement increases very substantially as a function of identification with the farm organization. Such a finding, however, must be immediately tempered by a glance at the scope of this influence across the farm community, which is remarkably narrow. A majority even of non-Southern farmers in our sample belong to no such farm organizations, and of those who do belong, the proportion willing to indicate "a great deal of interest" in the organization is small. In fact, members of farm organizations show almost exactly the same distribution of interest in those organizations as is reported by union members for their local union organization. Given the fact that union membership is notoriously involuntary, this similarity is in itself striking. We find further that the interested farm organization members are disproportionately constituted of part-time farmers who have an urban occupation as well, along with somewhat higher education. If we restrict our attention to the minority of full-time, non-Southern farmers who belong to farm organizations, only 26 per cent express great interest in their organization (base N of 34) as opposed to 44 per cent among union members (base N of 428).

The farmer's lack of enthusiasm about the farm organization is reminiscent of his lack of commitment to the political organization. It is relatively easy to imagine the farmer feeling remote from the national political process and the group structures it entails; it is a little harder to understand his aloofness from group structures erected in the name of his interest, unless it be that for one reason or another he has difficulty committing his interest to any continuing group enterprise that transcends the local setting. In this event, aloofness from the political party would be but a special case of a broader phenomenon.

We should not lose sight of the fact that "high" political involvement among farmers is "high" only relative to the farm community itself and would not necessarily appear intense against a broader social backdrop. For example, if we take the tiny group of highly identified members of farm organizations in the "revolt" year of 1956 we still find an aggregate pitch of interest somewhere near levels registered in 1956 by white-collar clerical workers, or those that characterized skilled and semi-skilled workers in 1952. Against the backdrop of the total society, the American farmer is without question somewhat indifferent to national political affairs.

THE ECONOMIC SENSITIVITY OF THE FARMER

If one dominant characteristic of farm political behavior is its variability, a second that has received much attention is its economic sensitivity. The farm vote is frequently described as a "pocketbook" vote.

In fact, this description is often accorded the status of a motivational explanation for the variability of rural voting. It does not in itself provide complete satisfaction: it does not make clear precisely why this vote should be more an affair of the pocketbook than some other vote. Let us survey the evidence that may be brought to bear upon the contention of peculiar economic sensitivity in the same spirit with which we explored the political motivations that seemed relevant to the farm problem.

We have noted that between 1952 and 1956 the economic situation of the American farmer deteriorated rather rapidly. Prices of many farm products had fallen off, and yet the cost of farm materiel was on the rise. The farm prosperity of the 1940's had faded, though boom times reigned elsewhere in the economy. The new Republican Administration, in an effort to discharge large farm surpluses, had challenged past Democratic farm policy. This was, in brief, the setting that led to expectations of a farm revolt against the Republicans in the 1956 election. Let us assess the partisan implication of this economic pressure.

One simple measure of degree of economic pressure from farmer to farmer may be based on a question asked in 1956 concerning the trend in prices that the farmer felt he had encountered in the four years since the previous presidential election. The experience of any farmer was dependent, of course, on factors such as his geographic location and the types of produce that he attempted to market. Few farm respondents, however, had felt any upward motion of prices during the 1952–1956 period. Some felt that the price picture had not changed much from their point of view; the remainder reported that their prices had gone down over the four-year period.

As Table 13-2 indicates, there was a very sharp relationship between price patterns that the farmer had experienced prior to 1956 and the partisan direction of his presidential vote in that year. We should not conclude uncritically that the direction of the farm vote was as thoroughly determined in the 1956 election by immediate experiences with prices as this table may suggest. On one hand, we have confidence that the perceptions of price trends depend on a solid reality base. That is, in the aggregate, the farmers' reports conform well with general trends shown by national statistics on farm income during this period.

It is plausible, however, that prices were in fact declining more sharply under farmers of Democratic leanings than under those of Republican predisposition, for political partisanship among farmers is related to various types of farm situations. Most clear is the link

*Table 13-2. Relation of Trend of Prices Received
by the Farmer, 1952–1956, to His 1956 Vote*[a]

	Reported Price Trend		
	Up a Little; Same; or Mixed Trends Balancing Out	Down a Little	Down a Lot
Proportion Voting Democratic	13%	39%	66%
Number of cases	27	36	29

[a] This table is based on non-Southern farmers only. In the South, the same pattern was present, although somewhat less distinctly. With prices for tobacco and fruit on the rise and cotton holding fairly well in the 1952–1956 interval, Southern farmers felt less beleaguered in general. Nevertheless, of 21 Southern farmers who saw prices slightly up or mixed, only 52 per cent voted Democratic. Of those 19 who saw prices declining, 84 per cent voted Democratic.

between the number of acres that the individual farms and his party preference in 1956. Undoubtedly, the fact that the small farmer looks with relative favor upon the Democratic Party is itself bound up with reactions to economic pressures in time past and the farm legislation of the New Deal period. But to the degree that the small farmer already held pro-Democratic views in 1952, and to the degree that the small farmer suffered more severe economic pressures between 1952 and 1956, some portion of the relationship in Table 13-2 would exist even if the current economic situation had no relevance in immediate political decisions.

Short-term economic pressures reflected in recent price trends continue to show a substantial relationship with the 1956 vote, however, even when farm size is controlled. Although it is not our custom to present data involving as few cases as the cells of Table 13-3, the great

*Table 13-3. Relation of Farm Price Trends and
Farm Size to 1956 Presidential Vote of Farmers*

	Southern Small Farm		Southern Large Farm		Non-Southern Small Farm		Non-Southern Large Farm	
Prices are . . .	Down	Up or Same	Down	Up or Same	Down	Up or Same	Down	Up or Same
Proportion voting Democratic	100%	55%	70%	50%	62%	33%	41%	6%
Number of cases	9	11	10	10	26	9	37	17

clarity with which the patterns match *a priori* expectations and the congruence between regional findings have led us to preserve all analytic distinctions here. We may evaluate these patterns over the table as a whole, without overemphasizing the absolute size of any single entry. In a general way, the table is striking in the degree that the farm vote appears accounted for by three factors of differing "time depth": (1) the long-standing traditions of rural northern Republicanism and Democratic voting in the South; (2) more recent trends presumed to be of New Deal–Fair Deal vintage, which have won support for the Democrats from the small farmer and Republican support from larger farmers; and (3) current, short-term economic pressures. Yet for our immediate purposes the table is most relevant as it demonstrates the strength of these current economic forces in affecting the farm vote.

Other aspects of the data also lead to the conclusion that the relationship between prices and vote in 1956 represents in no small measure a simple and direct reaction on the part of farmers to economic events since the preceding election. And our independent knowledge of the partisan fluidity of the farm vote makes this degree of rapid partisan change seem plausible. Farm people who voted counter to their normal party affiliation in the 1956 election appear to have done so as a function of their immediate economic situation.

The status polarization of the farm community as a function of both stable and short-term differences in economic fortune illustrates with great clarity the folly of treating the farm vote as unitary, in the group sense, even to the modest extent with which we earlier subscribed to this notion for labor unions, Negroes, and Jews. The farmer appears to respond to his own economic situation, with little reference to the manner in which others in the same occupational category are faring. Since prices and hence economic situations are tied to specific crops, economic winds frequently blow in several directions at once across rural America, leading to a variegated response. The "farm revolt," if represented by any gross unidirectional shift in farm partisanship, is likely to come about only when economic difficulty faces a large proportion of farmers at once.

The role of the economic in determining farm responses to political affairs, as well as its role in fragmenting the farm community as a political group, is convincingly demonstrated by attitudes of farmers toward key issues of governmental farm policy. In 1956 we asked all farm respondents to react to the following proposition, which seemed to strike at a major controversy extant with regard to the "farm problem": "If a farmer can't sell things he raises at a profit, the government should buy them and limit the amount the farmer can produce." Responses to the support issue are related to party identification. Democratic farmers tended to accept supports, and Republican farmers to oppose them, undoubtedly reflecting the national posture of the two major parties during this period. But this alignment is a confused one, since the smaller farmer is at the same time partial toward the Democrats yet hostile toward the Democratic position on the price support problem. If the smaller farmer seems drawn to the Democrats yet doubtful about their price support position, the larger farmer is caught in the same cross currents, exactly reversed. This conflict of forces sums up the difficulties to be encountered in treating the American farmer as a voting bloc. And the clear economic roots of these cleavages lend weight once again to the contention of particular economic sensitivity among farmers.

Economic Motivation and Turnout. We have already introduced evidence which implies that as economic pressure on the farm increases, the political involvement of the farmer, relative to an urban backdrop, increases as well. The suggestion is obvious that short-term economic pressures lie behind the spurts in vote turnout that mark the farm vote. Now that we have located focuses of economic pressure within the total farm community in 1956, we can attempt to document this proposition at a finer level of analysis.

As we have seen, the small rather than the large farmer was in most direct revolt against the Republican Administration in 1956. More specifically, the small farmer *who had perceived his prices to have declined* during the 1952–1956 period was most severely concerned. Now under normal circumstances we would expect that the *large* farmer, in view of his higher education and political involvement, would show a vote turnout higher than that of the small farmer. But if it is true that economic pressure leads to a surge in political involvement, we might expect some visible reversal of this normal expectation in 1956.

The data do in fact suggest that it was the small farmer suffering declining prices who was most motivated in his political response during the 1956 election. Without information on the same farmers over a period of time we cannot be entirely sure that the heightened motivation within this group is a *temporary* heightening. Yet the entire structure of our materials strains toward the conclusion that save for economic pressure, this group would not have pulled out of line in this fashion. The special economic pressure within this subset, defined by farm size and production of crops that were hit by price declines, was not present in 1952. It is present in 1956, and the group shows unexpected political involvement. We assume, then, that we witness here a spurt of involvement as a very simple reaction to economic pressure.

Economic Motivation and Farm Political Behavior. The fact that farmers react politically to economic pressure in no sense answers the problem posed by the peculiarities that surround such protest. Other groupings have pocketbooks, and other groupings experience economic hardship. Why does rural economic protest appear peculiar?

We are forced to maintain either (1) that farmers suffer economic pressures that differ in their intensity or quality from those suffered by other groups in the society; or (2) that farmers have, for whatever reason, a different political style of coping with pressures of the same generic type as those encountered elsewhere in the society.

Lipset *et al.*, recognizing that response to economic pressure is not in itself a solution of the farm puzzle, appear to pursue the first line of thought. It is argued that the farmer—and the one-crop farmer in particular—has a position in the social structure that is unique from an economic point of view. He suffers extraordinary insecurity of income, owing to the vagaries of weather on one hand and world or national commodity markets on the other; he is peculiarly dependent upon governmental action for regulation and maintenance of the markets that are his economic lifelines.[3]

Many of these observations have merit and undoubtedly have important bearing on the situation. Yet we are not convinced that this approach moves to the heart of the problem. We are not convinced, for example, that economic pressure as it bears upon the one-crop farmer differs in a critical way from economic pressure that has borne upon the urban laborer. Nor are we convinced that this approach copes with the most tell-tale peculiarities of rural political behavior. The explanation, as it stands, suggests that groups like one-crop farmers may turn out to be perennial troublemakers in the political system; but key facts, such as the transience of this troublemaking and its ideological fickleness or incoherence, are noted but are left unassimilated.

Let us, then, take the opposing fork of the argument. Let us assume that although economic pressures on the farmer and on the laborer exhibit many interesting qualitative differences, we shall be safe in conceptualizing economic pressure in very simple terms. We shall

[3] *Ibid.*, pp. 1128 ff.

presume that such pressure has but one dimension of variability that requires attention, and that is its intensity. If this intensity is the same upon farmer and laborer and the nature of the response varies, then we are called upon to explain this variation in terms of differences between farmer and laborer as political actors.

FARMER AND LABORER: REFLECTIONS ON THE MASS BASE OF PROTEST MOVEMENTS

We have already indicated some of the more notable similarities and differences between the political dispositions of the farmer and the urban laborer. Both are poorly educated, and one consequence of this fact is a lowered capacity to organize a steady input of political information. With restricted information goes a reduced sense of involvement in the outcome of political events. This psychological remoteness leads in turn to sporadic political participation.

Though there are broad similarities between farmer and laborer in these terms, the farmer if anything suffers by comparison. He shares the laborer's primary handicaps, but these have been compounded by the circumscribed provincialism of his rural life. In a simple physical way, he lies outside the flow of major political events. We find vestiges of this difference even in our current American data, where "normal" farm involvement, once education is controlled, does not compare favorably with the lowest reaches of the urban status hierarchy. If our views on sources of these lingering contrasts in involvement are valid, the discrepancies must have been a good deal sharper a century ago.

We presume that it is this physical remoteness that has led to the point of sharpest contrast between the farmer and the urban laborer, for despite gross similarities in the involvement dimension, there are marked differences in the way the two occupation types are bound into existing group structures in the society. That is, the farmer has a lower incidence of membership in social groupings than the urban laborer and, where membership exists, is more apathetic toward the group. This appeared to be true in terms of occupational organizations, and in terms of political memberships we have noted major contrasts between farmer and laborer in sense of allegiance to a political party and, as a consequence, in regularity of support for the party at the polls.

We can expand on some of these differences with our data from 1952 and 1956. There is good reason to question how much organizational "reach" the traditional parties have into the hinterlands. In the revolt year of 1956, when excitement about the election was off from its 1952 pitch in urban areas, there is evidence that party organization did extend its efforts into rural areas where there was believed to be heightened political ferment. In general only about one person in ten, in the adult population, reports having been personally contacted by a party worker in connection with the election, although this figure is somewhat higher outside the South, approaching a ratio of one person in five. In 1956, 23 per cent of our non-Southern farmers reported such contact, and 17 per cent of rural nonfarm persons had the same experience.

There was a good deal of focus upon the farm problem in connection with the 1956 election, and of course physical access to rural areas had been improving steadily for a century. In 1952, the principal campaign efforts were not directed toward any particular urban or rural segment of the electorate, as there were no notable economic lines of stress between city and country to prompt such attention. In this more normal setting, though patterns of urban contact were much as they were to be in 1956, party contact in rural areas was very slight indeed. Only 7 per cent of non-Southern farmers reported being contacted, and the comparable figure for nonfarm rural persons was 9 per cent. The likelihood of experiencing direct contact with a party worker seems to have been twice as great for the *unskilled* urban laborer in 1952 as it was for the farmer, and of course the probability was larger still for the semiskilled or skilled laborer.

Furthermore, a comparison of 1952 and 1956 data gives little reason to believe that when the farmer is more exercised about politics this involvement will receive expression in partisan group participation. In 1956 he was more likely to have been contacted by a party worker seeking his vote; but there is no sign of any increase in his voluntary participation in partisan activity. Even in terms of informal communication we get no sense of heightened activity. The farmer in 1956 was less likely to have attempted to influence the partisan intention of some other person than was the urban blue-collar worker (such attempts reported by 21 per cent of non-Southern farmers, as opposed to 29 per cent of urban laborers).

Data cited earlier in connection with membership in farm organizations raise the possibility that lack of firm bonds between the farmer and traditional political group structures is but a special case of a broader insulation of the farmer from group activity. In 1952 we explored the types of group participation in which a subsample of our respondents was involved, including both formal organizations and informal groupings such as poker clubs and sewing circles. Participation in informal group activity is less among farm people than it is among urban blue-collar workers, and, if church memberships are excepted, the same observation may be extended to more formal groupings as well.[4]

It is in this sense, then, that although both farmer and laborer are poorly educated and relatively uninvolved in the political process, the farmer is distinct in the degree to which he floats free of the group life of the larger society. Hence we need no unique explanation to cover the farmer's lack of commitment to either of the political parties; he appears to stand on the periphery of social process more generally speaking, and his low sense of commitment to a party is simply a case in point.

The urban laborer is little more absorbed in politics than the farmer. But he does find himself imbedded in a network of group contacts, and experiences a flow of informal communication on political matters that can fill some of the gap left by his lack of attention to published news. Furthermore, where there is membership in some secondary group having political norms, a rare occurrence in rural areas but common in the city, we have seen the urban worker drawn even more tightly into the traditional party structure. Beyond the one-party South, the greatest differences in strength of party identification emerge between the full-time farmer, apathetic toward farm organizations, and the urbanite, highly identified with a secondary grouping that transmits political standards in the name of group welfare.

Therefore the farmer and the laborer share some crucial characteristics but stand in sharp contrast on others. What happens politically when heavy economic pressures are brought to bear upon these different political actors? In both cases we would expect an upsurge in political involvement and greater turnout at the polls. It seems psychologically unsound to believe that the farmer, when subjected to a given degree of economic pressure, suffers more intensely or is more motivated to act than the urban laborer. What is peculiar to the farmer is not the sensitivity itself; rather, it is the manner in which *partisan meaning* is ascribed to economic pressure. For the urban laborer, be he Republican or Democrat, economic pressure prompts attitude formation and behavior within channels that are group-defined and of long standing. Where such loyalties to a party are lacking, as they tend to be among farmers, these channels are faint or simply do not exist. The farmer is psychologically free to march to the polls

[4] Ronald Freedman, unpublished data, 1952 Election Study, Survey Research Center, The University of Michigan, Ann Arbor, Mich.

and "vote the rascals out," whether or not he himself may have helped establish them in power in the first place. The result is political behavior that fluctuates sharply in its partisan character and, for the analyst, data that show spectacular links between simple economic pressure and partisan choice.

The farmer does not thereby behave as a man apart but simply as the political independent of low involvement behaves in any setting. Urban populations certainly contain individuals who, in the normal course of events, are apathetic toward political participation, yet who flow into the active electorate under sufficiently extreme provocation. These persons tend to style themselves as "Independents" and feel little allegiance to the traditional parties.[5] The critical point is that in the urban setting they are greatly outnumbered by committed partisans, most of whom vote with regularity. Thus their behavior is largely concealed, as it is not in rural areas.

Farm and Labor Movements in American Political History. These observations have rather clear implications when we examine past behavior of the farmer and laborer in this country. We propose that it would take long-unrelieved economic disaster before the urban laborer would begin to depart from the existing structure of traditional parties on any large scale. Yet, at the onset of economic difficulty in rural areas in times past, new parties have had nearly the same chance to capture farm indignation as the old, for the farmer has had little psychological anchor in the "normal" elements of the ongoing political process.

It might be argued that we have begged the question by confusing effect for cause. If the urban laborer is, in 1956, tightly bound into the traditional party structure, does this not merely reflect the direction in which the laborer has been led by his elites in times past? If the farmer floats free of this party structure, is it not because his leaders have more frequently drawn him toward third-party solutions for his economic problems?

---

[5] Although the interpretation is a popular one, there is no reason to believe that such people, rural or urban, stay away from the polls under ordinary circumstances because they are "alienated" from the system in any affective sense. If there is an alienation, it appears to be cognitive: such persons tend to be poorly educated or, if educated, interested in other things than politics. They are little aware of any effect which a remote government has upon their lives, except as events may suddenly go awry in a manner completely beyond their control. The fact that in crisis they turn to the polls itself seems an indication that they do not customarily fail to participate out of disgust at "the system." When events arouse affect, they participate; when things are going well, motivation is absent.

We do not believe that such an interpretation adequately covers historical facts. The major thrust of the modern American laboring movement did not come to rest within the traditional party structure because this was the initial reflex of radical labor leadership but because all attempts to draw the urban laborer into third-party ventures were dismal failures. The success of third parties in the agrarian setting, on the other hand, was remarkable. The record shows that the American West of the nineteenth century spawned third party after third party, not of the sort of fringe labor party that quadrenially in our day attracts a minute portion of the national vote, but vigorous social movements that, in their brief ascendance, captured astonishing popular support almost overnight in rural areas.[6]

Our interpretation of rural rebellion provides effortless explanations of a number of other peculiarities associated with these events. For example, it follows that as education among farmers comes to approximate that of persons in the urban setting, and as advances in transportation and communication bring him into closer contact with the traditional groups and forms of the society, the distinctive character of the farmer's political response should fade as well. For better or for worse, he becomes a more "socialized" political actor. We would profess to see such an evolution in the quality of rural political protest over the period since colonial times. Rural protest has become increasingly channeled within the guidelines set by the existing parties.

Our account sheds equal light upon one of the most perplexing features of rural protest at a mass level, its unique transience. This characteristic has often been obscured by scholarly preoccupation with the rise of totalitarian movements. Usually in these latter cases the guiding elite that has benefited from rural revolt has succeeded in acquiring full power. This has meant the suspension of further democratic process and hence the obliteration of clues as to subsequent rural reactions. Yet if we look at those cases in which democratic process has been sustained—and the farm revolts of the nineteenth century provide the most striking examples—it is consistently true that the mass base, *upon relief from the most immediate economic grievances*, has disappeared as rapidly and unexpectedly as it coalesced. Other economically insecure groups have, under pressure of repeated economic crises in the urban setting, slowly forged links with the

---

[6] Since 1860 only one "urban" state in one presidential election (Pennsylvania, 1912, for Theodore Roosevelt) has cast its electoral vote for a third party, and in this case the candidate was closely associable with the existing party structure. Yet during this time about two dozen agrarian states have, at one point or another, contributed third party electors in a presidential vote.

political process. Such movements have come thereby to enjoy continuing loyalty from a mass base that extends into periods of high
prosperity. None of the American farm outbursts has acquired such
continuity.

Our interpretation not only can accommodate this aspect of rural
behavior, but in an obvious way would demand it. The rural mass base
collapses as economic pressure is relieved for precisely the same motivational reasons that permitted its implausible formation. Its clientele is
overburdened with individuals whose ties with political parties are
extremely weak; and the proof of the matter is nowhere more clear
than in the fact that they were lured away from the traditional party
structure in such haste. The psychological function that party identification plays seems such that the first response of the party faithful to
economic storm is not the third-party solution but some attempt to
affix responsibility and look for succor in a manner best calculated to
preserve existing party loyalty. If pressure continues and none of the
traditional parties can effectively relieve it, then we might expect a
growing willingness to consider third-party alternatives. But this
would be a slow process even at the individual level; over the aggregate
of party faithful it would indeed be hard to imagine sudden inroads
of these massive proportions.

By the same token, the mass base that forms with great rapidity will
wither away quickly because it is saturated with individuals who do
not frequently participate in politics when "times are good." Such
persons, upon solution of the immediate problem, will resume their
normal posture of sporadic attention to politics, or will drift on small
pretext to some other party that catches their attention.

Ideology and the Mass Base of Protest Movements. It is the matter
of ideology that constitutes the final puzzle surrounding rural protest
movements. Though investigators have frequently left the transience
of rural protest unexplained, a great deal of effort and ingenuity has
been devoted to the search for plausible links between the pattern of
reforms proposed by the elite of the movement and needs imputed
to the rank and file.

Most discussions of this problem share an underlying assumption
that there need be some basic congruence between the ideology proposed by the elite and the motivations of the mass base in flocking to its
electoral support. Certainly such movements must have points of
strong attraction. But to presume that the mass base is endorsing the
ideology as the analyst conceives it is to presume that such programs—
which usually call for change in the pattern of political and economic

relationships—are in some real sense comprehended by more than a handful within the mass base. The argument developed in Chapters 8 and 9 tended to call this assumption into question even for the moderately educated and moderately involved voter. It should be clear that no commonly recognized political actor would be less likely to fulfill this assumption than the farmer.

We get some sense of the nature of the appeals that may attract farm support from our free-answer materials. Two interviews capture rather eloquently the modal farmer's view of the political situation.

The first of these interviews came from a small Mississippi farmer whose prices had been declining. There is the familiar profession of great ignorance about politics, with virtually no other content. However, Stevenson's name elicited the remark: "Now wait a minute—ain't he the one gonna give money to the farmers? My boys an' me needs that."

Much the same flavor comes through in the second interview, taken with the wife of a New Jersey farmer. She launched her comments about politics with references to the "good pay we used to get for our crops during the War, even when some went bad," and went on to talk about politicians as "slick." When questioned about Stevenson's good points, she indicated: "I haven't read about him. My husband and I don't care to watch the speeches on TV." But when asked if there was anything about Stevenson that might make her want to vote against him, she said, "Well, no. Maybe I should vote for him if he is going to help the farmers get more money."

It does not seem difficult to imagine the perception getting abroad that a candidate or party is going to "get the farmers more money" with little accompanying notion as to the changes in law or governmental relationships that such aid might entail. Not only are these people largely oblivious of the way in which their own aid might be implemented, they tend as well to hold an extremely narrow perspective on political process. They evince little awareness as to what is going on in other sectors of the society; their criteria for political decision are totally wrapped up in the tangible benefits that may flow to the farmer.

This paucity of anything resembling ideological comprehension in rural areas is vividly illustrated in another manner. If we assume that the elite that is thrust up by economic stress is itself rural, with at best a moderate background of political involvement or contact with sophisticated political views, then we are not surprised by those numerous traces of ideological incoherence among rural elites found in the historical record.

Once we assume that a rural elite generated by economic disaster is not apt to have the capacity to develop its own program or philosophy, the question whether or not any ideology becomes attached to the electoral outburst at an elite level depends on factors of cultural diffusion or, more simply put, upon what may be within sight at the moment. In the Saskatchewan case examined by Lipset, the farm population included an unusual proportion of recent migrants from industrial areas abroad. There was a large contingent of trade union members and erstwhile Fabian Socialists. It is not surprising, then, that this movement found an ideology quickly and that its elite was prominently populated by the sophisticated new arrivals.[7] In the American West, however, there apparently was little knowledge of urban ideas, and there were years of floundering before the rural elites who had been activated by economic stress even found that plausible bodies of ideas were available that might be borrowed.

Of course as we turn from elites back to a consideration of the mass base that supported them, we must water down our expectations accordingly. The development or even grafting on of an ideological program is a slow and painful process for those relatively capable individuals who have been drawn most passionately into the cause of protest. Therefore our assumption that an ideology *per se* is not likely, in the short span of a year or two, to have permeated a mass base that is less involved and less sophisticated than the elite seems sound indeed. Hence the question as to why this or that ideology was so irresistible that large numbers flocked to its support seems calculated to lead to blind alleys and contradictions.

It should be strongly emphasized that our argument is focused entirely on the nature of continuities between elite and mass base. We are not questioning the value of efforts to understand the transmission and diffusion of ideologies. Obviously, the nature of the ideology that captures such a surge of protest is of tremendous consequence for the history of nations. But we say that the character of the ideological superstructure, as the analyst conceives it, is normally irrelevant to the motivations behind any sudden mass base that it may achieve.

---

[7] Seymour Lipset, *Agrarian Socialism: The Cooperative Commonwealth Federation in Saskatchewan: A Study in Political Sociology* (The University of California Press, Berkeley, Calif., 1950), p. 25. This seems an inverse case of the "binding in" of rural populations.

★ *chapter 14*

Population Movement

The movement of peoples is a fascinating theme in American history. The commonplace fact of large scale migration to the West was transformed by Frederick Jackson Turner into a provocative thesis on the development of our modern culture.[1] More recently, and somewhat more narrowly, professional students of politics have turned to basic social and economic characteristics of the population for explanation of new developments in national politics. Arthur Holcombe made evident the extent to which urbanization replaced regional politics with the now familiar phenomena of the rural-urban conflict.[2] Of still more recent vintage are the arguments advanced by such observers as Louis Harris and Samuel Lubell.[3] Their understanding of political cleavage in mid-twentieth century rested in part on the perceptive realization that movement away from the central city and into the burgeoning suburbs had serious political implications beyond the mere redistribution of political partisans.

The winning of the West, the growth of the city, and the rise of suburbia have contemporary as well as historical interest for us in our present analysis. More than half of the present residents of our large cities grew up in other and smaller cities. Almost 40 per cent of the people who grew up in large cities have now moved to smaller cities, into the suburbs, or to a home in the country. At least one of every two members of the electorate of the 1950's had moved far enough

---

[1] Frederick J. Turner, *The Frontier in American History* (Henry Holt and Co., New York, 1921).

[2] Arthur N. Holcombe, *The New Party Politics* (W. W. Norton and Co., New York, 1933).

[3] Louis Harris, *Is There a Republican Majority?* (Harper and Brothers, New York, 1954). Samuel Lubell, *The Future of American Politics* (Harper and Brothers, New York, 1952), and particularly *The Revolt of the Moderates* (Harper and Brothers, New York, 1956).

from the home in which he grew up to be living in a place of different population size.[4] Four out of ten native White Americans have moved from one state to another since growing up, and three out of every twenty have moved from one of four major geographic regions to another. As of the 1950's almost half the voters in the Far West had grown up in the South or in the East and had moved west in their adult years.[5]

These gross views of population movement do not capture any change of residence within the same town or city, nor do they reflect intrastate movement which does not also involve a shift in population size of place of residence. Even without including such less dramatic movement in a description of change in residence, almost 60 per cent of the adult population can still be described as "movers."

At least three kinds of political effects may be identified as possible concomitants of population movement. The first is the aggregate change in political composition of areas that "movers" leave and into which they move. Another kind of political effect associated with change of residence occurs when the individuals who move undergo political change. Such changes may be categorized under two distinct headings. In one situation a common factor or set of factors puts into motion both the residential change and the political change. For example, a person's financial success may lead to changes in a wide range of behaviors and values, social and political. The second way in which individual change is related to a change in residence involves the hypothesis that political change is the later result of moving and of the social changes that moving implies. A change of residence, for whatever reason, places a person in a new environment and in responding to the new environment he undergoes political change. Thus in the classic contemporary example, the working man moves to the suburbs as a Democrat, but there associates with Republicans and with greater or lesser speed takes on Republican characteristics.

All three kinds of political change that can be associated with population movements and changes in residence are potentially im-

---

[4] Here and later in the chapter we mean to distinguish three categories for the size of place of residence: (1) metropolitan centers; (2) suburbs, smaller cities, and large towns; and (3) rural villages, open country residences, and farms. The categories are so defined that a change in the population size of one's place of residence cannot be the result of national changes in urbanization but occurs only by a personal change in residence as a result of geographical movement *and* the crossing of a boundary between places of different population size.

[5] U. S. Bureau of the Census, Series P-25, #198 (1959). In this chapter as well as elsewhere throughout the book we utilize the Bureau of the Census definitions of regional boundaries separating Northeast, South, Midwest, and Far West.

portant, in part because of the local base on which American politics rests. There have been major redistributions of members of the electorate that are important because they result in a shift in the balance of power both among and within political units. Changes in personal political predispositions are also in evidence in the national electorate. In our discussion we shall not always be able to distinguish empirically between political effects that are concomitants of change in residence and those political effects that are caused by the act of moving. Whatever their respective importance, their combined importance may be considerable and we shall review something of the net result.

Our discussion of population movement centers on two aspects of individual moving: (1) interstate movement, which will be analyzed largely in terms of regional population movements, and (2) movement from place to place that results in a change in the population size of one's place of residence. The time dimension embraced by our definition of a change in residence includes two points in each person's life history, the period in which "he was growing up" and "now" (1952 or 1956). The occurrence of moving is further pinpointed by some analyses of how long each person has lived in the community of present residence.[6]

INTERREGIONAL MIGRATION

The broadest class of political change—redistribution of the population with or without accompanying individual changes—will be discussed in terms of regional populations. The end result of all the moving to and fro that has gone on in the past half century or more finds about one out of every seven persons living in a region other than that in which he grew up. The proportion of native born in regional populations varies as shown in Table 14-1.

Who are the movers? As a single gross category they are men who tend to be somewhat better educated and who have considerably better jobs and higher incomes than the natives of the regions they leave. As this syndrome of characteristics strongly suggests, for some of these people, geographical mobility is associated with upward social mobility

---

[6] We will distinguish people who may have moved to their present home in the postwar period (having lived in the community ten years or less) from those who must have moved in earlier (because they have lived there for more than ten years). Between the time a person "was growing up" and "now" he may have lived in a dozen other states and in places of a dozen different sizes. This we do not know. We do know (1) where he grew up—by city size and by state, (2) where he now lives, and (3) how long he has lived there.

Table 14-1. *Regional Distribution of "Native Born"*

	Present Residence				
	North-east	South	Mid-west	Far West	Total
Grew up in region	92%	92%	89%	52%	86%
Grew up in another region	8	8	11	48	14
	100%	100%	100%	100%	100%

—professional and business men on the make and on the move, leaving home territory for greener pastures. To go beyond such generalities we must examine some of the larger categories of movers.[7] We shall examine three major groups: (1) people who have moved to the Far West, (2) those who have moved to the South, and (3) the remainder, those who have moved from the South or from a northern region into either the Midwest or the Northeast.

The West and How It Grew. Half of all the people who have moved to a region other than that in which they grew up have moved to the Far West. There, in turn, they constitute almost half of the total population of that region. They constitute a prime example of a massive redistribution of the population, and they provide us with a considerable potential for observing important political implications in population movements.

Our analysis allows us to identify two streams of westward migration, one from the South and the other from the North. Northerners who have moved West are relatively well educated (28 per cent have attended college) and they tend to hold white-collar jobs. They show a slight Democratic majority in their party affiliations and they vote with about the same diligence as their former neighbors in the Midwest and Northeast. There are at least two interesting points of political difference, however, between the movers and those they left behind. The movers' affinity for the Republicans nearly equals that of the other Northerners, but it does not depend on any pro-Republican advantage resulting from changes of party identification. This stands in contrast

---

[7] Even though almost 30 per cent of all Negroes have moved to a new home in a new region, they are too few in absolute numbers in our sample data to analyze within these categories. Consequently, Negroes have been excluded from the general investigation of regional movement and will be considered separately at the end of the discussion. Unless specifically noted, the following discussion pertains only to native-born Whites.

to the quite visible pro-Republican change reported by the natives of their home regions. The implication is, of course, that at sometime past these movers were markedly *more* pro-Republican than their former associates, who have since caught up with them. The second difference lies in their presidential votes of 1952 and 1956. The movers gave Mr. Eisenhower almost 75 per cent of their votes in these two elections—significantly more than the Republican proportion cast by those they left behind.

It is evident that this Northern migration to the West has meant the introduction of a relatively heavily Republican population into a region dominated by sentiments that were much more pro-Democratic. There is little evidence, however, that the incoming Republicans have been converted or softened in their Republicanism. Instead, their contribution to Western politics would seem to be more that of minimizing political differences between the Far West and the other Northern regions. They constitute a third of the Western population, and without them the Democrats hypothetically would outnumber the Republicans by more than two to one in the eleven Western States.

The second stream of Western migration, that from the South, constitutes about 14 per cent of the total Western population. (Northern migrants contribute 34 per cent of the total.) Both groups of Western immigrants are considerably older than any other group of movers or nonmovers we shall examine. Despite the age of the Southern migrants, their educational attainments are about the same as those of the Southern nonmover. However, they are somewhat lower than the average for the North, and markedly below the educational background of other migrants to the West. Although the income level of the Southern migrants is equivalent to that of the Northern migrants (and above that of the native South), their average occupational status is very low—lower than that of the South generally and much lower than that of their fellow migrants.

If these former Southerners now differ somewhat in socio-economic terms from the people still living in the South, they have retained a major part of the Southern pattern of political behavior. Their voting rate is low—only two-thirds voted in 1952 and 1956—and the vote that is cast is very strongly Democratic. Where native Southerners reported an average vote of some 56 per cent for Mr. Stevenson in 1952 and 1956, the Southerners in the West reported that 60 per cent of their votes had been cast for him—a truly remarkable record in those years of Mr. Eisenhower's dominance. Although they followed the national pattern in reporting a diminution of Democratic Party identification over the years, they still ranked only slightly behind the South in their continuing Democratic allegiances.

Thus, in their political behavior the former Southerners provide a marked contrast to the other newcomers to the West in the extremity of their Democratic predispositions. Moreover, as with the Northern migrants to the West, four out of five party identifiers among the Southern migrants report no change in party identification, and their reported Democratic partisanship does not depart substantially from that of the Southerners who had not ventured from home.

In short, the movement of an extremely Democratic group into a *relatively* more Republican environment appears to have resulted in virtually no individual change or dilution of Democratic allegiances. The North-to-West movement brought a relatively Republican group into a relatively more pro-Democratic region, where they remained as Republicans and, in like manner, showed little sign of political acculturation. Both movements contribute a significant portion of the political complexion of the Far West. Both must be described primarily as a redistribution of partisans and participants. The absence of the Northern emigrant would leave Western politics nearly as strongly Democratic as the politics of the Solid South. Their presence, however, gives the West an electorate that is to some extent an amalgam of North and South. With party identification as the vehicle for transmission of hereditary loyalties, it is not surprising to find transplanted partisans confounding some of the traditions of nonpartisanship once so strong in the coastal states.

Movement to the South. Northerners moving to the South are the second major category we shall discuss. Though a relatively small group, less than 2 per cent of the total White population and slightly less than 10 per cent of the Southern Whites, they are worth describing because of their possible strategic contribution to American politics. These migrants are also of interest because they are, in fact, quite different from the usual description of the Yankee who has gone South. In the first place they are not merely Northerners who have retired and moved to the sunny climes. They boast a very high current average income—certainly not merely the annuities of pensioners from the North—and two of every five are presently engaged in a professional or business career. A third have attended college and nine out of ten have at least some high school education.

As one might expect, their political predispositions do not strongly favor the Democratic Party—they divide about equally between Democratic and Republican allegiance—and their reports of changing party identification do not indicate they are succumbing to the appeals of Southern Democracy. In 1952 and 1956 they resembled Northern migrants to the Far West as they cast over two-thirds of their votes for Mr. Eisenhower. However, their contribution to the Republican effort in the South was limited not only by their restricted numbers but also by a modest rate of voting—only 68 per cent voted, despite socio-economic characteristics that would suggest a much higher rate.

These migrants would seem to possess considerable potential to influence Southern politics. Above all other groups in our population analysis they feel themselves to be politically effective. They also appear to possess an unusually well-organized set of political attitudes, showing more partisan consistency in their appraisal of national political objects than does any other group. Finally, they show little sign of being changed themselves by the environment around them. They report a change in party identification no more frequently than does the rest of the nation, and the changes they do report follow the national mode *away from the Democratic Party,* not to it.

The Invasion of the North. The third and last stream of regional population movement which we shall consider is composed of persons moving into the Midwest or Northeast. As with the case of the Far West, this immigration has two distinct parts, one from the South and the other consisting of movement within the North itself. The two parts are polar opposites on almost every social, economic, and political dimension we have considered. The Southern White migrants, a minuscule 4 per cent of the Northern population, are young (40 per cent under 35), poorly educated (40 per cent have not gone beyond grade school), and tend to hold low status jobs (60 per cent are blue collar). Nevertheless, their sense of personal political effectiveness compares favorably with all but one or two of our groups, and their level of participation apparently reflects their Northern environment. Their turnout rate is well above that of the other Southerners we have examined—72 per cent voted in 1952 and 1956. They predictably reflect their Southern origin in the Democratic nature of their party identifications and in their vote for President.

On the other hand, the Northerners who have moved from one Northern region to another are not particularly young. This group, constituting slightly more than 2 per cent of the Northern population, is well educated; over half of them are business and professional people, and they report an extremely high average family income. As fits the stereotype of people with such social and economic characteristics they are heavily pro-Republican in their political sentiments:

only 25 per cent call themselves Democrats, whereas 52 per cent identify themselves with the Republican Party. A share of this Republican predominance is apparently of relatively recent origin; some 18 per cent describe themselves as *former* Democrats, whereas only 7 per cent report they have left the Republican ranks. The members of this category of movers are highly motivated as citizens and manifest their sense of great political effectiveness: 89 per cent voted for President in 1952 and 1956. They voted three to one for Eisenhower.

The two groups that compose the Northern immigration are of interest because of the extreme differences between them. They do not, however, give us any new insights into the impact of moving on the politics of the movers. And, contrary to the situation in the Far West, these migrants comprise such a small portion of the electorates they join as to accomplish little in the way of an immediate reshaping of the regional politics in their new homes.

Negro Migration from the South. A quite different impact on local, regional, and national politics has resulted from the migration of Southern Negroes. We may first note that the attention given to the growing Negro vote in the North reflects the visibility and strategic location of that vote rather than its size alone. Even though the proportion of Negroes who have moved from one region to another is double the proportion of Whites who have changed regions (29 per cent of all Negroes against 13 per cent of all Whites), Negroes still constitute but one-fifth of all such movement. In absolute numbers the Negroes who have moved North are almost equalled by the Northern Whites who have moved South.

The social and economic characteristics of the migrant Negro provide an insightful commentary on the contemporary nature of the American dilemma. Compared to Southern Negroes who *have not* left the region, the immigrants now in the North are of about the same age, but they have received more years of formal education. They do not on the average hold higher status jobs, but their average income is much higher. Some 35 per cent report a family income of over $4000, whereas only 6 per cent of the Southern Negroes give a similar report. In both the North and the South the nonfarming Negro is a blue-collar worker in more than seven out of ten cases; he is a white-collar man in only one out of ten. The better education of the Northern Negro is thus likely to be associated with a much higher income, but not necessarily with a substantially higher occupational status.

In 1952 and 1956 three out of every four Southern Negroes who claimed a partisan allegiance described themselves as Democrats rather than as Republicans. And those who did vote voted just as heavily for the Democratic candidate as did the Southern White. Moreover, the *ratio* of Democratic to Republican Party identification was just as high among Southern Negroes as among Negro migrants to the North. Nevertheless, some contrast with the Negro who had moved North was still evident. Negroes in the South divided their votes for President in the two elections about equally between the two parties; Negroes who had left the South were much more strongly Democratic, giving over three-fourths of their votes to Stevenson. The sharpest contrast was provided, of course, in the extent of participation. Only one in six Southern Negroes reported a vote in 1952 and 1956, whereas four in six immigrants in the North reported voting. The greater political involvement of Northern Negroes was also evident on a number of attitudinal dimensions such as sense of personal political effectiveness and range of attention to national political events and objects.

The contrasts and similarities between movers and nonmovers among Southern-born Negroes become quite understandable when viewed in relation to the characteristics of Negroes who have lived all of their lives in the North. When the three groups of Negroes are compared, it is apparent that the natives of the two regions represent social, economic, and political extremes. The emigrants to the North occupy a position suggestive of partial but not complete transition from one subculture to the other.

Our inspection of four categories of travelers has provided evidence relating population movement to individual political change. Three of the four categories contain very few individuals who have changed to conform to their new environment. Northerners moving West and South and White Southerners moving West have retained or accentuated the distinctions that set them apart from their new neighbors. Only Southern Negroes moving North have showed any tendency to shed some of their traditional attitudes and thereby become more like their new associates and less like those who remained behind.

URBANIZATION, SUBURBANIZATION, AND POLITICAL CHANGE

In this era of urbanization it may come as something of a surprise to note that some 21 per cent of the total population has moved away from the city or away from larger towns and cities to smaller ones than those in which the movers grew up.[8] At the same time, three out of

---

[8] We shall not treat suburban areas here as a special population category. There are several reasons for this omission of special treatment of the suburbs. First, when we proceed with a comparison of persons who were brought up in metro-

five persons who have moved to a residence in a different population density category have moved into more densely populated centers.

Social Mobility and Political Change. The voters who have deserted the metropolitan centers in favor of suburbia have drawn much comment from the political commentators and analysts. One favorite theme has held that this change in residence is an indicator of upward social mobility and has been accompanied by a change in politics that has seen Democrats turned into Republicans. We shall not attempt to verify or deny this thesis as it applies to particular suburbs or even to the categories of suburbs in which this phenomenon has been reported. We will, however, move directly to a confrontation of the hypothesis that upward social mobility, outward geographical mobility away from the metropolitan center, and a turn away from Democracy to Republicanism are interrelated. It may be noted in passing that this analysis is a story with a more general moral as its conclusion. It illustrates how more appropriate data may affirm the accuracy of observations based on less appropriate data while at the same time disclosing a basic fallacy in the conclusions drawn from those observations.[9]

Many of the emigrants from big city living occupy the top rung of the social and economic ladder. They tend to be well-educated members of well-to-do families of professional people and businessmen. They are more often than not Republicans, and they reflected this in their voting in 1956. A full analysis of the problem, however, does not support the simple thesis that upward social mobility has led to a Republican surge among these ex-city dwellers. The first data to indicate a flaw in the theory concern the widespread occurrence of social mobility. Whether defined by occupational status or subjective social class affiliation, and whether described in terms of intergenerational movement or by the intragenerational mobility of the individual, upward social mobility is shared in identical measure among all of the relevant population groupings. Mobility cuts uniformly across all

---

politan central city areas but have now moved to less densely populated places, we cannot discern any substantial empirical differences between the subgroupings that are identified in our data. Second, the nature of our data does not allow us to investigate the many smaller categories subsumed under the single heading, "suburb." We can only describe as one group the residents of the heterogeneous category of places that share the general character of being suburban areas.

[9] All of the following data and the discussion they support refer only to native-born Northern Whites. Non-Whites and Southern residents deserve similar attention, but the available data are not adequate to do more than indicate the necessity for dealing separately with the three groups.

population categories except those involving persons who grew up on farms. The upward social mobility of the former urbanites is fully matched by that of the folk they left behind, as well as by all other groups of nonrural origin. Thus, even before turning our attention to questions of stability and change in political partisanship, it is apparent that any *differences* among the population groups in their movements away from the Democrats or to the Republican fold cannot be explained by differences in the incidence of upward social mobility.

The second relevant datum in this analysis concerns change in political partisanship. Our most direct indicator of this is the citizen's report of change in his own sense of partisan identification. Although the picture of change in party identification is not as uniform across all groups as was the pattern of intragenerational occupational mobility, it is so uniform as to undercut decisively the hypothesis that we are testing. Former metropolitan residents have indeed moved away from the Democrats and toward the Republicans in their party loyalties. A total net shift of 16 percentage points in their partisan division has been recorded in this group. There is, however, a 12-point shift in the same direction on the part of lifelong metropolitan residents. A Democratic to Republican switch by 2 per cent of the former metropolitan dwellers, or an Independent to Republican movement by 4 per cent, would account for all of the difference we observe between the two groups. This scarcely can be taken as evidence that the trend toward Republicanism is significantly greater on the part of the émigrés from the big city.

The further implication that upward social mobility is, in general, *not* associated with changes in party identification away from the Democratic Party may be tested directly. As Table 14-2 indicates,

Table 14-2. *Relation of Reported Changes in Own Occupational Status to Changes in Self-Identification with Parties, 1956*

	Occupational Mobility	
	Down	Up
Changes in party identification		
From Republican to Democratic	28%	24%
From Republican to Independent	8	12
From Democratic to Independent	32	29
From Democratic to Republican	32	35
	100%	100%
Number of cases	47	121

even among the people who report both a change in partisanship and a change in their own occupational status there is no suggestion of a relationship between the two kinds of change.[10]

If the validity of these data is granted, the logic of the argument follows quite readily. The hypothesis is that upward social mobility among émigrés from the metropolis has been accompanied by conversion to Republicanism. The implication has been that movement *out* from the city is associated with upward social mobility, whereas retention of a central city address means either downward mobility or at least an absence of change in social status. It appears, to the contrary, that upward social mobility has been experienced every bit as often by the nonmovers as by those who have traded convenience for space, and it is associated equally in both groups with pro-Republican changes in political partisanship. Moreover, the absence of a really unique change in political allegiance among ex-urbanites further indicates that movement out of the metropolitan centers cannot stand as the factor responsible for changes in partisan loyalties that cut across nonmovers as well.

We may speculate that the visibility of suburban politics has been responsible for explanations of political behavior that now must be qualified. The mushrooming colonies of former big-city dwellers are indeed properly described as containing a great many Republicans, many former Democrats, and many upwardly mobile residents. What has been missed are the similar movements away from the Democratic Party and upward on the social scale that have gone on, quite independently, in the less visible homes of the old central-city areas as well. Moreover, without actual knowledge about the political histories of the former urbanites, the extent of their traditional Republicanism could not be determined. With our reports of their own past behavior at the polls, we can now establish that much of their Republican sentiment is of extremely long duration, if not a matter of family heritage. The combination of a tradition of Republican sympathy

---

[10] Similarly, when we compare the occupational status of our respondents with that of their parents we find very little evidence that upward or downward changes in status from one generation to the next are associated with shifts toward the Republican or Democratic Party. Upward mobile people are slightly more likely to have shifted from Democratic to Republican identification than those people whose status has moved downward, but both types of status-changers are much more likely to have moved toward the Republican Party than away from it. Their changes in status appear to have very little relationship to their changes in partisanship.

and an "average" rate of defection on the part of the minority Democrats adds up, of course, to the formidable Republican strength that many of these communities brought to the political wars in the 1950's.

The Metropolitan Electorate—Past and Present. Two population groupings stand out as particularly interesting: one comprised of persons who grew up in a major city but have since moved to smaller cities or towns or to homes in the country, the other consisting of persons who were raised in rural hamlets or on farms and who have now become central-city residents of a major metropolis. These two groups stand at the polar extremes among the array of population groupings with regard to almost every social and economic characteristic. The urban emigrants enjoy the highest occupational status, boast the most substantial family incomes, and are individually the most likely to have received a college education. At the other extreme the immigrants from the country are not well equipped in terms of formal education (only one out of two has gone beyond grade school), and a generally low occupational status is reflected in the low proportion whose families had incomes in excess of $6000 in 1956.

On each count, the native of the metropolis stands roughly midway between the extremes, sharing his position with former residents of towns and cities. But when we turn to a study of the clearly political variables, this order among sometime metropolitan residents changes rather drastically.

Emigrants from the metropolis and migrants to it are arrayed in almost identical fashions on the party identification continuum. Despite great differences in their social origins, the former big-city dwellers and the onetime country folk are remarkably similar in the nature of their underlying partisan allegiances. Furthermore, members of both groups present a remembered history of almost unalloyed support for Republican presidential candidates. Their behavior in 1956 proved no exception: only two groupings gave Mr. Eisenhower more support than did the former metropolitan dwellers, and one of those was the immigrants from the rural areas. The latter group—although socially and economically the most disadvantaged of the three components of the metropolitan electorate—gave Mr. Eisenhower almost four out of every five votes they cast.

On the other hand, the lifelong inhabitants of the metropolitan centers constitute a sturdy core of Northern Democratic support. In 1956 they provided the strongest resistance to the Eisenhower sweep of the North. And even this was not commensurate with their predominant partisan loyalties, for they are even more heavily Democratic in their division of party allegiances than the other two groups are Republican in theirs.

There are, nevertheless, some expected political manifestations of the social and economic characteristics of the three groups. These appear in the area of political participation. The onetime rural residents had the poorest record of turnout in 1956. The former members of the metropolitan electorate shared honors with the neighbors they left behind in demonstrating their civic virtue. The low turnout of former farmers reflects the agrarian political heritage described earlier. It is also consistent with their presently relatively low sense of political efficacy. At the same time, the migrant from metropolitan living was supported in his participation by a sense of efficacy commensurate with his objectively demonstrated ability to attain the higher goals among those valued by our society.

Residential Mobility among Democrats and Republicans. Probably because they are *less* visible, people who have moved *into* the metropolitan centers have not been the object of extended scrutiny or comment. Nevertheless they are in some ways as unique as the urban-to-rural mover—and in their greater numbers (60 per cent greater than the number of outward movers) they constitute a category of considerable political importance. Before turning to a closer examination of these new members of the metropolitan electorate, we may draw attention to an interesting consequence of their Republican affiliation that we have already observed. When viewed in conjunction with the staunch Republicanism of the big-city émigré, they complete a picture of a preponderantly Republican circulation through the metropolitan center.

One corollary of the exodus of Republicans from the metropolitan centers lies in the heavy Democratic preponderance among the metropolitan residents who do not move. If a third of the emigrants are Democrats, over half of the metropolitan-bred nonmovers are Democrats. The striking extent of partisan differential in this movement out from the metropolitan center is highlighted by the discovery that 71 per cent of the Democrats raised in a metropolitan center still live there or in another similar central-city area, whereas only 46 per cent of the metropolitan-bred Republicans have resisted the movement away from these central cities.

The net result of the two streams of movement, in and out of the major metropolitan centers, apparently has been to leave the partisan balance within the metropolitan center almost unchanged. The Republican-dominated in-migration has almost exactly offset the out-migration. Among all persons who grew up in the metropolis, the division in party identification is 47 per cent Democrats, 25 per cent Independents, and 28 per cent Republicans; among the present residents of the same cities the division is 49 per cent Democrats, 24 per cent Independents, and 27 per cent Republicans. But here the balancing-out ends. Among Democrats who are sometime residents of a metropolitan center, 47 per cent are lifelong residents; among sometime metropolitan Republicans, only 28 per cent have spent their lives in a metropolitan home.

The definitive explanation of the greater residential stability of Democrats or the greater mobility of Republicans is not at hand. There are, however, two lines of speculation that may be suggested. In the first place, the Republican character of the movement into the metropolis seems quite reasonable. After all, the in-migrants come from farms, villages, towns, and smaller cities. The preponderance of Republican sentiment in these places is well documented in voting statistics.

To the extent that this argument is persuasive, the explanation of party differences among big-city emigrants is made more difficult. Despite a sometime Democratic-Republican division of 47–28 in the metropolitan electorate, the emigrants divide 33–37 in favor of Republican identifications. This situation occurs because, as we have noted, 53 per cent of the sometime metropolitan Republicans have moved out, whereas only 29 per cent of their Democratic counterparts have left for less crowded surroundings. But why the difference between 53 per cent and 29 per cent?[11]

The data pertaining to intergenerational occupational mobility suggest a promising line of speculation and future inquiry. Among persons whose occupational status is lower than that of their father's there are no party differences in the frequency of movement away from the big city. But among persons who have achieved upward mobility and have exceeded their father's occupational status, the differences are striking indeed. Among Democrats the proportion of nonmovers is 76 per cent (N = 62); among Republicans the same proportion is only 37 per cent (N = 40). Moreover, comparing the upward mobile with the downward, upward mobility *increases* the proportion of nonmoving Democrats, from 66 per cent to 76 per cent. Upward

[11] The difference does not appear to be a function of financial ability to move. Indeed, there is a tendency for the difference to be accentuated among higher income families where freedom to move is least limited by such factors.

mobility among Republicans decreases nonmoving or, stated positively, increases the frequency of movement out. Where only 37 per cent of the downward mobile Republicans move out, a full 63 per cent of the upward mobile follow the trail to suburbia, exurbia, and beyond.[12]

In the absence of needed data we can only speculate about the meaning of these discrepancies in partisan response to intergenerational mobility. It seems likely that fairly basic differences in social values are involved. It may be that the Republicans, despite their own metropolitan origins, are more often linked through enduring family ties to ancestral beginnings in small cities, towns, and on farms. The urban Democrat, on the other hand, may be the child of a thoroughly urban culture. Whether the metropolis of his family line once was Warsaw or Rome or Dublin, or Boston, Baltimore, or New York, he may accept more often the way of life of the metropolitan center.

Changing Electorates. The greater residential mobility of Republicans, in the setting of metropolitan politics, is in itself of considerable interest. But the implications are even more intriguing when we recall the greatly different social and economic characteristics of people who move into and out of the metropolitan centers. In aggregate group characteristics these two groups are similar politically but dissimilar on other dimensions. It remains for us to discover the extent to which the dissimilarities are particularly true of the Republicans (or the Democrats) in each group or the extent to which they cut across all political comparisons that we might make.

We are, of course, interested in the social and economic comparisons because they will indicate the extent to which the "circulation" of partisans out of and into the city changes the clientele to which each party must appeal. Let us consider education as the first social characteristic of interest and let us first compare movers with non-movers. People who have moved *out* of the central city are better educated than those who stayed behind. The extent to which this is true is reflected by the following measure of *differences in education level* within each partisan group:

[12] Intragenerational mobility does not appear to be at all related to change of residence for Republicans, although it is related to Democratic movement. Among Independents, both intergenerational and intragenerational mobility are sharply related to changes in residence. In all instances upward mobility is associated with movement away from the metropolitan center.

Emigrants compared to nonmovers among:

Democrats	+18 ⟶	(18% more with college education among
Independents	+28	emigrants, or 18% more with grade
Republicans	+32	school education among life-long
		residents)

People who have moved *into* the central city also differ from those already there, but they do so by virtue of being *less* well educated. The differences within each of these groups of partisans are:

Immigrants compared to nonmovers among:

Democrats	−5
Independents	−11
Republicans	−30

If outgoing Democrats were *better* educated than nonmovers by a mean difference of +18, and if incoming Democrats were *less well* educated than nonmovers to the extent of a difference of −5, the net difference between those moving in and those moving out is −23. For Independents, the difference in educational level is somewhat greater, expressed by a difference score of −39. For Republicans, the difference amounts to −62. The comparable data pertaining to income are as follows:

Emigrants compared to nonmovers on family income:

Democrats	+6 ⟶	(6% more with income over $6000
Independents	+31	*or* 6% fewer with incomes under $6000)
Republicans	+9	

Immigrants compared to nonmovers:

Democrats	−28
Independents	−20
Republicans	−58

Net difference between movers, immigrants compared to emigrants:

Democrats	−34
Independents	−51
Republicans	−67

As far as the background variables of education and income are concerned, the differences between incoming and outgoing citizens are greatest among Republicans and least among Democrats. The same is true with regard to the occupation of those citizens in the labor force. The following data refer to differences in proportions of white-collar jobs in each pair of groups.

Emigrants compared to nonmovers:

Democrats	−5	⟶	(5% fewer in white-collar jobs among
Independents	+30		emigrants than among nonmovers)
Republicans	+25		

Immigrants compared to nonmovers:

Democrats	−15
Independents	+10
Republicans	−10

Net difference between movers, immigrants compared to emigrants:

Democrats	−10
Independents	−20
Republicans	−35

Much the same picture is presented by data pertaining to the citizen's subjective social class position. There is virtually no difference between incoming and outgoing Democrats; the former include only 5 per cent fewer middle class people. Incoming Independents include 26 per cent fewer middle class persons than do Independents who have moved from the metropolis; the comparable difference among Republicans is 23 per cent fewer among immigrants than among emigrants.

Some of the consequences of the parade into and out of the metropolis are by now apparent. The movement involves Republicans more often than Democrats, and the social and economic differences between the pairs of Republicans are far more extreme than are those for comparable Democratic groups. It is fair to conclude that the nature of metropolitan Republicanism has changed rather dramatically during the recent decades. For example, instead of a onetime Republican metropolitan electorate composed of 35 per cent with some college education and only 18 per cent with no more than grade school behind them, metropolitan Republicans now have only 19 per cent with some college and a full 37 per cent with no more than grade school education. For Democrats the change has been from 11 per cent college and 20 per cent grade school to 11 per cent college and 27 per cent grade school. Among Republicans the change in occupational composition has been from 48 per cent white-collar to 29 per cent white-collar; among Democrats the change has been a much smaller decline, from 36 per cent to 32 per cent.

For politician and analyst alike the influx of relatively low status Republicans in metropolitan politics suggests fascinating potentials for political change. Most Democrats who have moved into the metropolitan center from elsewhere have been living in their present homes since before the Second World War.[13] Most of the incoming Republicans moved to their present residences after the war. Even assuming that these Republican newcomers may be unable to achieve complete insulation from the politics of their new neighbors, social integration (and the subsequent acceptance of community norms) appears to be a very slow process. It is a matter of critical significance for metropolitan politics, however, whether these Democratic influences may in time make themselves felt. It would seem we have discovered in these new members of metropolitan Republicanism an acid test for the durability of party identification.

The last point to be made concerns the phenomenon of status polarization in politics. Viewed in terms of status polarization, the newcomers to metropolitan politics constitute a major unpolarized segment of the electorate. The Republican newcomers are not of sufficiently low status to reverse the direction of status polarization when placed next to the new Democrats. They are, instead, merely similar—so similar as to contribute a depressing effect on the level of polarization within the total metropolitan electorate. Moreover, the changing of polarization within the metropolitan centers has been furthered by the nature of the movement *away* from the cities. Among the former metropolitan residents polarization is considerably more pronounced than among the nonmovers and, of course, much more accentuated than among the unpolarized newcomers. The three groups of sometime metropolitan dwellers thus display three distinctly different levels of polarization, ranging from high polarization among emigrants to no polarization among immigrants. Another consequence of population flow around the metropolitan center is thus observed in the reduction of polarization within the metropolitan electorate. The reduction has taken place, however, without necessary reference to class ideology, economic stress, or any of the other elements that were identified earlier in the analytic delineation of the components of polarization. The redistribution of political partisans has again been of major importance, even in the absence of individual political change.

[13] The reader is reminded that this analysis excludes Negroes.

chapter 15

The Electoral Effects of Other Social

Characteristics

In addition to the historical imprint of a region or the pressures of group interest that the voter reflects, other attributes he possesses as a member of the society contribute to an understanding of his political behavior. Most of the characteristics that we shall encounter in this chapter refer to sociological categories in the population rather than to self-conscious groups. They represent the elements of "life situation" that we took pains to cancel out of our calculation of group effects in Chapter 11. Persons fifty years old may differ in attitudes and behavior from those thirty years old. But we do not think of groups of fifty-year-olds or thirty-year-olds, which in some sense mediate these differences. Common age is not considered the reason for association, nor is there a sense of unity with unknown individuals of the same age in other parts of the country. Nevertheless, individuals who are located in a given category are likely to behave differently from those who fall in another category. We must consider the further types of intervening mechanisms that might lead to these differences. In most instances, such differences arise in one of two broad ways:

1. *As results of differential exposure to politically relevant experiences.* Social attributes tend to define certain unique experiences that people of given categories have undergone or are undergoing. To the degree that like experiences elicit like reactions, individuals with the same attributes may come to behave in the same fashion without any conscious reference to one another. People do not become alert to problems of pensions and fixed incomes until a certain age. But there are common elements to the pressures that people of this age bring to politics.
2. *Those differences based on socially defined roles.* In some cases cultural values exist that prescribe interests or behaviors for individuals belonging to specific social categories. A man is supposed

to know something about politics, for example, whereas a woman need not.

In the first case, like stimuli bring like responses. Various social categories are differentiated in their behaviors because they receive different stimuli. In the second, the same stimuli presented to members of different categories bring different responses, as a function of social prescriptions regarding appropriate behavior for the members of each category.

We shall attempt to spell out the political implications of a series of social attributes, seeking in each instance the intervening states that shed light on the reasons for the existence of the relationship. Our major emphasis will be upon variation in political participation. In general, social characteristics that do not tend to become bases for group action in a certain partisan direction show much more significant relationships with vote turnout and other aspects of political participation.

EDUCATION

Formal education has many striking consequences for political behavior that are independent of status implications and that undoubtedly remain constant in strength even in times when class differences lose most of their partisan importance. Some of these differences are matters of sheer information. The greater an individual's education, the more likely he is to attend to sources of political information and hence to know "what is going on." His view of political objects and events will be more specific and more highly differentiated. The educated person is distinct from the less educated not only in the number of facts about politics at his command, but also in the sophistication of the concepts he employs to maintain a sense of order and meaning amid the flood of information. In fact, it is psychologically sound to presume that the two phenomena go hand in hand.

Just as there are wide differences in cognitive structure as a consequence of differences in education, there are differences in motivation to participate in the political process that are of profound significance. Higher status people tend to take a more active role in politics, and, although education is secondary to occupation as a focus for partisan differences, it is the dimension of status that seems most central in matters of political participation.

Only a small fraction of the adult population engages in much political activity beyond the act of voting itself. But in the various other types of participation that we record, there is some visible upper status bias within this fraction. Generally, education serves as the best predictor of these forms of participation among status dimensions. Perhaps the strongest relationship with education appears in the tendency to talk informally with others with a view toward influencing their vote decision. The "opinion leader" role in political choice is not widely sought, but it is more likely to be sought by the more highly educated. Educational differences are less marked in some of the other forms of participation: membership in political organizations and campaign work are less clearly dependent on status lines.

The strongest evidence of educational difference comes, however, in the ultimate casting of a ballot, as Table 15-1 shows. Aside from geographical differences between the South and other regions of the country, no other social characteristic commonly employed in our research bears such a strong relationship to turnout in presidential elections.

Table 15-1. Relation of Amount of Formal Education to Differences in Presidential Vote Participation, by Region[a]

	No Education; Some Grade School	Completed Grade School	Some High School	Completed High School	Some College	Completed College
Non-South: per cent voting	70%	68%	77%	87%	92%	93%
Number of cases	334	365	455	720	230	179
South: per cent voting	32%	50%	50%	63%	80%	85%
Number of cases	301	113	193	185	92	68

[a] Figures in this table are based on a combination of data from the 1952 and 1956 election samples.

Our data provide a fairly clear picture of the types of motivation to participate that distinguish the more highly educated people and that hence may be presumed to intervene between education and higher turnout at the polls. We have indicated that interest and involvement in the outcome of the current election vary strongly as a function of education. We have assumed extensive interplay between these motivational correlates of education and the cognitive differences mentioned previously. The more meaning an individual can find in the flow of political events, the more likely it is that these events will maintain his interest. The person who makes little sense of politics will not be motivated to pay much attention to it. And, of course, the more interested the individual, the richer the cognitive background which he accumulates for subsequent political evaluations.

There is no significant relationship between strength of party identification and formal education, but the educated stand out with great clarity on the motivational dimensions we call "sense of political efficacy" and "sense of citizen duty." These highly generalized attitudes show strong relationships with education and with vote turnout. With more formal schooling an individual is more likely to feel that he has influence on political events. And he is more likely to feel a sense of civic responsibility about voting, however hopeless the cause and however small his vote against the total number cast.

It is not surprising, of course, that a well-educated person should feel greater confidence in his effect on the political process. He has only one vote, but in many other ways his education is likely to ensure him greater community influence. In part, this is a status matter. But the fact that political efficacy is more strongly related to education than to other dimensions of status that may symbolize equal strength in the power structure suggests that education contributes to the attitude in a more direct way. Undoubtedly we capture here some basic beliefs concerning the way in which the democratic process works, beliefs traceable to the educational experience.

Although feelings of involvement in the current election, sense of political efficacy, and sense of citizen duty appear to depend substantially on education and in turn help to predict which persons in the electorate will vote, this causal sequence alone does not exhaust our understanding of the motivational complex behind vote participation. The broad motivational attitudes lead to considerable differences in behavior even within narrowly defined educational categories. As Table 15-2 suggests, however, this additional predictive capacity

Table 15-2. Relation of Involvement, Efficacy, and Education to Vote Turnout, outside the South, 1956

	Grade School	High School	College
High efficacy, high involvement			
Proportion voting	96%	89%	96%
Number of cases	48	197	137
High efficacy, low involvement: or low efficacy, high involvement			
Proportion voting	81%	83%	87%
Number of cases	158	287	59
Low efficacy, low involvement			
Proportion voting	53%	68%	92%
Number of cases	156	173	36

itself varies systematically with education. Within categories of education, further knowledge of motivational attitudes improves our prediction of turnout substantially at the lower levels of education; but this increment wanes very notably at higher levels. People of college background tend to go to the polls however indifferent they may be to the election outcome and however cynical they may be about the importance of their participation.

This lack of symmetry between educational groups may reflect increased social pressure to vote, among higher educational milieus. At the lowest status levels involvement in politics is not widespread and voting is somewhat sporadic. There is a minimum of external forces on the individual to vote: any interpersonal expectations that would induce him to the polls despite lack of interest are attenuated. Whether such a person votes depends far more heavily, then, upon his internal value structure. In higher milieus, however, most people have some interest in politics, and voting is "the thing to do." Those few who do not share this interest are out of step. Their apathy is not a socially useful excuse for failure to vote. Hence the minority of well educated who lack interest go to the polls anyway.

OCCUPATION

A person's occupation can affect his partisan preference independently of simple status considerations. An occupation defines the group of people with whom the individual works and thereby delimits spheres of primary-group influence. Jobs that entail working with people rather than things add another dimension of experience, according to the nature of the clientele. In some cases the occupation imposes peculiar interests and values that may be of political relevance.

Occupations may be arrayed not only in terms of the standard status hierarchy, but also according to the sectors of the economy represented, close to what the Census Bureau calls "industries." There are administrators and clerical workers, for example, across a wide range of occupational milieus: government service, retail sales, manufacturing, transportation and communication, and professional services. Therefore "industry" may be thought of as a dimension fairly independent of the occupation status ladder.

The most distinctive industrial grouping in terms of 1956 partisan vote division is constituted by those private services that cater to financial or business enterprise. Included here are occupations in advertising, accounting, various forms of industrial consultation, banking, real estate, and insurance. Individuals in this general category voted over 75 per cent Republican in 1956, by contrast with the national vote division of 57 per cent. No other industrial grouping deviates as sharply. Of course, a portion of this Republican dominance may be simply attributed to the fact that occupations included in this category tend to lie at the higher status levels. But even after controlling the status factor, this grouping remains sharply Republican. It is likely that exclusive occupational contact with a business clientele builds particularly firm values concerning the proper role of government and private enterprise, sound fiscal policy, and the problem of government welfare activity.

Other important mechanisms operate within industrial classifications as well. A person's work situation may put him in closer contact with people at status levels different from his own than he is likely to experience otherwise in his day-to-day living. Within industrial groupings where lower-status workers predominate, higher-status people are less likely to vote Republican than they are at similar status levels in other industries. Likewise, clerical personnel in the sphere of services to private business are more likely to vote Republican than are clerical personnel in industries where over-all status levels are lower. In short, occupation, although a central index of status, can also provide a social medium in which status differences in political attitudes may become blurred.

SEX

The possibility of sex differences in political behavior remains a subject of interest in part because female suffrage is still disputed in some modern Western democracies and in part because our own acceptance of female activity in politics is of rather recent vintage. Women's right to vote did not become universal in the United States until 1920, yet sufficient time has passed to invite evaluation of its consequences.

The Nineteenth Amendment and the entry of women into high political office represent some of the clearer bench marks of changing sex roles in politics. Yet social roles are deeply ingrained in day-to-day assumptions about behavior in any culture, and these assumptions are not rapidly uprooted. Decades after the first successes of the suffragettes many wives wish to refer our interviews to their husbands as being the person in the family who pays attention to politics. Or the woman may say in so many words: "I don't know anything about politics—I thought *that* business was for men, anyway."

The vote participation rate among women in our samples is consistently 10 per cent below that of men, as an overall estimate. This 10 per cent difference is a gross summary at a point in a process of social change. Such change obviously does not occur at an even pace within all segments of a society. The gross differential in vote turnout conceals a good deal of variation among social groupings. It is in this variation that we may view the dynamics of social change; and imbedded here are the clues that help us to judge whether change is still proceeding or has run its course.

We would presume that a shift of role definition of this sort would have its genesis within the most educated strata of the society. Subsequently it would ramify slowly downward through the status hierarchy and outward geographically from the more cosmopolitan centers to increasingly remote areas of the nation. We would expect, too, that in some degree the progress of change would depend upon actual turnover of members of the society. It would be consummated as senior generations, schooled in older points of view, slowly faded from the population, their places taken by younger people for whom new arrangements are merely the "normal."

Table 15-3 permits us to examine the distinctiveness of political sex roles across region, education, and age levels. Sex differences in turnout are generally sharper in the South than at equivalent age and education ranges elsewhere in the country. This differential probably reflects a lag in sex-role change in this area, relatively sheltered as it seems to be from many modern cultural innovations. Though there are irregularities in the remainder of the table, there are substantial indications that sex differences in turnout are least at higher levels of education. This point is clearest in the South (note row labeled "Average Differences") but is visible at lower levels outside the South as well. These differences emerge independently of the strong background correlation, present for both sexes, between education and turnout. The increase in participation with education is steeper for women than for men. Although turnout rates are higher for both sexes at each succeeding level of education, the poorly educated woman is less likely to vote than her male counterpart; but the behavior of college women is very little different from that of college men. Vestiges of older political sex roles are most apparent, then, at lowest social levels.

To the degree that the South is a relatively rural area, Table 15-3 supports the prediction of sharper sex differences at greater distances from metropolitan areas. But there is further evidence favorable to the proposition within the non-South alone. Sex differences averaged across three categories of age and the two lower education group-

Table 15-3. *Relation of Region, Education, and Age to Sex Differences in Presidential Vote Turnout*[a]

Age	Non-South				South (White)[b]			
	Grade School	High School	College	Average Differences	Grade School	High School	College	Average Differences
Under 35	+16% (107)	+5% (460)	−2% (151)	+6%	+5%[c] (44)	+15% (152)	+1% (52)	+7%
35–54	+9% (326)	+2% (534)	+5% (188)	+5%	+53% (122)	+14% (106)	−8% (50)	+20%
55 or over	+16% (352)	+2% (222)	+7% (61)	+8%	+23% (103)	+28% (70)	+11% (47)	+21%
Average Differences	+14%	+3%	+3%		+27%	+19%	+1%	

[a] Figures in this table are based on a combination of data from the 1952 and 1956 election samples. The primary per cent entries in each cell represent a simple subtraction of the proportion of women within the category voting for President from the same porportion among men. Positive percentages indicate that men turned out a higher rate than women; negative percentages indicate higher female vote proportion. The entry in parentheses refers to the number of cases involved in the comparison.

[b] In view of legal and extralegal restrictions on Negro voting in the South, along with the distinctive age and education characteristics of the Southern Negro, this portion of the table is restricted to Southern Whites.

[c] There is an unusually low ceiling on this entry, as only 28 per cent of Southern White males of grade school education under 35 voted for President in these elections.

ings within type of residence outside the South reveal the following differences:

		Average Differences in Turnout Proportions of the Sexes
Non-South	Metropolitan	+5%
	City and town	+20%
	Village and rural	+28%

The evidence for differences in sex roles as a function of age are much less clear in Table 15-3 (note "Average Difference" columns). Hypothetically, most of the women over 55 at the time the data were gathered had "come of age" politically before female suffrage had been generally accepted. We would expect larger differences between the sexes in the bottom row of primary cells. In an absolute sense, the differences are largest for this row, but not significantly so. The hypothesis, however, may have some merit not apparent on the basis of this table alone. For there are additional barriers to vote turnout among younger women that are present for neither younger men nor older women.

Mothers of young children are consistently less likely to vote than are fathers of young children across all levels of education within both the 21–34 and 35–54 age groups. As usual, the differences are sharpest where education is least, and diminish to a small increment of 5–6 per cent in turnout rate of college fathers over college mothers. But the average difference of 11 per cent is substantially clearer than the same comparison among the childless. Furthermore, this dip in participation among mothers of small children does not appear to be matched by a slackened political involvement within this grouping. We pointed earlier to situations in which turnout rate may be surprisingly high among people with limited interest in the political situation. Here we seem to see an inverse case, in which voting is less frequent than the aggregate level of involvement would lead us to expect. The presence of young children requiring constant attention serves as a barrier to the voting act.

This barrier is not present for older women, yet sex differences in vote turnout do not diminish accordingly. We could account for this combination of circumstances by assuming that women who grew up before formal acceptance of female participation in politics have continued to act under some constraint not felt in younger generations. This is not to gainsay the fact that any age effect to be found in the current era is at best weak. If there once were strong age differentials among women in acceptance of new sex role definitions, it is likely that the resistant age cohorts have by and large passed from the population.

Education plays a double role in the causal nexus surrounding these sex differences. By controlling education in Table 15-3, we underscore contrasts between the sexes independent of differences in schooling. But we conceal the fact that women tend to show different levels of education than men, and that these differences, strongly related to turnout, are themselves undergoing change. The proportion of women receiving some college education has increased much more rapidly in recent decades than has the comparable proportion for men. But if newer political sex roles gain increasing acceptance at lower educational levels, and if the average education of women rises more rapidly than that of men, two forces will be acting to erode sex differences in turnout.

Sex Differences in the Approach to Politics. If we consider the motivational patterns underlying vote turnout, we find in the first instance that differences in current involvement between men and women are congruent with the turnout differentials already explored. That is, women are somewhat less likely to express a sense of involvement in the current situation. This discrepancy is clearest at the lowest levels of education, being fairly well obliterated or even reversed among college-educated men and women.

But there is substantial variety in the pattern of sex differences on other dimensions of motivational significance. There is no evidence, for example, that differences in intensity of party loyalty between the sexes help to account for sex differences in turnout. Women are about as likely to feel strong identification with a political party as men. Nor is there more than a marginal difference between men and women in the sense of citizen duty.

It is the sense of political efficacy that, with factors like education, age, and region controlled, differs most sharply and consistently between men and women. Men are more likely than women to feel that they can cope with the complexities of politics and to believe that their participation carries some weight in the political process (Table 15-4). We conclude, then, that moralistic values about citizen participation in democratic government have been bred in women as in men; what has been less adequately transmitted to the woman is a sense of some personal competence vis-à-vis the political world.

Belief in personal efficacy is one of the more prominent attitudes mediating turnout. Its weakness among women returns us directly

Table 15-4. Relation of Sex, Education, and
Region to Sense of Political Efficacy, 1956

	Men			Women		
	Grade School	High School	College	Grade School	High School	College
Non-South						
High efficacy	32%	47%	83%	13%	40%	68%
Medium efficacy	31	29	12	20	34	25
Low efficacy	37	24	5	67	26	7
	100%	100%	100%	100%	100%	100%
Number of cases	150	267	116	198	382	110
South						
High efficacy	16%	37%	78%	3%	31%	56%
Medium efficacy	12	28	15	20	36	22
Low efficacy	72	35	7	77	33	22
	100%	100%	100%	100%	100%	100%
Number of cases	89	82	55	90	147	27

to the question of sex roles. For this dimension of political motivation, more than any other, is relevant to role beliefs that presume the woman to be a submissive partner. The man is expected to be dominant in action directed toward the world outside the family; the woman is to accept his leadership passively. She is not expected, therefore, to see herself as an effective agent in politics.

It is our belief that sex differences in turnout rate fail to capture the full significance of sex role differentiation for the nature of the political response. Many women who manifest a clear sense of political sex roles by indicating personal indifference and dependence upon the husband's judgment, *do* respond nevertheless to civic expectations about vote participation. It is for this reason that a 10 per cent sex differential in turnout is misleading.

What is the significance of these sex differences for the electoral process? We have suggested earlier that a disproportionate amount of the partisan fluidity that is shown by voters from election to election may come from the politically unsophisticated. If this is so, it would follow that the addition of women to the electorate might have as a consequence greater variability in the partisan division of the vote over time. However, in the case of women, there is an added consideration. The wife who votes but otherwise pays little attention to politics not only tends to leave the sifting of information up to her husband but abides by his ultimate decision about the direction of the vote as well. The information that she brings to bear on "her" choice is indeed fragmentary, because it is secondhand. Since the partisan decision is anchored not in these fragments but in the fuller political understanding of the husband, it may have greater stability over a period of time than we would otherwise suspect. The independent woman, on the other hand, may well fill in a set of political concepts more parallel in quality to those employed by men. Hence the actual political consequences of sex contrasts may be rather small.

The dependence of a wife's vote upon her husband's partisan predispositions appears to be one reason why the entrance of women into the electorate has tended to make little visible difference in the partisan distribution of the national vote. Issues may arise from time to time to polarize the sexes: the Prohibition issue of the 1920's may have had some such consequence. In the current era, there is no reason to believe that women *as women* are differentially attracted to one of the political parties.

Women in our samples consistently show slight differences in vote partisanship by comparison with men, being 3–5 per cent more Republican. However, much of this discrepancy is traceable not to something unique in female political assessments, but to aggregate differences in other social characteristics between the sexes. For example, greater life expectancy among women means that their inclusion in the electorate increases the average age of the voter slightly. One of the current partisan consequences is a minor increase in the proportion of eligible voters of Republican disposition. Women are less likely to vote in the solidly Democratic South. Vote turnout for women slopes off more rapidly at lower levels of education than it does for men, and there is a mild tendency for voters at these levels, male or female, to be more Democratic. In general, if we take a large variety of other social characteristics into account, there are no residual differences in partisanship between men and women.

AGE

In treating the origins of party identification, we analyzed earlier the relationships between age and political partisanship. But differences in age have other consequences for the political process as well. Generally, older citizens are more likely to cast a presidential vote than are members of the younger generation.

Among active adults, the sharpest differences in participation occur in the earliest years after eligibility is attained. Under the conditions of motivation that existed in 1952 and 1956, for example, only about half of the quadrennial crop of newly eligible actually voted in their

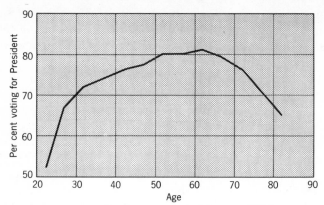

FIG. 15-1. Relation of age to voting participation.

first presidential elections. There follows a visible increase in vote participation as a function of age throughout the period of active life. As Fig. 15-1 indicates, however, turnout does not increase steadily as we move up the age scale. In fact, among the aged it actually declines again, undoubtedly due to infirmities that make trips to the polling place more difficult.

This relationship between age and vote turnout is of more than normal interest, for the increase in turnout among older citizens is totally independent of education. In fact, it runs at cross grain to the education factor, for the older generation of the adult population has had considerably less formal education than the younger. When we add income to education as a second explanatory factor for turnout, we do not gain much additional accuracy; when we add age to education, however, the increase is substantial. This fact is dramatically underscored in Table 15-5, where we summarize the relationship between a number of the social characteristics treated in this chapter and vote turnout. The oldest group of high school and college males in the South shows a decline in participation by comparison with the middle-aged cohort. Otherwise, there is a steady and at times spectacular increase of vote participation as a function of age.

Not only is age independent of education as a correlate of participation; it appears that the motivational differences that arise as a result of education are not the same as the processes that draw disproportionate numbers of older people to the polls. The final behavior —increased participation—is the same for older citizens and better-educated citizens alike. But the motivational picture is quite different in the two instances. The sense of political efficacy and the sense of

Table 15-5. Relation of Age, Education, Sex, and Region to Presidential Vote Turnout[a]

	34 or Less			Age 35–54			55 or Over		
	Grade School	High School	College	Grade School	High School	College	Grade School	High School	College
Non-South									
Male	60% (52)	78% (175)	88% (81)	80% (156)	87% (222)	96% (103)	87% (179)	93% (96)	100% (31)
Female	44% (55)	73% (285)	90% (70)	71% (170)	85% (312)	91% (85)	71% (173)	91% (126)	93% (30)
South									
Male	19% (32)	55% (69)	81% (32)	55% (87)	80% (54)	88% (33)	63% (72)	71% (21)	82% (11)
Female	13% (47)	41% (111)	74% (23)	22% (97)	56% (86)	82% (38)	31% (75)	58% (33)	86% (22)

[a] The primary entry in each cell indicates the proportion voting for President within the category. The number of cases involved in each proportion is indicated in parentheses. Figures in this table are based on a combination of data from the 1952 and 1956 election samples.

citizen duty, both of which show significant variation with education, fail to show any systematic pattern of age differences whatever.

What motivational processes, then, can account for increases in vote turnout as a function of age? The only elements that distinguish the motivational system of the older voter from that of the younger have to do with perceptions of and affect toward the parties. In the first place, although the more elderly citizen directs about the same volume of comment toward the candidates and the issues as the younger person, he communicates a significantly fuller image of the parties. The current *dramatis personae* of the political world and the issues over which they strive are not visibly more familiar to the older generation than to the younger. But the older person has observed the parties over a longer period of time and appears to have built a richer set of connotations concerning them. For the young voter the Democratic Party is, for better or for worse, the party of Stevenson and Truman. For the older voter the Democrats represent not only this but Roosevelt's leadership through the Second World War and the Depression as well.

An apparent corollary of this fact has been examined earlier. Individuals become increasingly identified with their political party the longer they have remained committed to it psychologically. If something causes a shift in party allegiance, the pattern is broken and identifications start again at a weak and hesitant level. Since most individuals hew to a single party throughout their lives, strength of party identification increases with age. Strong commitment to a party increases the probability that a person will vote. Therefore, we may presume that one reason why older people are more likely to vote lies in their stronger sense of party allegiance.

Young people not only vote less, then, but appear less securely bound to the existing party system as well. They are less likely to evaluate political objects in party terms and show less affective involvement in the fortunes of any particular party *qua* party. A political party signifies little more to them than its current leaders, be they attractive or unattractive. Like farm people, they are rather free psychologically to shift their vote from party to party and to move into and out of the electorate as well. In time of crisis they may suddenly flock to the polls in proportions that create great surges in the electoral support of a party promising salvation. And they may in crisis depart from the traditional party structure entirely. They have little base for the suspicion with which older voters may view the lineage of the *parvenus* among political parties. They have little feeling for the lineage of any of the contestants.

These observations have significance for political practice. It is probable that movements to reduce the voting age in effect imply a more fluid electorate.[1] Whether such fluidity is a matter for concern or a desirable source of "flexibility" in the political system depends upon our various normative persuasions. Likewise, any system of compulsory voting, which would drive an unusual proportion of very young people into the active electorate, would have similar consequences.

---

[1] We hesitate to make the statement more categoric, because it is conceivable that some of the observed age effects are functionally linked to the minimum age of eligibility. That is, if citizens did not receive the franchise until age 50, they might show the same behavior patterns in their fifties as people in their twenties under existing voting regulations. In fact, we would predict such an outcome if there were reason to believe that under these conditions adults under 50 would pay as little serious attention to political events as American adolescents do in the current era. However, we suspect that the adult would feel the weight of political events in a manner that would contrast with the adolescent whether or not he were yet eligible to vote.

★ ★ ★ ★ ★   SECTION V

THE ELECTORAL DECISION AND THE
POLITICAL SYSTEM

This book has sought primarily to show the influences on individual voting behavior. Taking the individual's voting act as a starting point, we have moved backward in time and outward from political influences to trace the intricate pattern of causality leading to behavior at the polls. Keeping to this task has limited our view in two respects. In the first place, fixing attention on the individual voter has kept us from accounting for the decision of the electorate as a whole. Certainly voting is an individual act; yet it is the collectivity of voters that makes the electoral decision, and we should use what we know of individual motivation to describe the forces on the decision of the total electorate. In the second place, confining our view to the *antecedents* of voting has kept us from assessing the place of the electoral process in the full political system. Voting by the American electorate occurs within a broader political order, and we should add what we know of electoral behavior to theories of the more general system in which it is set.

In two final chapters we extend our view in each of these directions. Chapter 16 shifts the terms of reference from the voter to the full electorate and from individual choice to the collective decision. The discussion deals first with the elections of 1952 and 1956, reorganizing the data of Chapter 3 to show the attitudinal components of the electorate's decision. It then moves to a somewhat broader consideration of American presidential elections, proposing a system of classification within which they may be understood. Chapter 17 returns to a question asked in the opening chapter of this book: what aspects of the wider political order can be traced to the character of voting behavior as we find it in the American electorate? Our final chapter examines the impact of electoral behavior on political leadership, its influence on party strategy, and its effect on the nature of the party system.

chapter 16

The Electoral Decision

The difficulty of knowing what motivates the electorate has not lessened popular interest in diagnosing the factors causing the outcome of a national election. The day after a presidential election a national inquest opens into the causes of the result. In political circles, in the mass media, and among the general public a host of explanatory factors is examined and the responsibility of each for the outcome is assessed. Despite the universal interest in what has influenced our elections, interpretation has scarcely risen above the simplest impressionism. The explanations offered for an electoral result are astonishingly varied; they depend typically on the slenderest evidence, and disagreements are commonplace even among knowledgeable observers. The plain fact is that there has not been an explicit means of assessing the relative importance of several influences on an election and of assessing its character in a wider set of elections. Yet a way of assessing these things ought to be within reach. We are able to account for the behavior of the individual voter, at least within tolerable limits. If we understand the forces on the individual citizen, we should be able to sum their effects and resolve the winning majority into its component elements.

COMPONENTS OF THE DECISION

We have seen in Chapter 3 that the individual's voting act is profoundly influenced by his feeling toward the objects to which this act relates. Indeed, we have seen that if we measure the partisan direction and intensity of his attitude toward six discernible elements of the world of politics we are able to predict quite well his behavior at the polls. To say whether any given person will vote Republican or Democratic we need to know where he falls on these dimensions of partisan feeling, that is, whether his attitude toward each political object is pro-Republican or pro-Democratic and with what strength.

Knowing the direction and intensity of the attitude forces on the individual we would have little difficulty telling which of these forces had pulled him more strongly in a given partisan direction. And just as the votes of individual people are added together to reach a collective decision,[1] so we may sum the attitude forces on persons in a sample of the electorate to assess the impact of these forces on the national vote decision.[2] As a result, we are able to decompose an election outcome into a set of attitudinal components.

When the vote of the Eisenhower years is resolved into its components, these methods lead to findings of considerable interest, which are summarized in Fig. 16-1. In the design of this figure the direction in which a bar goes out from the midline indicates which party the corresponding dimension of attitude has helped more. If the bar extends to the left, the factor has been generally pro-Democratic. If it extends to the right, the factor has been pro-Republican. The length of the bar indicates the relative magnitude of a factor's influence on the two-party division of the vote. The greater the bar's length, the greater the importance of the dimension of attitude in enlarging or lessening the winning majority. It is readily apparent that in both these years the sum of the lengths in the Republican direction is greater than the sum in the Democratic direction.

An inspection of this figure suggests that the Eisenhower victory of 1952 resulted from the combined effects of three factors. The Republican majority in that year appears to have been formed, first of all, out of the strongly anti-Democratic attitude toward the performance of the parties. The second Truman term was characterized by a growing criticism of the President and his Administration on the question of honesty in government. Revelations of irregularities, ranging from minor peccadilloes of patronage and favoritism to serious malfeasance in the Bureau of Internal Revenue, raised doubts as to the moral fibre of the federal Administration. Although none of the accusations involved such high crimes as those with which the Harding Administration was entangled in the Teapot Dome scandal, they appear to have had a much greater political impact.

The second factor that appears to have moved the electorate in the Republican direction was the favorable response to Eisenhower as a person. General Eisenhower's record as a military hero had developed

---

[1] For simplicity we assume here that a popular majority elects a President.

[2] A description of the methods used appears in Donald E. Stokes, Angus Campbell, and Warren E. Miller, "Components of Electoral Decision," *American Political Science Review,* LII (June 1958), 367–387.

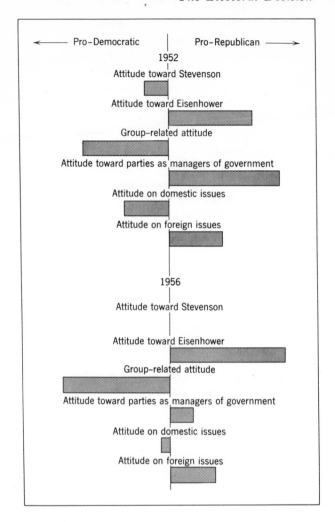

FIG. 16-1. *Attitudinal forces on the presidential vote.*

a strongly positive feeling toward him in all elements of the population before he had become associated in any way with partisan politics. Moreover, the Eisenhower candidacy seemed extraordinarily well suited to the demands of the time. Eisenhower's unparalleled reputation as a successful military leader gave promise of an answer to the desperate question of Korea. And his freedom from association with the seamier aspects of party politics and his widely acknowledged personal integrity carried a special appeal to many people who were disturbed at the level of political morality in Washington.

The third factor that contributed to the Republican majority of 1952 was the public's response to issues of foreign policy. The Korean conflict and other aspects of America's role in the cold war had generated attitudes that were decidedly favorable to the Republicans. Frustration and resentment over the stalemated Korean War, which had never been well understood by the American people, were widespread and intense. As the action in Korea dragged into its third year, it became an increasingly partisan issue, with the Republican leadership arguing either that this country should never have been involved in Korea in the first place or that the Democratic Administration should have brought our involvement there to a successful conclusion. It was an argument of great popular appeal that the Democrats apparently did not effectively answer.

This combination of factors appears to have overwhelmed the effects of several factors that tended to reduce the size of the Republican majority in 1952. The most important of these was the feeling that the Democrats were more favorable than the Republicans to the welfare of certain groupings within the population. But the magnitude of the Republican victory seems also to have been diminished by the pro-Democratic response of the public to issues of domestic policy and by the public's response to the new Democratic candidate, although the net effect of popular attitudes toward the personal qualities of Mr. Stevenson was relatively slight.

Although the election of 1956 seemed in many ways a rematch of the contest four years earlier, Fig. 16-1 shows how different were the components of the Republican victory in the two elections. In the latter year the popular appeal of Eisenhower was unquestionably of paramount importance. The public's approval of Mr. Eisenhower as a person was even greater in the second of these elections, and it seems to have contributed more to the Republican majority than did two other pro-Republican factors together. The strongly pro-Democratic sense of group interest appears to have been virtually the sole force reducing the size of Eisenhower's victory. The image of the Democratic Party as the friend of the common man, the Negro, the farmer, and the laborer still shone as brightly as before.

The paramount importance of Eisenhower's personality in the Republican victory of 1956 makes quite clear why it was that the Republicans, in winning the presidency, were unable to win control of Congress. Eisenhower's personal appeal was not completely without force on the congressional vote, since the practice of straight-ticket voting carried the choice that many people made between presidential candidates over to their choice between congressional candidates. Yet the influence of his appeal undoubtedly was much less on the vote for the House and Senate than it was on the vote for the presidency, whereas the other components of the Eisenhower victory probably had very much the same influence on the congressional vote as they had on the presidential vote. The result of this difference was that Eisenhower captured 57 per cent of the two-party vote for President, yet the Democrats won both houses of Congress.

ELECTORAL COMPONENTS AND PARTY IDENTIFICATION

We have noted many times that most Americans have an enduring partisan orientation, a sense of party identification, which has wide effects on their attitudes toward the things that are visible in the political world. Were party identification the sole determinant of the psychological forces on behavior, the attitudinal components of the vote would agree in their partisan direction with the party loyalties of a majority of the electorate. But we know that party identification is not the sole influence on how the voter appraises the things he is acting toward. In some elections the public's evaluations of the current elements of politics may not agree with its predominant partisan allegiances, and when they do not, in a system where the standing balance of party identification is not too uneven, the difference between evaluations of current political objects and long-term partisan loyalties may be wide enough to elect the candidate of the minority party. Indeed, one of the most telling characteristics of any election is how much other influences have caused the components of the decision to depart from those we would expect to find if party identification were the only determinant of the forces immediately governing behavior.

The reality of such a departure can be shown by an example within the span of our studies. Let us consider the election of 1952. The distribution of party identification in that year favored the Democrats by about three to two, although the Democratic advantage in the loyalties of those who voted was not quite so marked. Yet we know from Fig. 16-1 that the actual components of the 1952 vote were more pro-Republican than pro-Democratic. Other influences had deflected the forces on the vote from what we would have expected on the basis of party identification alone. The nature of this departure is seen more clearly if we redraw the components for the election of 1952 in Fig. 16-1 in order to show the relative force of each dimension of attitude in moving the electorate not from an even division of the vote but from

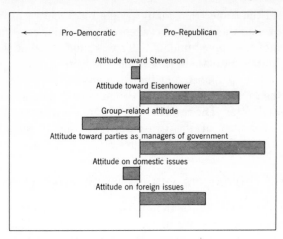

FIG. 16-2. Attitudinal components of the vote with effect of party identification removed, 1952.

the division we would have expected if the electorate's predominantly Democratic Party loyalties had been the sole influence on its appraisal of the elements of politics. The components of the 1952 vote, redrawn to "take out" the influence of party identification, are shown in Fig. 16-2. The bars of the reconstructed figure make clear how strongly other influences in 1952 were moving the electorate in the Republican direction.

A CLASSIFICATION OF PRESIDENTIAL ELECTIONS

A good deal of the meaning of an election for future years can be indicated by comparing the force of basic partisan attitudes with the electorate's long-term partisan loyalties. We propose now to reach beyond the recent elections and apply our theory of political motivation more broadly, using it to develop a more generalized system of classification of presidential elections.

We propose to classify American presidential elections into three basic types, which we may call maintaining, deviating, and realigning.[3] A *maintaining* election is one in which the pattern of partisan attachments prevailing in the preceding period persists and is the primary

---

[3] This classification is an extension of V. O. Key's theory of critical elections. See V. O. Key, Jr., "A Theory of Critical Elections," *Journal of Politics*, 17 (February 1955), 3–18. See also V. O. Key, Jr., "Secular Realignment and the Party System," *Journal of Politics, 21* (May 1959), 198–210.

influence on forces governing the vote. In this sense many, if not most, presidential elections during the past hundred years have been maintaining elections.

Among more recent elections we would describe the contest of 1948 as a maintaining election. The events surrounding the campaign of that year seemed signally devoid of circumstances that could generate forces running counter to existing partisan loyalties. In 1948 the total popular vote was 48.4 million, the lowest turnout in relation to the size of the total adult population since 1928. No compelling political issue stirred intense reaction throughout the electorate. The attempt of the short-lived Progressive Party to arouse public interest in issues of foreign policy proved a failure. It was, in other words, an election in which no overriding issue intruded to deflect the electorate from voting with its standing partisan allegiances.

Neither was it an election in which significant numbers of voters were activated by the personalities or accomplishments of the presidential candidates. Neither President Truman nor Governor Dewey stirred the enthusiasm of the general electorate. On the contrary, they were both criticized for presumed inadequacies and were undoubtedly seen in highly partisan terms; Truman and Dewey both drew their support primarily from the most highly committed followers of their parties. Neither was able to swing the independent vote in any significant way, attract any sizable number of defectors from the opposition party, or stimulate any important fraction of the in-and-out vote to go to the polls in his behalf. These are the marks of strong candidate appeal, and they were not present in the 1948 election.

It is likely, then, that in 1948 the electorate responded to current elements of politics very much in terms of its existing partisan loyalties. On election day the Democrats turned out to support Truman and the Republicans to support Dewey. Neither party marshalled its forces at full strength. But Mr. Truman was fortunate in representing a party whose followers considerably outnumbered the opposition, and the electoral decision maintained his party in power.

In a *deviating* election the basic division of partisan loyalties is not seriously disturbed, but the attitude forces on the vote are such as to bring about the defeat of the majority party. After the personalities or events that deflected these forces from what we would expect on the basis of party have disappeared from the scene, the political balance returns to a level that more closely reflects the underlying division of partisan attachments. A deviating election is thus a temporary reversal that occurs during a period when one or the other party holds a clear advantage in the long-term preferences of the electorate.

In the previous pages we have described characteristics of the Eisenhower victory of 1952 that establish this election as a deviating one. The election of Woodrow Wilson in 1916 suggests itself as an additional example. There seems little doubt that during the period of the Wilson elections the electorate was predominantly Republican. In 1920 and the two elections following, the minority status of the Democratic Party was again convincingly demonstrated.

The definition we have given of a deviating election implies that in such an election more people than usual will cross party lines in casting their votes. As a result, the events of a deviating election can easily suggest that traditional party loyalties have become less important. To be sure, they have—in an immediate sense. But if our view of the motivational basis of voting is correct, a deviating election should not be taken as evidence of a secular decline in the importance of party identification. Demonstrating a lasting decline in the role of party identification needs more evidence than that which one or two deviating elections can supply.

Key has pointed out that there is a third type of election, characterized by the appearance of "a more or less durable realignment" of party loyalties. In such a *realigning* election, popular feeling associated with politics is sufficiently intense that the basic partisan commitments of a portion of the electorate change. Such shifts are infrequent. As Key observes, every election has the effect of creating lasting party loyalties in some individual voters, but it is "not often that the number so affected is so great as to create a sharp realignment."

We have said that changes in long-term party allegiances tend to be associated with great national crises. The emergence of the Republican Party and its subsequent domination of national politics were the direct outgrowth of the great debate over slavery and the ultimate issue of the Civil War.

The most dramatic reversal of party alignments in this century was associated with the Great Depression of the 1930's. The economic disaster that befell the nation during the Hoover Administration so discredited the Republican Party that it fell from its impressive majorities of the 1920's to a series of defeats, which in 1936 reached overwhelming dimensions. The program of welfare legislation of the New Deal and the extraordinary personality of its major exponent, Franklin D. Roosevelt, brought about a profound realignment of party strength, which has endured in large part up to the present time.

In order to describe with confidence the movement of part of the electorate from the Republican to the Democratic Party a generation ago, we would need to know when it was that these people formed a stable emotional attachment to the Democratic Party. If we had this information we might well find that an attachment of this kind appeared in some of the changers as early as 1928, whereas it appeared in others only in the late 1930's or early 1940's, after they had voted Democratic several times. It is worth noting that the Democratic harvest of votes continued through the midthirties. Although Roosevelt's margin of victory in 1932 was large (59 per cent of the two-party vote), it was not until 1936 that the Democratic wave reached its peak. The long-entrenched Republican sympathies of the electorate may not have given way easily in the early years of the Depression. From this point of view we might speak not of a realigning *election* but of a realigning *electoral era*.

What is more, it is clear that the changes of such an era arise not alone from changes in the party loyalties of those who are past the age of socialization to politics. It comes as well from the relative advantage of the party that dominates the era in recruiting new identifiers from among those who are first developing their political values. The past histories of persons we have interviewed in the 1950's indicate that the New Deal–Fair Deal era produced a lasting change in party strength primarily by attracting to the Democratic Party most of the age cohort entering the electorate during the 1930's and 1940's.

One other aspect of change has been evident in most periods of lasting displacements of party strength. We have said that the distinguishing characteristic of a realigning era is a shift in the distribution of party identification. By this we mean that a *net* shift occurs, benefiting one party rather than the other. But it is clear that a net shift in the party balance does not imply that individual changes have been in one direction only. Such a shift may result from partially compensating changes of party loyalties in several population groups. For example, one party may gain strength overall from a greater polarization of politics along class lines. Lasting changes in the party balance may also accompany political realignments along regional lines. This was what happened in the elections after the Civil War. And, as Key has made clear, the realignment accompanying the election of 1896 moved the industrial East toward the Republican Party and the West toward the Democrats, giving our presidential politics a regional cast that persisted through subsequent elections. If the Republicans gained from this dual sectional movement, it was largely because the East was by far the more populous region.

We do not mean to say that changes in the political loyalties of groups are an indispensable part of long-term displacements of party strength. Yet there are two reasons why a change in the group basis of politics is likely to presage a lasting shift in the party balance. First, changes in the political loyalties of groups tend to be associated with issues that persist through time. Second, changes in party loyalty occurring on a group basis tend to be reinforced by group opinion processes. Attitudes rooted in social groups are likely to be more stable than are attitudes that are denied the status of group norms.

In view of all that we have said, how are we to characterize the two elections for which we have adequate survey data? The Eisenhower elections were clearly not maintaining elections. Neither were they realigning elections in the sense of a profound shift of the nation's party identifications having occurred in this period. Yet the question might well be raised of whether they were not the early elections of a realigning electoral era. We believe they were not, for reasons that a brief review of our findings may serve to make clear.

The most immediately relevant information that we can draw out of these studies is the fact that in both 1952 and 1956 the number of people who called themselves Democrats outnumbered those who identified themselves as Republicans, and this ratio showed no tendency to move in the Republican direction between the two years. What is more, the Republican Party did not recruit a heavy majority of young voters who were coming into the electorate, although these years did see the Democratic proportion of new voters reduced to something like half.

A second important item is the evidence that for the most part those Democrats and Independents who voted for Eisenhower at the time of his two elections preferred the man but not the party. This is dramatically demonstrated by the high proportion of ticket-splitting reported by these people. Three out of five in 1952 and three out of four in 1956 were not willing to support the Republican slate even though they voted for its presidential candidate. It is especially significant that this separation of the candidate from his party was greater in the second Eisenhower election than in the first. If we compare 1952 to 1932 it seems probable that the potential for shift created by the Democratic victory in 1932 was realized in 1936, whereas whatever readiness for shift was present in the electorate in 1952 seems to have largely faded out by 1956. There is evidence from our 1956 survey that without Eisenhower's coattails the Republican candidates for Congress would have fared even more poorly than they did.

We may observe, finally, that political change in the Eisenhower years was not accompanied by a marked realignment of the loyalties of groups within the electorate. The factors in these years that deflected the vote from what we would have expected on the basis of party identification alone acted quite generally across the electorate and were all of a relatively brief duration.

These considerations lead us to the conclusion that the Eisenhower elections did not presage a critical realignment of partisan attachments. They did not seriously threaten the prevailing Democratic majority, and the factors that made them possible seem not to have been of a long-term character. One may ask how long a party can hope to hold the White House if it does not have a majority of the party-identified electorate. There would not appear to be any certain answer to this question. The unfolding of national and international events and the appearance of new political figures to take the place of the old hold the potential for unforeseeable political consequences. We should expect, however, that the circumstances that keep a minority in power would tend over time to increase the proportion of the electorate whose loyalty it commanded. If this increase does not occur, the minority party cannot hope to continue its tenure in office over a very extended period.

chapter 17

Electoral Behavior and the Political System

Studies that look only to the *determinants* of voting fail to consider a number of problems for which systematic knowledge of electoral behavior is of great importance. We have said that popular elections are one of several means of decision making in the political system, that this system coheres largely because its decision processes are bound together by relations of mutual influence, and that, as a result, decisions of the electorate are of interest for their influence on what occurs elsewhere in the system. Our quest of understanding should not end with the discovery of the causes of electoral decisions; it should extend to their consequences as well.

Tracing the influence relations between the electorate and those who play other roles in the political system is a task for research that fixes its attention explicitly on these relations. But the substantial absence of such studies ought not to prevent our saying what we can on the basis of research that is oriented primarily toward behavior within a single decision process. A great deal has been learned about the impact of electoral decisions by those who have studied legislative or administrative bodies. In the same spirit—but from a very different perspective—we offer here some comments on the relation of the electoral process to other elements of the political system.

In describing this relation, voting research can make a unique contribution by suggesting the significance for politics of *psychological* aspects of the electorate's behavior. The significance of broad social variables or other influences that we conceive as causally antecedent to psychological factors is generally easier to see. The presence of psychological elements of voting is established only by research directly focused on them, and this research can enlarge a good deal our understanding of their implications for the larger political order.

What psychological dimensions of voting are of greatest importance for the political system? Our discussion will focus on the low emotional involvement of the electorate in politics; its slight awareness of public affairs; its failure to think in structured, ideological terms; and its pervasive sense of attachment to one or the other of the two major parties. These properties of the electorate's cognitive and affective orientation to politics can be shown to have profound consequences for other elements of the political system. Three consequences of this sort will concern us here. The first of these has to do with the situation of elected leadership in American politics; the second, with the problem of party strategy; the third, with the structure of the party system itself.

ELECTORAL BEHAVIOR AND THE PRESSURES ON LEADERSHIP

In the practice and normative theory of democracy elections are important largely as a means by which the acts of government can be brought under the control of the governed. And yet, as a formal matter, the electorate does not vote on what government shall do. The public's explicit task is to decide not what government shall do but rather *who shall decide* what government shall do. If the two decisions are bound together, as they are in the practice of every democratic state, it is because candidates for office are judged partly for the position they take on public policies, while policies are judged partly for the impact they have on the electorate's choice between candidates.

The fact that public policy is tied to public opinion by the perceptions policy-forming elites and the electorate have of each other deserves the fullest appreciation. It means at the very least that the relation between governors and governed depends on the intellective processes by which the electorate reviews and expresses its judgment of public affairs. Commentaries on democracy often assume two basic facts about the electoral decision: first, that the public is generally in possession of sufficient information regarding the various policy alternatives of the moment to make a rational choice among them (that is, that it has clear goals and is able to assess what the actions of government mean for these goals), and, second, that the election in fact presents the electorate with recognizable partisan alternatives through which it can express its policy preferences. Let us review the evidence as to the policy awareness of the electorate.

Our detailed inquiry into public attitudes regarding what we took to be the most prominent political issues of the time revealed a substantial lack of familiarity with these policy questions. Our measures have shown the public's understanding of policy issues to be poorly developed even though these measures usually have referred to a general problem which might be the subject of legislation or (in the area of foreign affairs) executive action, rather than to particular bills or acts. Neither do we find much evidence of the kind of structured political thinking that we might expect to characterize a well-informed electorate. The common tendency to characterize large blocs of the electorate in such terms as "liberal" or "conservative" greatly exaggerates the actual amount of consistent patterning one finds. Our failure to locate more than a trace of "ideological" thinking in the protocols of our surveys emphasizes the general impoverishment of political thought in a large proportion of the electorate.

It is also apparent from these protocols that there is a great deal of uncertainty and confusion in the public mind as to what specific policies the election of one party over the other would imply. This fact reflects the similarity of party positions on many issues, as well as the range of opinion within parties. But it also reflects how little attention even the relatively informed part of the electorate gives the specifics of public policy formation.

We have, then, the portrait of an electorate almost wholly without detailed information about decision making in government. A substantial portion of the public is able to respond in a discrete manner to issues that *might* be the subject of legislative or administrative action. Yet it knows little about what government has done on these issues or what the parties propose to do. It is almost completely unable to judge the rationality of government actions; knowing little of particular policies and what has led to them, the mass electorate is not able to appraise either its goals or the appropriateness of the means chosen to serve these goals.

The quality of the electorate's review of public policy formation has two closely related consequences for those who must frame the actions of government. First, it implies that the electoral decision typically will be ambiguous as to the specific acts government should take. The thinness of the electorate's understanding of concrete policy alternatives—its inability to respond to government and politics at this level—helps explain why efforts to interpret a national election in terms of a policy mandate are speculative, contradictory, and inconclusive.

The second consequence of the quality of the public's review of policy formation is that the electoral decision gives great freedom to those who must frame the policies of government. If the election returns offer little guidance on specific policies, neither do they generate pressures that restrict the scope of President and Congress in developing public policy. To be sure, the fact that the wider public has so little to say on specific policies strengthens the position of special publics and particular "interests" in making their demands on government. Yet in important respects the latitude of government decision makers in framing public policies is enlarged by the fact that the details of these policies will be very largely unknown to the general electorate.

However great the potential ability of the public to enforce a set of concrete policy demands at the polls, it is clear that this power is seldom used in American politics. Yet it would be altogether wrong to suppose that the electoral process does not profoundly influence the course of government. Unquestionably it does. The decisions of the electorate play a role primarily in defining broad goals of governmental action or very generalized means of achieving such goals. Because these tend over time to become matters on which there is consensus in American society—e.g., since the 1930's, economic prosperity as a goal of public policy—this function of the electoral process may go largely undetected. But even a rough comparison of our system with one in which a regularized expression of popular opinion is not possible suggests how important is electoral behavior for stating broad objectives of government.

The importance of the public's concern with certain broad objectives of government is quite clear in our studies. We have seen in the preceding chapter that the electoral decision results from a comparison of the total image of one of the candidate-party alternatives with the image of the other. A good deal of the public response to these political actors simply expresses feeling, or affect. Many people see this party or that candidate as "honest," "dependable," "capable," or, more generally, as just "good." In a similar way, a large proportion of the electorate sees the parties or candidates as good or bad for this or that segment of the public, often referring to the group with which they themselves identify. But our examination of public attitude shows that certain generalized goals of government action enter the image of the parties and candidates and that these goals play a major role in electoral change. In the years of our studies, the generalized goals of peace and prosperity, rather than specific acts or policies in pursuit of them, were important in coloring the image of the parties and in shaping the electoral outcome.

Our conclusion that the major shifts of electoral strength reflect the changing association of parties and candidates with general societal goals rather than the detail of legislative or administrative action is affirmed by what we know of the voters most susceptible to change. The segment of the electorate most likely to alter its image of these political actors is not the part that is best informed about government but the part that is least involved in politics, psychologically speaking, and whose information about details of policy is most impoverished. Change is not limited entirely to people of low information and involvement, but they are more likely than others to respond to the wars or economic recessions or other gross changes in the political environment that may generate substantial shifts at the polls. The extraordinary fact that these people supply much of the dynamic of politics makes it clearer why the behavior of the electorate imparts a concern for broad goals of policy or generalized means of achieving these goals more than for the specific content of public policy.

If government is influenced by the broad policy concerns that enter the electorate's decision, it is influenced too by public attitudes that have little immediate relationship to specific candidates or parties. Large areas of public policy do not enter into political discussion because there is broad consensus that they lie outside the range of tolerance. These largely unspoken but widely accepted injunctions may have far greater significance in the electoral mandate than such issues as may become the subject of partisan controversy. They set the limits within which the parties offer policy alternatives.

Of course, parties and candidates also are inhibited from offering "extreme" policy proposals by the fact that political leaders share many of the value beliefs of the electors to whom they appeal. Because these beliefs are shared, the stands on issues of those seeking office are kept within acceptable limits not by their reading of public attitude but by their own internal values. Yet the significance of their readings of public opinion should not be discounted. The fact that political leaders are sensitive to how the electorate would react to policies that are not now—and may never be—issues between candidates in any actual election establishes an important additional link between public opinion and government.

The limits of what is acceptable differ in different parts of the electorate and at different points in time. There are broad national issues that lie outside the range of tolerable discourse. The nationalization of industry, governmental control of the press, the compromising of national sovereignty in world federations—such proposals are not now discussed in political campaigns because it is generally agreed that they go beyond public tolerance. But the range of opinion that is seen to fall within tolerable limits is not altogether rigid; the pressure of ongoing events can force very considerable changes. For example, the orthodox philosophy of private enterprise, which was largely unquestioned in American politics during the 1920's, became the subject of very heated controversy during the 1930's. And although there is still considerable difference of opinion as to the proper character of the nation's foreign relations, the advocacy of full-blown isolationism, which was not uncommon during the 1920's, now to all intents and purposes lies outside the range of controversy.

ELECTORAL BEHAVIOR AND PARTY STRATEGY

One way of describing a party's strategic problem in securing an electoral majority is to say that it must assume positions of greater acceptance than its opposition on the dimensions of political controversy that influence electoral choice. If an electorate responds to public affairs in terms of one or a few well-defined and stable ideological dimensions on which there is little movement of opinion, political controversy will be relatively tightly bounded and the possibilities of party maneuver—and alternation in office—relatively circumscribed. But if an electorate responds to public affairs in a less structured fashion, politics will be more fluid, party strategy will include or may consist primarily of exploiting new dimensions of opinion, and the likelihood of party alternation in power will be greater.

All this suggests important consequences of the lack of ideological structure in the political thought of the American electorate. We have seen that the stable qualities of the public's response to political affairs have to do primarily with long-term loyalties to the parties rather than ideological commitments against which current acts or policies of the parties could be evaluated. The forces not based on party loyalty that influence the decisions of the American electorate appear almost wholly free of ideological coloration. As a result, their impact on the party balance is much more variable than would otherwise be the case. This may perhaps be seen most clearly in the importance for the vote of popular reactions to the personalities of the changing figures nominated for President. The major role played by candidate appeal suggests the absence of overriding public concern to judge the policies of the candidates and their parties against the standards received from well-elaborated political ideologies.

An awareness of this situation is reflected in the strategies of American political parties. Despite the common tendency to impute more structure to popular thought than it actually has, American party leaders show by their willingness to exploit new and relatively temporary dimensions of popular feeling that they know the public's response to politics is not dominated by fixed ideological dimensions. Especially is this evident in the tendency of the party out of power to conceive its problem not as one of winning adherents on an established dimension of political controversy but rather as one of developing new dimensions of opinion, on which it can overcome its competitive disadvantage. The difference in these strategic outlooks expresses much of the difference in what the Taft and Eisenhower forces urged the Republican Party to do in the convention of 1952. The Taft view was that the party should take a plainly conservative position on the left-right dimension that had emerged out of the struggle over the New Deal by nominating a candidate whose conservative stand was unquestioned. The belief that such a course would lead to majority support at the polls was based on the assumptions that the electorate was moving to the right and that the party had previously failed to attract its full potential vote because of non-voting among those who felt it was aping the Democrats. The strategic view that implicitly was endorsed by a majority of the Republican convention was that the party should exploit quite different dimensions of opinion, especially by nominating a war hero of enormous popular appeal. The slogan "Corruption, Korea, and Communism," with which the Republican Party went into the campaign, suggests nicely the free-wheeling character of this strategy. Each of the elements of the slogan referred to a subject of public concern, real or imagined, that was relatively new and transitory; and none of the three bore much relation to the others, except for an alliterative one.

ELECTORAL BEHAVIOR AND THE PARTY SYSTEM

Few aspects of a political system are of greater importance than the number of parties having a realistic chance to control government. Certainly the number of parties competing effectively in the electoral process is a tremendously significant aspect of the context in which the electorate must reach a decision; the influence of a two-party system on American electoral behavior has been implicit in every chapter of this book. Yet this influence does not move in one direction only. The electorate's response to politics is part of the context in which political parties operate, and the behavior of the electorate can have important effects on the party system itself. We feel that this is specifically true of American politics. Our studies lead us to believe that the persistence of a national two-party system in the United States depends in some measure on the way in which the American electorate reaches its decision.

To account for the persistence of a two-party system we must be able to say, first, why there are not *more* than two parties and, second, why there are not *less* than two. An important answer to both these questions lies in the electorate's profound loyalty to the existing parties.

Our studies regularly have shown that three quarters of the adult population grants outright its allegiance to the Republican or Democratic Party and that most of those who call themselves Independents acknowledge some degree of attachment to one of the parties. These partisan identifications typically extend far into an individual's past —if not into the past of his forebears as well—and appear highly resistant to change. The individual's partisan choice at the polls does not invariably follow his sense of party loyalty; we are able to specify the conditions under which he will vote against that loyalty. Yet the effects of party identification are so pervasive that the decision of the electorate to a great extent expresses its attachment to the two established parties. The conserving influence of party identification makes it extremely difficult for a third party to rise suddenly and with enough popular support to challenge the existing parties. If the forces on the vote were formed wholly anew in each campaign, new or minor parties would be able to establish themselves fairly easily as serious contenders for power. But these forces are not made anew; they are formed in large measure by the political past, in which a third party has not had a place.

If party identification tends to limit the number of parties to two, it tends also to strengthen the second party by stabilizing the electoral competition of the parties. The substantial effect of long-term partisan loyalties on the vote reduces the amplitude of the swings from one major party to the other. We are accustomed to accepting as a great victory the outcome of a national election in which the winning party attracts not 20, 30, or 40 per cent more than an equal division of the vote but a mere 10 per cent more. Since the strength of the two parties is not uniformly distributed geographically, the moderate extent of fluctuations in the vote means that the minority party is never deprived altogether of office in our federal system of government. Even in the face of a "landslide" the party out of power nationally will hold many seats in the Congress, and it will also retain control of a number of state governments. But if the damping effect of party identification were removed and the electoral tides were to run at full strength, the second party might well be forced into a minority position everywhere at once and be deprived of the forum and leadership it requires to return to power in national government at a later time.

The action of party identification in moderating electoral movements explains why a minority party is not destroyed overnight. Yet it cannot explain why a second party is not shut out of power indefinitely. Why is it that the party vote oscillates about an equal division over time rather than developing a persistent, and perhaps increasing, margin for a majority party? The answer to this question is really far from obvious.

Undoubtedly a number of factors are at work. Yet our studies suggest a hypothesis about the public's response to politics that may supply a key to understanding: the party division of the vote is most likely to be *changed* by a negative public reaction to the record of the party in power. If true, the hypothesis accounts simply enough for the attribute of party competition we seek to explain. A majority party, once it is in office, will not continue to accrue electoral strength; it may preserve for a time its electoral majority, but the next marked *change* in the party vote will issue from a negative response of the electorate to some aspect of the party's conduct in office, a response that tends to return the minority party to power. The greater the majority party's share of the underlying identifications of the electorate, the greater is the probability of its winning elections and holding office. But the greater also is the probability of its losing strength by being in office when a calamity occurs that arouses the public's ire against those in power. Hence, the greater the majority party's strength, the greater the likelihood of its strength being reduced.

One aspect of this hypothesis needs to be specified very clearly. Unfavorable feeling toward a party that is being turned out of power may well be coupled with favorable feeling toward the party that follows it in office if the latter copes successfully with problems the public feels were mishandled by the preceding administration. This sort of positive attitude may well play an important role in fixing or augmenting a change in party strength resulting from the public's negative reaction to the record of the other party. But *new* positive attitudes, unrelated to the issues that brought a turnover of party control, are not likely to initiate a shift in the party balance.

Why should the electorate be more likely to punish an incumbent party for its mistakes than to reward it for its successes? Part of the answer almost certainly lies in the low salience politics has for the general public. Because of the slight political involvement of the electorate, very little crosses the threshold of public awareness and becomes associated with the image of the party holding office. (Of course, even less becomes associated with the image of the minority party when it is out of office.) As long as public affairs go well, there is little to motivate the electorate to connect events of the wider environment with the actors of politics, and the successes of an administration are likely to go virtually unnoticed by the mass public. But when events of the wider environment arouse strong public concern, the electorate is motivated to connect them with the actors of politics—typically, with the incumbent party. An economic or military or other form of calamity can force events across the threshold of political awareness, to the detriment of the administration party. And because these matters have gained broad public awareness, the party coming to power may attract considerable positive feeling by coping successfully with the problems that have driven its predecessor from office, whereas the new administration's later successes in other areas of policy may evoke little public response. Caught by the fact that the electorate is more likely to be moved by their mistakes in office, the two parties continue to alternate in power, with neither developing such a commanding edge that its opponent is excluded permanently from winning the presidency.

What of the states? If the nature of electoral response makes it probable that the national party division of the vote will tend to oscillate about an even division, why is it that year in and year out many of our states are firmly in the hands of one party? Of course, even in strongly one-party states the division of the vote often reflects the shifts of party strength that bring a turnover of control in national government. But it is clear that the dominant party in many states does *not* suffer a continuing, secular decline in strength until effective two-party competition is restored. How is this fact to be reconciled with the argument of the preceding pages?

The answer depends on the fact that the nation as a whole is a self-contained political system in a sense that a state is not. The forces generating, maintaining, and altering the party identifications that keep one party in power in many states have primarily a national focus. Our most deeply one-party area—the South—was delivered into the hands of the Democratic Party by the Civil War and Reconstruction Era, as many northern areas were delivered at the same time into the hands of the Republican Party. And the forces that have prevented a serious erosion of the Democratic Party's hold on the South have had to do chiefly with struggles over national policy, particularly affecting racial questions. Indeed, in many ways the Southern states are one-party states *only* in national politics, with intraparty factions serving more or less adequately as political parties at the state level.[1] Paradoxically, the fact that we have one-party as well as two-party states, which has often been cited to show that the states are distinct political systems, is evidence that in vital respects we have a *national* politics. Since the forces that are most important in fixing and chang-

---

[1] The classic statement of this view is given in V. O. Key, Jr., *Southern Politics in State and Nation* (Alfred Knopf, New York; 1950).

ing long-term party loyalties are primarily national in character, the fact that a party may remain in power in state government over a great many years does not undermine our hypothesis.

From all this it should be clear that the response of the electorate to politics is a major determinant of the structure of the party system —as it is a determinant of the strategies of the parties and of the behavior of policy-forming elites. To be sure, electoral behavior offers no simple or sovereign theories of politics, and we do not arrogate to voting a primary role in the political system. Even to establish the effects of voting behavior treated here we have had to accommodate institutional factors such as the nature of the executive, the separation of powers in national government, and the federal character of our political system. And if we were to write comprehensively of the political order we would have to consider a great many things lying outside the electoral process.

Yet an understanding of electoral behavior throws a good deal of light on the political system. By vesting in a mass public the power to make a critical type of decision, our form of government implies that the public's orientations to politics will have wide influence throughout the political order. We have explored here some effects of the electorate's slight involvement in politics and limited awareness of public affairs; of the nonideological quality of its thinking; and of the pervasive character of its partisan commitments. If our argument runs true, these qualities of the prevailing response to politics account for important elements of American government. Indeed, their power to do so suggests that important additional connections are to be found by a closer mapping of the influence relations binding the electoral process to the other means of decision making in the political system.

Index